Carole and

THE GIFTED TRAP

You are both beautiful
bright Lights
Allow them to
shine and ...

Be Great!

♡

"Annie"

Anne's masterful manual, **The Gifted Trap,** is a compelling play-book that breaks down, spells out and offers success strategies to help you manage the challenging opponents and hurdles of perceptions, beliefs and judgment that we all must manage in order to win in the game called life.

James Brown
CBS Sports & News

. . . .

The Gifted Trap is a fabulous guide to completing the journey to self-realization and to the fulfillment of one's destiny using the gifts and talents that we consciously or subconsciously suppress.

Anne shows us how often we are obstacles to our own success, and gives us the formula for "getting out of our own way" in order to be who we were meant to be. Read it, enjoy it, live it!

Van Coots, MD
Brigadier General, US Army

. . . .

Anne Palmer's guide to self-fulfillment stands out from the plethora of such books for the clarity of her instructions, her honesty about the obstacles, and her capacity to make you feel that your most deeply-held ambitions are within reach.

Joel Dreyfuss Veteran Journalist & Editorial Director
USA Today, Washington Post, The Root

. . . .

The Gifted Trap is a transformative message, delivered through the voice of an impressive inspiring leader who boldly and courageously stepped on the stage as a top finalist in the eWomenNetwork "North America's Next Greatest Speaker" contest and modeled what it means to own your voice with a powerful presence.

Now it's your turn! This insightful book will empower and guide you to embrace the "extra" in front of your ordinary ... so that you, too, can joyfully claim your greatness!

Sandra Yancey
CEO & Founder eWomen Network

. . . .

Faith is a gift. It is a discovery of what is possible for you in your life. **The Gifted Trap** represents an opportunity for you to tap into your light within and see how faith has dawned in your life. It reveals a new vision of the role faith as you respond to your call to greatness. Walk now into where that light is leading you—into new discoveries of who you are and what your life is really all about. Allow this insightful book to illuminate your way.

The Very Reverend John Sanders
Former Dean, St. Phillips's Cathedral of the Episcopal Diocese of Atlanta

. . . .

This insightful book affords you, the reader, permission to let your individual light shine and, in doing so, you will undoubtedly free others to do the same. In an age when too often mediocrity is the order of the day, and where far too many gifted peopled lack the courage and encouragement to stretch beyond that which is in their immediate reach, **The Gifted Trap** is especially needed. It is beautiful and powerful. Enjoy it!

Dr. Carolyn Meyers
President, Jackson State University

. . . .

The Gifted Trap is a superb book. An engaging and enlightening wake up call for all those dedicated to accelerating their personal leadership—A personal and professional must-read for executive leaders around the globe who seek to claim their greatness and unleash their potential."

Elizabeth van Geerstein PhD, Master Certified Coach
Adjunct Professor Personal Leadership Development
Rotterdam School of Management, Erasmus University,
The Netherlands

. . . .

Our mission at the International Speakers' Bureau is to seek out and promote talented speakers. As the founder of ISB, immediately upon hearing Anne speak, I recognized her as the "real deal". She has a rare and special gift—her presence is commanding. She is like a breath of fresh air!

Michelle Lemmons-Poscente
Founder, International Speakers Bureau

. . . .

The Gifted Trap ... is a wonderful call-to-action for leadership development. Anne Palmer has done a great job illuminating a new pathway for talented people from all walks of life to emerge. She has done an amazing job!

Stedman Graham
Author, Educator, Entrepreneur

. . . .

The Gifted Trap is a blessing of a tool to use as you want to move away from other peoples' perceptions of who they think you are and move toward the knowing, and the purpose, of who you know yourself to be.

It offers the opportunity for you to liberate yourself and stand in your own greatness ... defined by you. When I think about the joy the book brings ... it brings an opportunity, or the space, to no longer ask the world who you should be, or take on someone else's perceptions ... but to give the world notice as to who you choose to emerge to be.

Anne skillfully outlines, not only the beautiful stories and poems, but she examines her own life, as she calls you to examine your life – to examine the places where you've fallen prey to Perceptions, Beliefs and Judgments and then offers you a way out.

Anne is a profound orator, gifted speaker, anointed and blessed teacher and coach. She is sure to give you nuggets, tools, systems and knowledge that will inspire you, encourage you and give you that piece of hope and understanding that we all look for ... Truly one of my favorite people.

Lisa Nichols
Global Transformational Speaker
CEO, Motivating the Masses

ANNE PALMER, NANGS finalist and author of *The Gifted Trap* invites you to

JOYFULLY CLAIM YOUR GREATNESS!

What Sandra Yancey says about *The Gifted Trap*
CEO & Founder, eWomen Network

" ... A transformative message, delivered through the voice of an impressive and inspiring leader who boldly and courageously models what it means to own your voice with a powerful presence. Now it's your turn ... to embrace the "extra" in front of your ordinary ... so that you, too, joyfully claim YOUR greatness."

THE GIFTED TRAP™
E.M.E.R.G.E. FROM GIFTED TO GREAT™

To claim your greatness is not arrogant... To ***not*** claim it is!

SO...
CLAIM YOUR COPY TODAY

1 Book: $19.95
2-5 Books: $17.50/per copy
6 or more: $15.00/per copy
Bulk book pricing available

Also available –

"The Dawn of A New Day" CD...
Soothing Sonnets for Your Soul
CD: $20.00 | Book & CD Bundle:$30.00

Books _____

Bundle _____

Shipping _____

Total $ _____

THE GIFTED TRAP™

E.M.E.R.G.E. FROM GIFTED TO GREAT™

1 Book: $19.95
2-5 Books: $17.50/per copy
6 or more: $15.00/per copy
Bulk book pricing available

• • • • • • • • • • • • • • • • •

The Gifted Trap … offers you an opportunity to give the world notice who you choose to emerge to be.

A profound orator, gifted speaker, anointed and blessed teacher and trainer, Anne gives you nuggets, tools, systems and knowledge that will inspire you, encourage you and give you that piece of hope and understanding that we all look for … Truly one of my favorite people."

Lisa Nichols – Global Transformational Speaker / CEO, Motivating the Masses

Also available – "The Dawn of A New Day" CD … Soothing Sonnets for Your Soul CD $20.00 | Book & CD Bundle $30.00

PAYMENT & SHIPPING INFORMATION:

Date: _____

Cash _____

Check # _____

Credit Card#: _____

Exp _____ Cvv#: _____

Name: _____

Address: _____

City: _____ Zip: _____

State: _____ Zip: _____

Phone: _____

Email: _____

Signature: _____

THE
GIFTED TRAP™

E.M.E.R.G.E. FROM GIFTED TO GREAT™

ANNE PALMER

The Gifted Trap™
E.M.E.R.G.E. FROM GIFTED TO GREAT™
©2013 by Anne Palmer

Pure Presence Publishing, LLC

ISBN: 978-0-9884931-0-0

Printed in the United States of America

DEDICATION

Thank you to all my angels on high, especially...

Augustus L. Palmer, Sr.

My father, "Daddy," known to many as "Big Gus," for embodying excellence and modeling the true meaning of faith. Your courage, and that of your Red-Tailed Tuskegee wing brothers, left an indelible imprint on this earth.

Augustus L. Palmer, Jr.

My brother, known affectionately as "Little Gus" for the brilliant light that radiated from your soul. Your struggle was not in vain. Many will benefit from the lessons gleaned from your premature passing with far too many songs still in your trapped heart. Sing from heaven, my brother... sing!

Herbert Nathaniel Hardwick, Jr.

Herbert Nathaniel Hardwick, Sr.

To my gifted gentle giants, "Uncle Herbie" and "Big Daddy" (my best friend) for modeling dedication and devotion as you stood tall and strong in stature with loving, caring and compassionate hearts.

Walter Lester Henry, MD

To my "Uncle Lester," for your steady, measured, prolific gifts and commitment to medicine...and to mankind. Your legacy as a Master Physician, Buffalo Soldier and mentor lives on. Your belief in me never wavered.

TABLE OF CONTENTS

Dedication ix
Acknowledgements. 1
Foreword. 5
Introduction 9
   Why I Wrote This Book. 10
   Letter From President Obama 17
   Acclaim From a Friend 18
   'Just Trust'. *20*

PART ONE : WAKING UP IN THE DARK

CHAPTER I – WAKING UP IN THE DARK **23**
CHAPTER II – WHAT IS THE GIFTED TRAP?. **25**
   How Does It Feel to Be in the Gifted Trap? 28
   Emotional Entrapment – Stuck in Quicksand 29
   How Do You Know You're Entrapped? 30
   What Is Joy? 30
   The Shadows Within Us 32
   Total Package…Triple Threat 33
   Manifestations of Emotional Entrapment 38
   Symptoms of Emotional Entrapment 40
      Why Bother?. 40
      Am I Good Enough?. 40
      What Makes You Think You Can?. 41
      Gifted Looks Easy … But It Takes Effort 41
   Breaking Free Is Hard To Do. 41
   "Vision These Words". *45*
   You Are Gifted **46**
      Giftedness Defined 46

Everyone Has Genius Within 47

Gifted Children Grow Up. 48

Identifying Gateway Gifts. 49

    The Gift of Athleticism. 49

    The Gift of Intelligence. 50

    The Gift of the Arts and Creativity 50

    The Gift of Communication. 51

    The Gift of Innovation 51

    The Gift of Beauty 51

The Challenge of Giftedness 52

Your Unique Gifts. 54

Unconventional Gifts 55

Gilded Golden Gifts 58

Being At Peace With Your Gifts. 61

Imagine If You Were Invisible 61

CHAPTER III – THE BAIT THAT LURES YOU

INTO THE TRAP **65**

PB&Js™ – Nourishment or Sewage? 68

Perceptions 68

    Internal and External Perceptions 70

Beliefs 75

    Beliefs on Professional Playing Fields 77

    Beliefs in Athletic Arenas "Just Do It". 77

    Putting On and Taking off Beliefs. 79

Judgment. 80

Destination by Default **84**

    Withering On The Vine 86

    At The Pinnacle of Success 87

Mastering and Managing Excellence. 89

Disappointment and Desperation –

    The Most Likely To Succeed Syndrome. 91

    "If". *94*

CHAPTER IV – THE BURDEN OF GIFTEDNESS **97**

Characteristics and Symptoms **98**

High Self-Confidence, Yet Low Self-Esteem 98
Alienation and Loneliness. 100
Perfectionism – The "Disease to Please" 101
Walking A Tightrope 103
Living a "Less-Than Capable" Life 104
Determination/ Exhaustion /Burnout. 104
Struggles Inside The Trap **105**
Self-Doubt 105
Sabotaging Behavior – Being a Victim 108
Searching For Joy In All The Wrong Places 109
Being Discredited By Others. 111
Play Small Or Be A Target 112
Misunderstood 113
Two Greatest Fears 116
What You Long For From Inside The Trap **118**
Love 118
Acceptance 119
Validation. 119
Knowing You Are Not Alone 120
"This Space Called Grief" 123
CHAPTER V – THE VOICES WITHIN **125**
"The Beauty In Miss B" *127*
The Most Common Voices. **129**
The Voice of Doubt – "No Way .... You Can't!" 132
The Voice of Perfection – "You'd Better Do
It Perfectly!". 133
The Voice of Skepticism –
"Better Not ... That's Not Possible!" 134
The Voice of the Protector – "Be Careful" 135
The Voice of Criticism – "You Aren't All That!". 136
The Voice of the Guards At the Gates "What Are You Here . . . .
For? And What Do You Want?" .137
The Voice of the Image Consultant – "Is That
Appropriate?" 138

The Voice of the Wounded Child – "Is It Safe To Come
    Out To Play?" 139
Know Your Voices. 143
    Getting to Know All of You : Identifying the Voices 144
    Active Imagination 146
    Chatter That Matters : Negotiate and Co-create With
    Your Voices 150
The Voice and Choice. 152
Initiating Healthy Chatter. 154
    Recording the Chatter – Journaling 155
    "Fear Too Has A Purpose". *156*
CHAPTER VI – YOUR GIFT, YOUR LIGHT 159
Are You Too Good For Your Own Britches? 159
    How Do You Know If You Are Too Good? 163
    Balancing Confidence and Compassion 166
    "Claiming Voice". *168*
How Bright Is Your Light? 170
    Is Your Light Too Bright? 170
    Sharing the Spotlight 172
    Broadcasting Your Brilliance 173
    Permission To Let Your Light Shine 174
Out of the Trap And Into The Light 176
    "Stepping Out of The Trap". *176*

**PART TWO : EMERGING
THE DAWN OF A NEW DAY – A NEW WAY**

"The Dawn Of A New Day" **181**
CHAPTER VII – E.M.E.R.G.E. 183
Embracing The Emerge Process. 183
Finding Your Freedom 183
    Conventional Psychological/Medical Pathway. 185
    Holistic Spiritual Pathway. 186
    Plugging Into Source 187
    Acknowledging Your Greatness. 189

"*Martyr Wisdom*". *193*

The E.M.E.R.G.E. Process **195**

"*Expanding Your Heart*". *196*

E-xamine **196**

Awaken. 197

Acknowledge. 198

Accept 200

"*A Truthful Stance*" *202*

M-aximize **204**

E-ngage. **211**

R-eframe. **214**

G-ain **220**

Gaining The Courage and Clarity You Need To Soar 220

An Exclamation Mark About PB&Js™ 222

E-merge **224**

Emerge With Clarity. 224

Authentic Alignment 225

Staying in Authentic Alignment, Body, Mind
and Spirit. 225

A Shout Out To My Lifelines. 227

"*A Shift In State*" *232*

CHAPTER VIII – AS YOU EMERGE. **235**

Surviving Life's Storms

An Umbrella Offering. 235

"*A More Delicious Way of Being*". *236*

Smooth Sailing 239

Riding the Inevitable Emotional Waves. 240

The Undertow – Guts and Grief 240

Evolving Authentically. **249**

Gratitude 249

Thank You God For My Ten Toes 253

Grace – Rolling Waves 255

Faith 255

"*Relinquish Control*" *259*

Soulful Surrender – The Calm After The Storm 260

Restoration, Renewal and Rejuvenation 262

"Sleep". 264

Sabbath Time 265

Loving Yourself. 268

Power of Prayer – Wind Beneath Wings 269

Stay In Integrity With Your Truth. 271

"Visceral Desire". 274

CHAPTER IX – OWNING YOUR

POWERFUL PRESENCE **275**

Self-Care 275

Style 278

Stature 279

Self-Confidence 281

Self-Mastery 283

"Be All You Are Meant To Be" 284

CHAPTER X – THE PB&J DIETARY SHIFT **287**

"Emerge From The Trap". 288

CHAPTER XI – LIBERATE YOURSELF FROM

THE TRAP **291**

"Our Greatest Fear" – Excerpt from A Return To Love

by Marianne Williamson. 291

Invest In You 292

Integrate Your Head and Your Heart 292

Plug Into Source 292

Leave a Legacy. 293

Be Unapologetic About Your Giftedness... 294

Your Indelible Footprint... 295

APPENDICES

INTERVIEW PROFILES **297**

RESOURCES. **305**

ACKNOWLEDGEMENTS

T HE JOURNEY TO PEN THIS BOOK WAS ONE FOR WHICH I take little credit, for I was called to deliver this message and it has been a labor of love. The sequence of life events that led me to this place could not have been coincidence. There is but one explanation… and therefore the ONLY place to start my gratitude is with my ultimate source of strength, God. I add to that credit the choir of my ancestral angels, for they joined God in guiding me through life and chose me to deliver this message. It is clear to me that I am a vessel through which wisdom from on high flows. Thank you for seeing to it that I am always mindful of the needs of others. It is because of the deep connection that I have with you, God, and my other trusted sources that I am able to live in alignment with my higher purpose.

After God, I thank my parents, Augustus "Gus" and Mercedes "Dees" Palmer, for giving me the two greatest gifts of all—*life and faith*. Exposing me to church as a child left on me an indelible mark and instilled in me a spiritual structure that has fortified me. That structural underpinning has been a continuous thread that has sustained me through my most turbulent times. Father John and his wife Frances Sanders were the first pastoral family in a series that have nurtured and nourished my soul throughout my life— strengthening my spiritual spine so I am able to stand tall in my faith.

Those who know me personally know that my family, both immediate and extended, is far too large to name names. Suffice it to say, that it is a wonderfully eclectic and colorful tribe that provided the breeding ground for many of the life lessons shared in these pages. This story would not be a story without my family, my friends, and my ex-husband having each contributed to my life lessons. Those lessons turned out to be true treasures that challenged me to confront myself, own my gifts and emerge using the blessings that God gave me.

To my mentors that coaxed, coached and cajoled me to keep stretching and growing, I mention many of you in this book and want to thank you here as well. My journey was like a masterfully choreographed relay, with the baton being passed gently from one hand to the next. Each leg was synchronized to do exactly what was needed to get me to the finish line. So to "Dr. Bob" Filewich, Bill Mayer, Marcia Wieder, Tim Kelley, Jeffrey Van Dyk, Suzanne Falter, Dike Drummond, Marie Guthrie, Lisa Nichols, and Melissa Evans, I thank you for being an Olympic-quality relay team. The first leg with Erline Belton gave me a strong lead, one that was sustained throughout the relay.

Erline, you entered my life as my executive coach and handed me the baton at the beginning of my transformational journey. You have remained on the sidelines throughout this process, always believing in me and encouraging me to never give up—reassuring me that I am "good enough." You inspire me to keep living my life, just as you suggest in your book, *A Journey That Matters*, in a way that will leave a lasting legacy. You and I are eternally linked as "soul sisters."

Special gratitude goes to my personal Yoda, Arthur Samuel Joseph, whose brilliant Vocal Awareness Method™ served as an incubator in the final stage leading up to this book enabling me to complete the gestation and emerge from my own gifted trap as a healthy, whole, authentic and confident Voice to deliver this vitally important message. Arthur, you taught me to embody all of my gifts unapologetically. You encouraged and empowered me to be my Self, (fully integrated as in Jungian Psychology with a capital S), with grace and "in stature" to know that—using the Vocal Awareness mantra—*"I am an extraordinary person and I do extraordinary things."* I thank you for being not only my mentor, but most importantly, for being a very dear friend.

To my eWomen Network family, thank you for being the nurturing system of support for entrepreneurial and executive women that you are. I thank Sandra and Kym Yancey for creating eWomen Network's North America's Next Greatest Speaker (NANGS) contest as an international platform for talented speakers to step forward. It was through that experience that I truly claimed my voice, and gained the courage to transparently speak my truth so that others may benefit from this message.

The enticing cover of this book and many of the photos of me throughout my journey are a result of the talented Siddiqi Ray. Using her unique "soul portrait" process, she captured my true essence and my joy through her gifted lens.

I applaud each of the brave warriors who agreed to be interviewed for this book. You each revealed the truth of your "gifted trap" experiences so that others could benefit from your stories. My interviews with each of you enriched this work and brought life to philosophical paradigms—shifting them from theory to reality. Thank you for graciously and courageously stepping forward. You are each listed individually with a brief profile in Appendix A.

Rounding the bend to the finish line, I extend my heartfelt appreciation to Melissa Evans for being the link to Mia Redrick, the talented and gifted midwife of this book. Mia, you and your team at Finding Definitions exhibited such patience and support through the process—that itself was an amazing gift to me. You knew when to gently whip me, and always knew how to lovingly guide me to get this done. I might have miscarried along the way had it not been for your steadfast hand. Instead we collaborated to birth a healthy baby. Thank you for recognizing, owning and sharing your gifts with the world.

I cast my net of gratitude also to my support system of loving friends who have traveled this journey with me, reading and editing my drafts, giving honest feedback, holding me in prayer, or wiping my tears every step of the way. If I start to name you individually, I risk leaving someone out and I value each of you way too much to do that. If you are in my circle of friends, you know who you are, because I make a point to tell you regularly how much you mean to me, whether you are around the corner or on another continent. Some of you have known me for a lifetime and others for just a little while—and all of you are cherished treasures in my life. Whether you are part of my Monday morning meet-up group, a Sunday Soul Sister, part of my FedEx virtual office team, or a Dreamer with a True Purpose who is Vocally Aware, spiritually aligned in my community of Grace where we practice yoga and stay IN-Shape—you are part of my chosen family and <u>I love you for loving me</u>.

And finally I thank my now adult children, Brad and Kelsey, who gave my life meaning and purpose to be the best mother...and best person I could be. In my imperfect way I did the best I could with the information I had from the second you were each born. My motivation every step of the way has been my unwavering and unconditional love for the two of you. May the words within this book help you to heal from the inevitable wounding I may have caused, as well as from the PB&J™ (perception, belief and judgment) sandwiches that I may have fed you unknowingly. The greatest gift I was given was to be your mother. You light up my life and bring me unfathomable joy!

FOREWORD

By Arthur Samuel Joseph
Creator of Vocal Awareness

SUPPORTING GIFTED AND TALENTED ARTISTS, ATHLETES, exec-utives, politicians and people from all walks of life to discover and embody all of who they are capable of being is my life's work. Traditionally, our habit is to <u>present</u> who we are, but the goal of Vocal Awareness™ is to enable us to <u>"be"</u> who we are. In everyday conversation, whether we hold our breath or tighten our jaws or tongues, whatever we do to impede ourselves prevents others from truly knowing who we are. All tension, fear, and unconscious behavior also disempowers us. A key Vocal Awareness axiom, "We are not our behaviors," comes to mind.

Most of us believe that we know who we are, and that may be true. We often think that we have defined ourselves, when in fact, we also allow others to define us. We have been named by society—by oth-ers—through our behavioral process. It is simply the way the human condition works. Life imprints itself on us and, all too often, as Anne illustrates within these pages, it traps us.

Language defines us too. As Anne clearly states in this book, and you will learn as you study her marvelous work, the way we speak and interact with one another every day—including the voices within—also define us. Vocal Awareness teaches Mastery through Communication so that we learn to be in charge of the *message* and the *messenger* and *choose* how we want to be known.

So, understanding who you truly are and breaking free from any lim-ited definition of your Self that may exist requires that you be willing to embark on a courageous journey to claim all that is possible.

That journey is never outward toward the achievement of a goal, but always and only inward toward the discovery of the Deeper Self. It is a journey to discover and claim your Persona and then to master Self.

Along the way you will inevitably encounter one or both of the two greatest fears—fear of abandonment and fear of claiming your own greatness.

One of my students, Susan Purnell, emphasized this point eloquently in her interview with Anne as she spoke about an experience she'd had. Just before she was to be ordained as a priest at the hand of a Bishop, she heard a voice within her deliver these words:

"Do not give away what I have given you."

Those very words are the essence of what this book is all about. This book is a call to action to claim your unique giftedness and inherent greatness. That's really what life is about—are you going to claim it or not?

We all invariably fall into the gifted trap, as it is like quicksand in the jungle. We don't see it until we are in it, and then it is too late. Anne will teach you critical skills that lead to *Conscious Awareness* and, ultimately, your ability to extricate your Self from the quagmire of your very existence.

The finding of *your* Voice is a critical step in getting out of that *Gifted Trap*. Finding your voice and having the courage to speak up— even when it may not please others—is getting in touch with your most powerful Self. Tapping into the power of your Voice is an essential element for helping you move out of the entrapped spiritual/emotional state you may have been in.

My experience of Anne is as both a student and friend. I witnessed her as she found her Voice through her process of emerging. She is one of the most courageous people I know, being willing to do the WORK necessary to confront her Self and claim her Voice. I am so honored to write this foreword because it is a privilege to know and teach a woman of such integrity who lives the mind/body/spirit essence of the Work and thus embodies true Mastery.

So my friends, this book is a gift—a true treasure waiting to be revealed. Within its pages, Anne provides access to wisdom that will introduce you to an enlightened world—the fulfillment of possibilities and joy. When you do the Work, you create the opportunity to emerge with the ability to truly embody personal sovereignty at the completion of the journey.

Another basic tenet of Vocal Awareness is that life revolves around two things: *choosing* to do something or *choosing* not to do something. Even in not making a choice, you have effectively chosen. Make the choice to read Anne's book—the choice, in other words, to passionately commit to extricating your Self from the Gifted Trap.

INTRODUCTION

LIKE SO MANY TALENTED PEOPLE, I HAVE BEEN A VICTIM OF the Gifted Trap. It is a widely experienced, yet rarely openly discussed, emotionally uncomfortable existence—an existence that you get lured into unconsciously. Like me, you probably got into this place by default and didn't even know it.

Getting into the trap is an unconscious process. Getting out of it requires conscious awareness. That is what this book is designed to do—awaken and liberate you.

This book represents an opportunity for you to become aware of, and philosophically enlightened about, three of the most powerful influencers in your life—perceptions, beliefs and judgments—and how you have been impacted by them. During my own awakening, I came to refer to them as PB&Js™, and realized that they are, in fact, the very premise of why and how you are either emotionally empowered, or get emotionally trapped.

The amazing "Aha!" during my transformation was that these three influencers form the same acronym as a staple of American childhood diets—peanut butter and jelly sandwiches. While PB&J sandwiches can be a form of nutrition, they can also create a gooey, sticky, mess inside a child's lunchbox. The PB&J influencers, too, can be either yummy or yucky in the lunchbox called life. This realization changed my life.

Just like the sandwich, the influencers have the capacity to either nourish you, or limit you. They can impact you positively or negatively, and the reality is that **if you don't learn to manage them, they will manage you**.

In the pages that follow, we will explore the impact that Perceptions, Beliefs and Judgments have had on my life and the lives of those who generously shared their stories in this book, so that you might benefit and draw parallels in your life.

This conversation and the tools you will be given will illuminate new possibilities for you. The goal is to help you manage how these influencers impact your ability to use your gifts, so you are able to emerge from the trap that limiting PB&Js have lead you into.

So you see, your decision to read this book may well prove to be one of the most pivotal moments of your life.

In reaching this point you may have identified a latent need to make a change in your life—a need to heal something deep inside of yourself or to manage a major shift or crisis occurring in your life. It may be a heartfelt desire to transform the situations and emotions that suppress you. Or perhaps you are going through an emotional transition caused by a change in your circumstances professionally or personally. Often, it is simply an unspoken inner prompting that something is awry.

Whatever the reason, you have made the first courageous step towards throwing off the emotional shackles that prevent you from emerging into the person you are destined to be—the shackles that prevent you from shining as you have always been meant to shine.

Why I Wrote This Book

I have been asked what inspired me to write this book, and I want to share that with you.

The inspiration for this book came as a result of the tragic, premature, and possibly preventable, death of my oldest brother, Augustus Lindsay Palmer Jr., affectionately known as "Little Gus." My brother was an extraordinarily gifted and beautiful soul. After decades of doing emotional calisthenics to live up to expectations, and vainly attempting to discern his true purpose, became overwhelmed by the pressure of life. Like so many, he succumbed to self-sabotaging behavior as a way to numb his emotional pain. He sank deeper and deeper into the whirlpool of debilitating emotions that held him back and prevented him from claiming his full greatness. He neglected his health and abused himself physically until his body rebelled violently. The result: Gus passed away at the young age of 57 after suffering a massive stroke.

He was a victim of the Gifted Trap. His premature departure from this earth has left a void in my life and a need to reach out to other souls who find themselves caught in traps like my brother's.

Living in authentic alignment with the gifts you have been given and honoring all of who you are capable of being is a central theme of this book. The Gifted Trap represents an opportunity for you to become aware of all that life has available to you. You get to make a conscious choice to release yourself from the bondage that so often results from limiting Perceptions, Beliefs and Judgments that hold you back and imprison you emotionally.

> *"When you find that your life is out of alignment with your grandest idea of yourself, seek to change it."*
> **Neale Donald Walsch**

Once I consciously opened my mind to "realize with my real eyes—the eyes of my soul", it became clear to me that emotional entrapment is a state of being for far too many highly gifted and talented adults.

Almost daily I see evidence of people either "playing small to stay safe" or suppressing their feelings of isolation and emptiness. Many people play small to stay safe by underutilizing their talents, thus diminishing their brilliance. At the other end of the spectrum, I find highly successful people hiding behind perfect facades out of fear that admitting to their "sense of isolation" or feeling of not being "good enough" might result in a fall from the high perch of success they have worked so hard to create. In both cases, people's lives are out of alignment with the truth of who they really are. It's a painful existence—a gifted trap. The good news is that there is a way to break free.

It's time to pull back the curtain on this widely experienced, yet rarely openly discussed, state of being that plagues so many people.

It's time to shift narrow-minded perceptions into expansive possibilities. Time to reframe limiting beliefs into empowering beliefs. Time to replace unhealthy judgment with life-enhancing joy.

My ultimate goal and prayer for this book is to liberate people just like you from living under the burden of the Perceptions, Beliefs and Judgments that hold you back in one form or another. This book is for you, whether you are:

- At the top of your game professionally, questioning how good you really are, wondering what's next, and feeling that there must be more; OR

- At the other end of the spectrum, simply playing small to stay safe, wondering if you will ever achieve what you know in your heart you are capable of but have held yourself back; OR

- Transitioning out of a well-supported environment where you were labeled "gifted" as a result of your talent and are embarking on a new frontier where you will have to erect your own scaffolding to support your brilliance; OR

- At a point of desperation, frustrated that you just can't seem to figure out how to use the gifts and talents you have to get what you want out of life.

Whichever of the above scenarios resonates with you, I understand the emotional quicksand you feel you are in. My desire is to cast you a lifeline that will lead you to a more joyful life in which you fully embody your own unique giftedness.

The intention behind this book is to equip you with valuable tools to help you emerge and transition to a vibrant place of wholeness. A place where you are fully healed and at peace with who you are, free from the need to live up to the constricting expectations that have been haunting you—living instead with beliefs that empower you.

In the pages that follow, may you find wisdom in the words and courage from the concepts that will empower you to break free. May you release yourself emotionally from judgment, fully express your giftedness, and claim a more passionate, purposeful life filled with JOY!

You deserve the freedom to just BE YOU—that special you, that real, unique you. And my deepest desire is to awaken you to that new way of being!

There is an amazing transformation available within you when you allow your light to shine without reservation. I hope to awaken you to what is available to you, so that with each new day you embrace and celebrate your light. Today is the dawn of a new day… let it be the dawn of a new way of existing for you.

Take your first steps toward true freedom today as you discover the truth about where you are, decipher the code to unlock your trap door, and take action to EMERGE from your own Gifted Trap so that you will leave your indelible footprint.

My Father's Indelible Footprint…

This book chronicles and highlights episodes in a remarkable journey—one I traveled as the daughter of a legendary Tuskegee Airman, Augustus L. Palmer, Sr.

Daddy, like many of his Redtailed wingmen, lived an extraordinary life. Despite enduring unimaginable judgment during his lifetime, he managed to leave an indelible footprint and set a standard of achievement for the generations that followed him.

What makes this story about my father worth sharing is its relevancy to the theme and basis of this book. He taught me what it means to be gifted, to know that you have been called to use your gifts, to be faced with odds against you, and to still step into your greatness. It is a story of both the challenge and the opportunity that is before each of us. The questions are:

What will you do? Will you answer your call?

When I was growing up, my father would often say to me,

"Do it right, or don't do it at all."

As a Tuskegee Airman, a business executive with high integrity, and a committed husband and father, Daddy exemplified the true meaning of those words. He lived a life of extraordinary faith. He was dedicated to being the best he could be, and gave credit where credit was due—to God.

In case you are unfamiliar with the story of the extraordinary men known as the Tuskegee Airmen, let me share a bit of history about them, as summarized on Wikipedia.

The Tuskegee Airmen were the first African-American military aviators in the United States armed forces. During World War II, African-Americans in many states across the US were still subject to the Jim Crow laws that mandated the segregation of public schools, public places, and public transportation. Restrooms, restaurants and drinking fountains were all segregated – one for whites and one for blacks. The American military was racially segregated, as was much of the federal government. The Tuskegee Airmen were subjected to racial discrimination both within and outside the Army.

Despite these adversities, they trained and flew with distinction. It was reported that no bomber escorted by the Tuskegee Airmen had ever been lost to enemy fire. Yet for decades these men, who had overcome unconscionable ridicule and achieved extraordinary results, went uncelebrated and continued to be subjected to racial injustices at home.

It wasn't until March 29th 2007 that the Tuskegee Airmen were finally collectively awarded a Gold Medal by Congress. It had taken sixty years for the Airmen to be recognized for the incredible contributions they had made in World War II to defend the United States.

On January 8th 2009, I traveled to Washington, D.C. to see my 85-year-old father. He had accepted an invitation to attend the first inauguration of President Barack Obama along with the other surviving Tuskegee Airmen.

Needless to say, being present at the inauguration of America's first African-American President was a long-awaited honor for my father, and his historic wing-buddies.

When I arrived in DC and entered the apartment where my mother and father were living, I found Daddy in a slumped and weakened physical state, requiring immediate hospitalization. Within 24 hours, he was diagnosed as being in a state of advanced cancer. The prognosis was dim and it was recommended that we make him as comfortable as possible by engaging at-home hospice care.

Over the course of the next ten days leading up to the inauguration, Daddy stopped breathing six times and then started breathing again on his own. It was torture for our family to see him struggle and we couldn't understand why he was holding on.

On the morning of the inauguration, instead of witnessing it first-hand from the steps of the Capitol, seated near the newly-elected President Barack Obama, my father lay in his Hospice bed, hanging on to life by a thread as I held his hand. He and I watched the ceremony on television. After the official swearing in, my mother arrived to switch places with me to watch the inaugural parade.

When the final float passed before the White House and the formal inaugural festivities were complete, the United States of America had its first African-American President. A momentous event in American history was imprinted on the hearts and minds of people around the globe—and Daddy had lived to bear witness to it.

Just as that final float passed, my father looked out of the window at the American Flag being buffeted by the breeze, turned his head toward my mother, to whom he had dedicated sixty-two years of his life as a devoted husband...and then shut his eyes and left this Earth.

It was as if he was saying to us, "I'm going to the real Inaugural Ball now—the one in heaven."

At that moment, it was clear as a bell why he had been holding on for those last ten days. My father had lived his life with so many other Tuskegee Airmen in a proverbial gifted trap. They had overcome the most oppressive conditions to achieve greatness. They had served this country honorably in World War II, yet for most of their adult lives they had gone unrecognized for their contributions to our nation's history.

As African-American men they were seen as inferior, were believed to be incapable of flying a plane, and were judged by the color of their skin rather than by their intelligence, integrity and actual ability. It took six decades for them to be publicly honored and celebrated for their gift-edness and accomplishments. What emotional endurance those brave men exemplified!

The day after my father's death, on the President's first day in office, I wrote to President Obama about the dedication of the Tuskegee Airmen and my father's commitment to this country. I shared the story of how he held on to see history made. It was as if the very act of an African-American President being inaugurated validated what he had dedicated his life to. It was confirmation for him that his living had not been in vain. I felt that Daddy would have wanted the President to know how proud he was of his country and of the man who now was the Commander-in-Chief of the highest office in the land.

One week later, on the morning of January 27th, just hours before my father's memorial service was to take place, I received the following letter from the President:

THE WHITE HOUSE

WASHINGTON

January 27, 2009

Ms. Anne Palmer

███████████

█████████████████

Dear Anne:

It is with a heavy heart and a deep sense of gratitude and honor that I offer my condolences and join you in celebrating the life of your father, Augustus L. Palmer. I understand that he passed away on Tuesday and was unable to attend the Inauguration, and so I am especially grateful for the opportunity to extend my appreciation for his legacy of service and sacrifice.

The debt owed to men like your father is immeasurable, and can only hope to be repaid through service on behalf of generations to follow. The Tuskegee Airmen were genuine trail blazers, and I am one of the humble many who stand on their shoulders.

Once again, please accept my sympathies for your loss. When I lost my mother, and most recently my grandmother, I took comfort in knowing that they would stay in my life so long as I remained committed to the values they imbued in me. I hope the same holds true for you. As you honor your father's life, may his memory bring you great joy.

Sincerely,

While the public perception of my father is impressive, and I am indeed proud to share that perspective with you, in my mind the true character of a person is best communicated from the personal perspective of a friend.

Acclaim From A Friend –
Written by Dr. Carolyn Meyers – President, Jackson State University – Jackson, Mississippi

Having known the author Anne Palmer since she was born and having had the privilege of watching her grow into the lovely and brilliant woman she is, writing this preamble for this book is a special honor for me. What's more, I knew her father before she did and adopted him as my Uncle Gus. My memories of him are vivid and wonderful, as Uncle Gus was as much a part of my life as any "real" uncle could have been.

Besides running in and out of their home as a child, I can most vividly remember my father talking about Uncle Gus' family's impending move to Houston, Texas. The two of them had discussed it and my dad agreed that it would be a great opportunity for Uncle Gus. Being a child, I asked my dad why he was sad, if this move was such a great thing. I can still remember his answer: he was losing the physical closeness of a friend. He reassured me that they would always be friends, and they were. Most vivid is the memory of Daddy telling me that one day I would go to many places and meet many people. I should always remember to look for the princes and princesses, both very rare; they were to be treasured. Uncle Gus was a prince among people.

One of my favorite literary pieces is *Return to Love* by Marianne Williamson. It talks about being "...brilliant, gorgeous, talented and fabulous" like Uncle Gus, while reminding the reader of something Uncle Gus never forgot—that he was a "...child of God ... born to manifest the glory of God." This passage describes Uncle Gus, his talents and abiding faith. However, the last two lines of this passage at once portray the impact Uncle Gus and princes like him have on others, as well as the importance of *The Gifted Trap*. Williamson enlightens us that ...

"As we let our own light shine, we unconsciously give other people permission to do the same. As we are liberated from our own fear, our presence automatically liberates others."

So it's no surprise to me that Uncle Gus' daughter Anne would write this lovely book. I just wonder what took her so long. But on reflection, growing up with the "prince" would have been normal to her, and Anne probably thought everyone had the same experiences as she'd had.

The Gifted Trap is needed especially now, in this age when too often in our daily lives mediocrity is the order of the day. As a career educator I see young people who have "it all," so to speak, but lack the courage and encouragement to stretch beyond that which is within their immediate reach. What's more, I encounter erudite faculty who contain themselves and modify their talents to accommodate the limitations of others around them.

The Gifted Trap will afford you, the reader, permission to let your individual light shine, and through this permission you will undoubtedly free others to do the same. We need more princes and princesses!

The Gifted Trap is beautiful, powerful, and needed. Enjoy it!

Let Your Light Shine and Just Trust

The genuine and treasured letter from President Obama, along with the profound and affirming message from my brilliant and beautiful friend Dr. Carolyn Meyers, epitomize what this journey called life is about—*using your gifts to leave a legacy, while finding joy and fulfillment in living a purposeful life.*

My father did just that. I owe him a debt of eternal gratitude for teaching me that most valuable lesson. I wrote, and now share, this book with you with the sincere hope that you take away from our exchange my wish and mantra for you: let your light shine and Just Trust!

Just Trust
by Anne Palmer

Joyfully embrace each day you are given
Up-level your life with blessings and gifts from heaven
Stand in stature with your values all aligned
Tune energy, tighten core to support your spine

Take time to intuit, integrate and listen real deep
Respond to the call after messages have time to steep
Use your Voice as a precious tool to share what you know
Spread love from your heart everywhere that you go
Tuning in to Source for guidance is always a must

To EMERGE from the Trap...and Soar...You Just Trust!

PART ONE:

WAKING UP
IN THE DARK

Waking Up
In The Dark

IT WAS PITCH BLACK…THE MIDDLE OF THE NIGHT.

Suddenly I was jerked awake, gasping like a deep-sea diver whose oxygen had run out, reaching the surface, seeking fresh air, my heart was pounding in my chest. Endless thoughts ran through my head in an incoherent haze. What was happening? Who or what had awakened me? Was there an intruder in the room? The thunder of my pounding heart drowned out every other sound as I struggled to breathe, reaching out helplessly in search of a light.

In my dazed, dark, stupor I felt it, that sensation of hands around my throat, that overwhelming sense of near strangulation. I gasped for air, my breaths coming short and shallow.

"Breathe, Anne, breathe," I told myself, trying desperately to gain a sense of calm.

In the velvet cloak of blackness, the truth of what was happening began to sink in. As I came to grips with the reality that I was alone in that room—that it wasn't an intruder strangling me—I realized with my real eyes (the eyes of my soul) the truth of what was happening.

It was my divine higher power—God—shaking me at my core, urging me to literally wake up, and to understand that the life I was living was not what I had signed up for. I had been given an extraordinary package of talents—my mind, my body and an abundance of gifts— and God expected me to do something more with them.

"To whom much is given, much is expected," had been the mantra in my home growing up. And now it was clear…

There was something more for me to do—
something much more.

In the darkness I heard a voice clearly challenging me:

"Are you going to stay in this place and suffocate, or are you going to stand up, put a stake in the ground, and make the changes necessary for you to do what it was you came here to do?"

And in that darkness I KNEW… it was crystal clear that I had to shine a light on exactly who I was and wake up to where I was. It was a scary night…alone in the dark inside the "Gifted Trap."

That was my very first wake up call—the first of many that would change the course of my life.

"The morning breeze has something to tell you.
Do not go back to sleep." – Rumi

What Is The "Gifted Trap"?

EVEN THOUGH THIS IS THE FIRST YOU HAVE ACTUALLY heard about it, the Gifted Trap is a widely experienced phenomenon.

Like any trap, you cannot begin to move out of it without truly understanding that you are in it. Unlike a hunter's trap that is set with bait and snaps abruptly shut around its prey, the "Gifted Trap" is one that you are seduced and lured into. Over time, the intricate web of bars appears and before you know it you are ensnared, with little understanding of how you got into this space.

As I mentioned in the Introduction to this book, getting into the trap is an unconscious process. Getting out of it requires conscious awareness.

Becoming aware that Perceptions, Beliefs and Judgments (PB&Js™) are common bait that lure you into the trap is fundamental to understanding what the gifted trap is.

Reading about PB&Js throughout this book may conjure up memories of your childhood lunchbox filled with a peanut butter & jelly sandwich made with gooey or crunchy Smucker's peanut butter coupled with sweet, sticky Welch's grape jelly, nestled between two slices of Wonder bread. Yummy memory, right?

For many of you, PB&J sandwiches were a dietary staple of your childhood, as they were for me. You grew up, consuming those symbols of parental love in your lunchboxes and probably have fond, positive memories of those experiences. While those PB&Js were filling your belly, other invisible PB&Js fed your emotional diet as well.

The PB&Js that were a staple of your emotional diet as a child were perceptions, beliefs and judgment that you were exposed to by your family, and your environment. They served a purpose. Just like the sand-wiches fed and fueled your body, the other PB&Js fed your psyche and were cornerstones for the development of your emotional foundation. How you were perceived, what you believe, and how well you discern and form judgments all began in your formative years and became the basis for how you show up in the world today.

Positive perceptions, affirming beliefs, and virtuous ethical judg-ment were, and are beneficial to you. They help you to discern and understand the world you exist in and determine what will serve you well in your life. As both food and fuel, they nourish your emotional health and well-being.

That is a perspective on PB&Js that is absolutely true. There is, how-ever, another perspective that has equal merit and truth that is the basis for the conversations we will have together in this book.

The other perspective on PB&Js is that negative, narrow-minded perceptions; disempowering, limiting beliefs; and rotten, restrictive judgment are detrimental to you. They inhibit you from moving freely in the world you exist in. Like sewage that has been deposited inside an enclosed bin for a long time, these other PB&Js may well have left indelible "smelly scars" in your mind unconsciously. These confining PB&Js are the bait that lures you into the Gifted Trap. They may be self-imposed or societally-imposed—and either way, they keep you emotionally enslaved and imprisoned within "The Trap."

We will delve into the concept of PB&Js in greater detail a little later in the book. For now, let's get more clarity about another impor-tant premise of this book: the concept of being gifted.

Everyone possesses a quality or qualities that make you unique—qualities that are special to you and differentiate you from others. For some, it is crystal clear; for others, the water is muddy or murky and you aren't quite sure. The degree to which you are clear about your giftedness may well be a direct result of how the PB&Js have impacted your life.

In writing this book, I had the pleasure of interviewing former football cornerback Troy Vincent, who since retiring from playing professionally advanced off the field to become the NFL Senior Vice

President for Player Engagement. I asked Troy in our interview about when he first knew he was talented. His answer speaks volumes about how PB&Js can positively influence your life:

> *My mother, grandmother and grandfather would always say, "You're beautiful, you're an artist," and I believed them...they spoke life into me, and they made life believable. They made my gifts and talents believable. So as I transitioned from elementary to middle to high school into college there always was a sense or a voice of "How great I am" and "What a special talent" I was. I always remember Grandma saying, "When God made you, he made something special." Those times and those voices—I always go back to the voices—it was just a constant reminder of who I am. My purpose is about recognizing—and more importantly, maximizing—my gifts and talents. I would say that throughout my entire life's journey there was a constant voice, that sweet voice of who I am...*

So in the case of Troy, the PB&Js served him, reinforced for him, and helped him to know how gifted he was. He was perceived as being talented. His family believed and caused him to believe that he had special abilities.

Throughout the book I will share excerpts from Troy's interview and the interviews of others to illustrate the correlation between your gifts and the impact of PB&Js on your awareness and self-actualization of your giftedness.

My father and his Tuskegee brothers were able to use the racially limiting Perceptions, Beliefs and Judgments of the time in a healthy way as fuel to empower them to become the best they could be—as motivation to achieve excellence.

There are many variables that come into play and determine the degree to which you: (1) become aware of your gifts and (2) have the environment and circumstances to support you in cultivating your gifts. Too often you are either unaware of your gifts, or have environmental circumstances that do not nurture your giftedness.

Therein lies the dilemma and the challenge to claim your greatness, even when circumstances or Perceptions, Beliefs and Judgments may have caused you to fall into the abyss. There is a disconnect that is created because deep inside you know that you were created for a reason and that you have the gifts to fulfill your purpose.

There is a space of disconnection between what you know intuitively that you are capable of, and how you feel emotionally about your ability to fully live into and up to what you are capable of. That space is called The Gifted Trap!

How Does It Feel to Be in the Gifted Trap?

So you might be wondering what it feels like to be in the trap?

Allow me to paint a picture for you of how it feels. Imagine that you are trapped in a prison cell, held securely behind solid metal bars, with no chance of escape. Take some time to visualize that situation now. Spend a few moments immersing yourself in that reality.

Can you sense the dankness of the prison walls? Do you feel the penetrating chill of the cell bars as you grasp them tightly in your hands, the bars that restrict your ability to move freely?

Perhaps you can even see through those bars to a life and freedom you yearn to have. You watch wistfully as people pass by in the distance. Outside the trap they inhabit that utopia that exists only in your dreams.

You know that if you could only reach beyond those bars and unshackle those chains you would be free—free to pursue a life lived true to yourself—but for some reason you can't. You are trapped, emotionally paralyzed, stuck and unable to move forward.

Now look at the people passing you by who are looking in at you. What do they see? They don't see your cage. Your bars are visible only to you.

Perhaps they see an intelligent, beautiful person who they believe has everything in life. Perhaps they see someone who is a reliable and trusted friend who seems capable, in control and apparently content with his or her lot in life.

You may be a multi-talented, multi-gifted high-achiever with the world seemingly at your feet. You may, on the other hand, be wondering how you are ever going to make your way out of the situation you find yourself in to claim the personal fulfillment you are seeking.

Perhaps your reality as you see you contradicts what the rest of the world sees. You are drained, listless and void of emotion. You are empty inside and long to feel whole. Yet you just don't know how.

You, my friend, are in the Gifted Trap. That's the bad news. The good news is that I'm here to tell you…there is a way out!

Emotional Entrapment – Stuck in Quicksand

Many people are highly gifted, yet within them lies an insurmountable emotional void—an abyss within their soul. It's hidden so deep that it often goes unacknowledged. It festers inside until it becomes a sense of despair and feeling lost. Without an adequate outlet or focus that is aligned with innate talents, emotions become entangled and one's whole outlook is dominated by an indefinable sense of malaise. It is then that general feelings of discontent and unhappiness take over.

Before long, you become caught in a self-imposed or societally-imposed emotional trap. You've been lured into that trapped space I described earlier. Then you notice that the ground beneath you is not firm. Rather, it is like quicksand—emotional quicksand sucking you in and pulling you deeper into the abyss. No matter how hard you try, you can't find a way out of the trap. You can't seem to find the emotional equilibrium you long for.

Emotional entrapment is a subconscious feeling deep inside of you. It is that place of feeling disconnected and insecure. It is also a place of fear, where your focus is on what you lack rather than on gratitude for what you have. You become so focused on what you don't have that it is impossible to see what you do have.

When you're in that place of emotional entrapment, the metaphorical magnifying glass that examines the minutiae of your life identifies only what is wrong, with little regard for the good—in effect dispensing with the positive. It is important to note something positive always exists to focus on. Unfortunately, from inside the trap the default lens is negative and cloudy.

If you find yourself focusing on a "deep rooted longing for something" beyond your current experiences that seems unattainable rather than focusing on the positives in your life, you are emotionally entrapped. A deep entrenchment in emotional entrapment leads to confusion, dissatisfaction and a diminishing sense of joy.

You are quite literally out of alignment with yourself.

How Do You Know You're Entrapped?

I recently came across a startling statistic, quoted by Joel Osteen, the revered American author and televangelist, that puts this situation into perspective. According to Joel, a **startling seven out of ten people that you will encounter every day are unhappy, and it's possible that the true figures are even higher than that**. I believe that this unhappiness is symptomatic of an underlying emotional entrapment that is prevalent in our society.

With staggering statistics like 70%, there is a strong probability that at some point you have experienced, or are experiencing emotional entrapment yourself.

To understand what emotional entrapment is, you need to first have your own working definition of what joy is. That will give you a framework or point of reference to compare and contrast emotional entrapment against.

What Is Joy?

Joy is a state of great happiness, delight and/or pleasure. Hopefully, we all know what it feels like to be joyful. Joy fills us with a sense of energy and power, a certainty that we can conquer anything, no matter what life throws in our path. It brings with it an optimism that is infectious and we yearn to share it with the world.

While writing this book I interviewed one of my mentors, executive coach and organizational healer Erline Belton. Here, Erline emphasizes the importance of joy and how easy it is to lose it when we are caught up in the Gifted Trap:

> *A fundamental element to moving yourself out of the Gifted Trap is to be able to laugh at yourself, have fun and commit to bringing joy into your life. So many people aren't having fun anymore. There's no laughter or joy. There's only that need to be perfect. The childlike qualities all get lost in the mix. When we play we bring out the best in ourselves, and when we try to be perfect we're not playing because the creative part of ourselves is caught up in the quest for perfection. Playing, laughter, and joy are really important parts of moving into another space that allows the person to be more than just a grown-up.*

Joy Is Elusive in the Gifted Trap

Emotional entrapment, on the other hand, presents itself as a feeling of being unbalanced and off-center. It thrives in, and feeds on, darkness, dominated by unidentified lingering shadows just waiting to take hold of you.

When you're caught in emotional entrapment, your whole life becomes a permanent roller coaster ride. You imagine being hauled to the top and have no idea what's awaiting you in your descent back down to the bottom or what the ride will be like to get there. It could be joyful, it may be traumatic—but either way, you feel like you have no control, no sense of what it is going to be.

Emotional entrapment is exactly like that; you have no idea of what will happen next, no focal point, no center, no grounding. Yet the shadows are omnipresent, lingering, waiting to catch you off guard, filling you with doubt, question marks and perhaps even fear.

This state of feeling utterly lost in the shadows, wandering along a path in the dark, unable to distinguish between shapes and figures and not knowing which direction to take or where your next steps will lead you…

is emotional entrapment, my friend.

In emotional entrapment you are out of alignment. To clarify this further, let's use the analogy of a car.

When the wheels of your car are out of alignment and you take your hands off the steering wheel, it will veer off course. When the car needs an oil change, lubrication and filter, it is sluggish and doesn't run very well.

Emotional entrapment is a lot like a car in disrepair. It is that place where you can't seem to align the wheels of your life. You need an oil change, a filter change and some good lubrication to get spark back in your life. Staying on your path takes effort. This is what emotional entrapment feels like.

Can you relate?

The Shadows Within Us

We all have some darkness lurking inside of us, in the deepest recesses of our soul. Those shadows are the result of the PB&Js – the Perceptions, Beliefs and Judgments. We'll look at those in more detail later, but these PB&Js lurk in two forms, those imposed by society and those of our very own making.

PB&Js are responsible for our sense that whatever we do will <u>not be good enough</u>, keeping us caught up in that delicate balance of always <u>striving for perfection and excellence to satisfy others</u>. They promote an overall sense of <u>unworthiness</u>, a feeling that you have failed to meet standards that have been set either by you yourself or by the world in which you exist.

It is frustrating to know that you have what it takes to live a joyful balanced life, yet you lack the ability to make it happen. It's like grasping for something that you can't reach. You know what you need to do and have all the pieces of the jigsaw puzzle there in front of you, yet you can't assemble them to create the picture of your life the way you would like it to be.

In the midst of what you consider to be your failures and shortcomings, you are caught in a paradox. On the one hand you feel you are capable and worthy of joy and happiness. On the other hand there is a cloud of doubt, those shadows that linger in the back of your mind, always haunting you.

You feel as if you are in a perpetual game, a game that resembles a mental tug-of-war. Neither side is willing to concede, leaving you in a constant battle with yourself—you are quite simply exhausted.

Allow me to share my own experience of emotional entrapment.

Total Package…Triple Threat

I have been blessed with what some refer to as the "Total Package." I have been gifted with:

- *Beauty* (physical attractiveness);
- *Brains* (an ability to think on my feet and communicate with clarity); and
- *Brilliance* (creativity, charisma, and compassion to boot).

On top of that I am domestic, athletic, maternal, yet powerful. All this seems to be such a generous blessing, RIGHT? But it ain't necessarily so!

This "Total Package" is perceived by many as a "triple threat," and as a shamanic astrologist once told me, "All too frequently, your atomic bomb intimidates people."

The most visible gift I have is the blessing of beauty—being physically attractive. No doubt you are aware of, and at some point have experienced for yourself, what happens when an attractive woman or handsome man walks into a room.

One of two perceptions are formed. Half the people in the room will gasp and admire his or her beauty. The other half will be intimidated by it. Some people's reactions border on disdain with a "Who does she, or he, think she or he is?" response to a gift that was naturally bestowed at birth.

Reactions, whether positive or negative, are typical examples of PB&Js—Perceptions, Beliefs and Judgments.

The interesting thing to note is that whatever the crowd's reaction is, there is absolutely nothing that the beautiful or handsome person can do about it. It is a reaction to him or her that is rooted in where each individual person is coming from. In other words, if you happen to be the one walking into the room—the handsome or beautiful one—you need to know that what is happening in the minds of others who are sizing you up and judging you before you even open your mouth has NOTHING to do with YOU. It's their "stuff," in their heads, to manage…not yours.

I shared this perspective about how people respond to an attractive person because I possess that gift and have lived it first-hand. I share this not to be arrogant and impress you, but to emphasize an important point. In fact, because of the gift of beauty, I spent many years of my life altering who I was to make other people feel more comfortable around me. I expended so much emotional energy doing mental gymnastics, thinking there was something I needed to do to me to get other people to accept me for who I really was.

Does that sound crazy? Well, it is the truth. Those mental gymnastics are symbolic of, and the essence of, what happens within the mind of someone who is wrestling with emotional entrapment.

You see, I felt that if I dressed and presented myself in a way that played down my physical attributes, I would be perceived by others as less threatening and therefore more approachable or likeable.

Often I would pull my hair back severely in a chignon rather than wearing it down. Rather than choose clothes to flatter my body, I purchased conservative loose-fitting styles. I've been told that my legs are one of my strongest attributes, but I would often wear pants instead of skirts to play that attribute down (for the sake of women, as much as for men). The women would be jealous; the men would be lustful. I couldn't win either way.

Yet in doing that I was doing myself a disservice. I was underplaying my gifts—being "less than" who I had been designed to be. In effect, I was rejecting the blessings that I had been given by God.

This was a form of emotional entrapment for me, and it's a fundamental emotional challenge that attractive, intelligent women and handsome, smart men around the world experience on a daily basis as a result of those gifts.

I was trying to be something that I wasn't to fit in, to be accepted and loved—not for who I was, but for a diminished image of myself. I worked hard to alter my natural gifts in order to be perceived as more ordinary and approachable.

Another of my gifts is my vision and intuitive sight. I am blessed with the ability to visualize great potential in a situation. When I see what is possible to make things better, I can't resist the urge to take action and "fix it." I am inspired and driven to transform the ordinary into something extraordinary.

However, in my excitement, I sometimes forget that others don't always see the situation from my point of view—and often they simply don't see possibilities at all. Consequently, my enthusiasm, my optimism, my incredible zest for life and my desire to make situations as good as they can possibly be may be perceived by others as me trying to take control.

Can I get a witness on this? Do you get accused of being "the General," that take-charge person who can see how to get things done and just wants to do it? Whew! Yes, I knew there were more of me out there in the world! Thank you for not leaving me out here all alone.

However, in the process of trying to effect positive change, sometimes the waters become muddied. You may attract negative comments from colleagues, family, friends and finish in a "Catch-22" situation. If you go ahead and utilize your gifts and talents, your way might be hampered by people who are threatened by your "take charge" presence and ability. Because they are coming from a place of feeling threatened by you, others do things to sabotage your goals, whether consciously or subconsciously. They find a way to cut you off and shut you out!

If you are nodding in agreement, you get this and now know that you are not alone.

Carole Martin Wright[1], currently working as a senior consultant, was previously a VP of information systems with a Fortune 100 company. Carole recalls *"playing concert-level repertoire on the piano at the age of 14"* and *"a life filled with fast grocery lanes and green traffic lights,"* yet she sensed resentment from the people around her because of her natural gifts and abilities.

> *"Some were resentful and felt I had an unfair advantage because of my reasoning abilities. I remember as a young student in class where I had the highest results on the board, one girl said in disgust 'I'm going to drop out until she's through with school.' The professor was sensitive enough not to announce the results in the class after that."*
>
> *"Similar things happened in the workplace as I advanced professionally. I have a very polarizing personality. Some people are really glad to know me, have a relationship with me, and see me as a 'poster child' for what we should be doing, and some others think I have an unfair advantage."*

Carole is not alone in experiencing this phenomenon. Successful executive Natasha Phoenix found herself isolated and alienated by her boss, who was threatened by Natasha's brilliance. Natasha says:

> *"It's happened a couple of times. In this particular circumstance, this person came in who was out to prove himself. He had a military background. Sometimes people emerge from the military with the right lessons. They learn about leadership and camaraderie. If I were a colonel,*

---

1   Carole Martin Wright and Natasha Phoenix are both pseudonyms at the request of the interviewees.

I would get nothing done without my team. On the other hand, some have a very direct style. They are used to people doing as they are told. In these instances, if people have their own ideas, it can be seen as a challenge to their authority, and that was what happened in this particular case. I had a very high profile within my province and I think he perceived this as a threat. As a leader I appreciate people challenging and questioning me, but not everyone treats it the same way. That was the most adversarial that I've ever seen it, and I do attribute it to his military background.

"Interestingly enough, that wasn't an isolated, rare thing to see. I've sadly run into that with women in executive positions who don't promote each other. I've typically run into situations where you have women above you, or your peers who challenge you on that level."

I also spoke at length with Melissa Evans, who enjoyed a soaring career in corporate America, being appointed to the role of director at the age of 24 and venturing out into her own business to become a millionaire by the age of 31. Yet in the following excerpt from my interview with Melissa she reveals how she was forced to suppress her giftedness in order to enable others around her to feel comfortable. Melissa is candid in talking about how she dealt with her emotional dilemma, knowing that she had so much to give but feeling pressured to dilute it to make the rest of the business world comfortable.

"I felt like a fake. I was growing fast in that industry. I'd attend conferences and make speeches. I would always feel I was using my gift, but it was so underutilized for my life purpose. I suffered inside because I knew that I had a responsibility, from a spiritual perspective, to be the best I could possibly be. I felt that if my parents could come this far, I could go that much further. I had that responsibility, but I had to follow the rules of the game, which were rooted in settling for mediocrity.

The feeling that she was in a "less than" place encouraged Melissa to find a way of using her gifts:

"I eventually set up my own business. The rule in the corporate world is either you don't break out or, if you do, you're a target. I only had one brilliant relationship with a woman who was my manager. Often times, men were easier to work with because they were less intimidated. I would be giving a speech for a client and my own colleagues would want to attack me with questions in an attempt to discredit me, while I was serving the client. That happened more than once."

You are not alone, but where does this leave you, the one with the vision to make the world better? You are out on the limb on your own.

This is an example of the emotional entrapment and alienation that sometimes comes with being gifted with "vision and intuitive knowing".

Emotional entrapment often yields a sense of isolation, leaving its victims in a state of confusion. One moment you feel you know who you are, and you celebrate your gifts. In the next moment, you feel that the world shuns your gifts and you are alone, an outcast, thrown off balance by the very gifts intended to bring joy to others and to you.

There you are, the victim of your giftedness, **misunderstood and isolated**.

Manifestations of Emotional Entrapment

As outlined above, emotional entrapment often stems from how the world reacts to your giftedness and how you in turn respond emotionally to those reactions. Deciding how you choose to respond to the reactions is the pivotal point at which entrapment begins to manifest. It can occur as a result of any type of gift you possess and it starts developing its roots often at early ages. A childhood story about my son illustrates this point very effectively.

My son is a gifted and handsome young man. He is personable, charismatic, athletic, smart—all around "gifted," and not because he's my son. (Although of course I would feel that way!) He possesses an abundance of natural gifts, which I've always encouraged him to appreciate, develop and use to the fullest.

When he was around 10 years old, our family moved to a new community. As a way of helping him adjust and meet friends quickly, I signed him up for Little League baseball. It was his first experience of playing the sport in a competitive way. Before long, he discovered he truly had natural ability and was darn good at it. With encouragement, he gave it his all. He practiced relentlessly, learning how to be a big hitter and acquiring the skills that would enable him to play at the top of his game in multiple positions.

Like so many young boys, he was passionate about being the "best" and set his sights on making the All-Star team at the end of the season. He dedicated his every available minute to learn every necessary skill to earn that distinction. He worked on perfecting his natural talent, allowing his athleticism and ability to shine through. By the end of that season he was one of the best baseball players on that team, and by all accounts was poised for being selected for the All-Star team.

Despite being the best player on the team (again, I'm not just saying this because I'm his mom), the coach didn't select him for the All-Star team. He was devastated... and so were his father and I.

When I approached the coach, what I came to find out further exacerbated the situation. The reason the coach gave for my son's ineligibility was that the coach had assumed that my son was too old for the team simply because he was tall for his age. The coach based this assumption on my son's height, never for one moment taking the time to ask. It was exactly that—an assumption—that he used as an excuse for not having selected him for the team. By the way, interestingly enough, the coach's own son made the team with skills that were less than All-Star quality.

I share this story as a perfect illustration of how the Gifted Trap snaps shut because of the sometimes unfair perceptions of others and their reaction to your giftedness. ***Life is not always fair.***

My son's gift wasn't "recognized," and in fact he was actually penalized for being too good. This "too good thing" is a concept we will explore in more detail later. His shining talent and gift—a natural ability to excel at a sport he loved and played with passion—was not acknowledged, respected, or honored.

I can't emphasize enough the indelible mark that incident—that cavalier and careless decision on the part of the coach—had on my son. To my knowledge, my son has never again picked up a baseball bat.

This is a classic example of the ***potential consequences that limiting Perceptions, Beliefs and Judgments of other people can cause that lead to emotional entrapment.***

Misguided PB&Js play out on professional playgrounds and playing fields daily. How often have you seen this in your professional lives, where you strive to acquire all of the skills necessary to showcase your gifts, only to be overlooked at the final hurdle? In Chapter VI you'll find an example of my own personal experience of just that.

As you will see, it is the limiting Perceptions, Beliefs and Judgments that lead you into and bind you in emotional entrapment. PB&Js are often both self-imposed and societally-imposed.

Symptoms of Emotional Entrapment

It is a frequent phenomenon for a victim of the Gifted Trap to reach a point when emotional exhaustion takes over. When you succumb to a combination of self-imposed and societally-imposed limiting perceptions and judgments, you begin to hold yourself back in an effort to protect yourself from feeling rejection or pain.

- ***Why Bother?*** – You begin to ask yourself "Why am I putting myself through this again?" You already know the outcome based on your previous experience and your heart sinks in anticipation of the emotional battle ahead.

- ***Am I Good Enough?*** – Another classic symptom of emotional entrapment is that question you repeat to yourself over and over again that epitomizes self-doubt: "Am I good enough?" or "Will I ever be good enough?" The irony is that from the perspective of the people around you, you may actually appear to be "too good." We will examine that side of the coin fully in Chapter VI.

- ***What Makes You Think You Can?*** – "What makes you think you can do that?" Additional aspects of the Gifted Trap are the various facets of your inner self that play a role in your individual decision-making process. The Doubter in you is emotionally battered by your emotional entrapment and the negative Perceptions, Beliefs and Judgments that constantly bewilder you. The Protector will respond defensively, reminding you that you don't need to prove yourself, you don't need to step out into the firing line again with a target on your back. "Stay below the radar this time," it whispers. "You don't deserve that judgment." Although well-meaning, the Protector will hold you back in an attempt to keep you safe.

- ***Gifted Looks Easy… But It Takes Effort*** – It is an interesting irony that "gifted" often shows up and looks effortless to the rest of the world. Yet managing giftedness in the maze of your individual emotional entrapment takes a high degree of emotional energy. The rest of the world takes it for granted how much effort goes into you showing up as "gifted."

Breaking Free Is Hard to Do

To the rest of the world, I appeared to be living the "perfect" life. Not only did the outside world hold that perception, but despite my acute unhappiness, I was participating fully in that perception as well. However, if I was ever to achieve true happiness for myself, I had to wake up and fully acknowledge the state I was in with regard to my life.

The most difficult reality to accept was that I had played a significant part in creating my situation. I had played into the PB&Js—both the good ones and the bad ones. In response to the PB&Js that I had experienced, I modified and adjusted myself until I was barely recognizable to me. I no longer knew who the authentic Anne was.

In that dark place of not being true to me, I finally understood that I had altered and adjusted myself, and my psyche, so many times in so many ways. I had contorted myself into an emotionally and physically unhealthy state. So there I was, trapped in an unhealthy marriage, in an emotionally lonely existence, allowing parts of my psyche to run my life, hold me back, and limit me. (We will discuss that in more detail in the chapter on Voices.)

As I began to awaken with the help of my behavioral therapist, Dr. Bob, who understood the mental manipulation and havoc that my psyche had reaped, I became aware that I was allowing behavioral patterns I had established as a child to govern my life as a grown-up. Later in my process of emerging I learned to recognize the behavior patterns that with the help of my "internal parts" were created as defense mechanisms as a way to protect me.

Many of you will identify with my predicament. As a child, the word "NO" was very familiar to me. I was part of a very large family. My parents were juggling the needs of so many children, and often out of concern for my safety or because of family responsibilities that were assigned to me as the oldest girl, they would not allow me to hang out with my friends. In my parents' defense, their "NO" was usually because they needed my help with chores, to look out for my younger siblings, or to do things for my grandfather.

The "NOs," however, became so common that I reached a point where I simply didn't ask. Assuming I knew already that the answer would be "NO," I stopped asking for what I wanted.

This pattern continued throughout my teenage years. When I was invited to sleepovers and parties—the typical teenage social events—rather than ask for my parents' permission, I made up excuses to tell my friends as reasons for my absence. It hurt too much to be told NO.

Let's fast-forward two decades ahead when I began to recognize that the same behavior pattern of "not asking for what I wanted" was showing up in my marriage. I had simply stopped considering my own passions and desires within my marriage. I stopped asking for things that would allow full expression of my talents and bring me joy. My husband's desires and vision for our life together took precedence over mine. Every ounce of my energy was poured into his vision, and I became numb to what I needed for myself. I stopped dreaming about what would make me happy. The echoes of the parental "NOs" in response to my childhood requests permeated my adult life—creating an enormous emotional abyss.

Accepting the part I had played in this "life conspiracy" was the biggest challenge of all for me. Deep inside I knew it had not been my parents' intent to saddle me with this limiting behavior pattern. It was a way of being I had embraced on my own. Faced with the seemingly insurmountable truth of where I was, juxtaposed against where I wanted to be, I crumbled. How had I gotten here? What did it all mean? How could I begin to turn my life around?

Emotionally, I shut myself down. My horror at the reality of my life deepened and was unfortunately reinforced by my husband. When I shared how depressed I was, he simply informed me that this problem was mine to deal with.

He explained that he was happy…the kids were fine…and this life worked for everyone but me, so (in his words) "You go figure it out!"

There I was, left on my own to figure it out for myself…alone.

In the midst of that solitude, the acceptance process began. I began meditating, writing and journaling in an effort to *tune into the truth within me—the truth that was longing to express itself.*

As I tuned into that truth, one phrase emanated from the darkness, penetrating it clearly—shining through like a bright spotlight:

"To whom much is given, much is expected."

I understood with crystal-clear clarity that the PB&Js—the narrow-minded perceptions, limiting beliefs and unhealthy judgments that were running my life—had the potential to be reframed. They could be shifted into expansive possibilities, empowering beliefs and life-enhancing joy if I was willing to do what it took to emerge from the Gifted Trap I was in.

I woke up and realized that to emerge in authentic alignment, I would have to totally dismantle what had taken all of my adult life up to that point to build. My decision to change for my own well-being would impact not only me, but in the process, my whole family. After years of altering myself in response to limiting PB&Js, I would now have to open myself up to even more challenging Perceptions, Beliefs and Judgments: ridicule, scorn, and even contempt.

Like many women, my number one desire was to be a good mother. In making this life-changing decision to be true to myself, I had to acknowledge that I could potentially be demolishing that other vital piece of who I was, or who I had always strived to be, the "perfect mom." At the end of this section, I have included a poem that I channeled through my divine power—or Source—during a dream, which communicates the love I feel as a mom.

Somewhere in the midst of these conflicting emotions and desires I made the conscious choice to stand firm. Building my life as it existed at that point had taken two decades—twenty years of building something that I was now admitting to myself was fundamentally dysfunctional. Despite my inherent inclination to put everyone else's needs before my own, for the first time in my entire life I was making myself—my emotional health and well-being—a priority. I realized that at the end of each day, I had to live with me. It was time for me to honor myself. I couldn't remain in that trap knowing that the life I was masquerading in wasn't authentic.

> *The stakes were enormously high, and I chose the path of being true to me, fully acknowledging the potential ramifications of such a huge decision.*

At this point, some of you may be reflecting on just how long it has taken you to reach the point where you are. Some of you may be evaluating how long the journey ahead of you might take to get where you want to be. It might seem so massive that you choose to turn away and remain where you are, "comfortably uncomfortable." And if that is your choice, I pass no judgment.

If on the other hand, however, you are committed to living a "no regrets" life, I encourage you to put a stake in the ground and claim your greatness. I want to be fully transparent and share with you that it most probably will not be an easy road (at least not at first). But I urge you to stay the course, look around you for the inevitable lifelines available to you, and embrace them. They will enable you to emerge from your emotional entrapment. On the other side of the process lies a golden state of being called … Authentic Alignment.

VISION THESE WORDS

by Anne Palmer

Only a mother could possibly know
What it means to have you stand always beside and show
What unconditional love means and is
It comes from the heart—shows outwardly as
smiles & sometimes as tears
I've been blessed to feel it—this love of which I speak
The kind of love that we search for and seek
A love so deep it can traverse oceans & miles
It supports you through life's troubles and trials
Whenever things go a bit awry, it's of you I first think
Knowing your love can be there as fast as I can wink or blink
No matter the distance, whether near or far
Physical distance matters not, for wherever I am… you are
Your heart is always packed to take flight if need be
To offer support, be an anchor and hold lil' ol' me

You Are Gifted

As I stated earlier, a foundational principle in this discussion is that everyone is gifted in some way. Everyone possesses a gift, a talent that is unique to you that makes you special.

If you are reading this and beginning to wonder where your giftedness lies, or are feeling like you have no gifts at all, I want to reassure you. You **ARE** gifted!

Let's explore in more detail what it means to be gifted.

Giftedness Defined

According to dictionary definitions, giftedness means:
- being endowed with great natural ability, intelligence or talent
- revealing special talents.[2]

I also want to share with you two different perspectives of giftedness, first from Dr. Cherie Clark, whose pioneering efforts led to the design of revolutionary transformational learning environments called Total Learning Environments™ in prisons and in drug treatment programs.

Dr. Clark's career has been built on teaching people <u>how</u> to think, not <u>what</u> to think. She signs every email with the Albert Einstein quote as follows:

"Everyone is a genius. But if you judge a fish on its ability to climb a tree, it will live its whole life believing that it is stupid."

In my interview with Dr Clark, she shared her perspective on giftedness:

---

2   Taken from www.thefreedictionary.com

*"My favorite philosophy is one I learned from one of my mentors, R. Buckminster Fuller, who discovered the principles he named '**synergetics.**' Fuller states and believed that 'every person is born a genius, designed by that greater-than-us power with all they need to succeed, to prosper and to grow. Over the course of growing up we get de-geniused' by experiences and well-meaning adults around us. So we have some myths that are beliefs in our culture that say mistakes are wrong, that they are something you should be ashamed of."*

The second perspective comes from Marie Guthrie, CEO of The Legacy Track, an organization that develops consciousness strategies for business leaders in both small and large companies. Here, Marie shares her own view of what giftedness is:

*"Here's what I know to be true. Each of us has an '**Inner Genius**' and it is what our soul came to do on this planet. Yes, we have all of these other talents. We may be smart, artistic, athletic, whatever our gift is, but true giftedness occurs when we can take those wonderful abilities that we have and align them with our soul's contribution and desire. We then allow our 'Inner Genius' to come forth into this world. That's what giftedness means. How do we put all of this together and serve the greater good? That's giftedness, that's inner beauty, that's genius."*

Everyone Has Genius Within

Part of being trapped in the Gifted Trap is our confusion over what our gift is. You may be multi-talented, but to escape the Gifted Trap you need to specialize in that one area where you are uniquely blessed.

To help you to better understand how to tap into your giftedness, we provided the quote below from Rocamora School:

"Even if you have doubts about the extent of your giftedness, you will really bring your talents to life if you will embrace your drive to become, serve, create, achieve, and contribute. Self-recognition is not to fuel egotism or elitism, but to align with a more powerful, creative part of you that will let your heart, your knowledge, your talent loose on the world."

On its website, which is included in the Resources section in the back of this book, you will find access to a test you can take to determine your own talents and giftedness.

Another resource in the back is a link for *The Passion Test* (taken from the book of the same name written by Janet Bray Attwood and Chris Atwood). I hope you will find it useful in defining your own giftedness. Additionally, later in this book you will have an opportunity to do some self-excavation exercises that I offer to help you identify your gifts.

Gifted Children Grow Up

Giftedness in children, of course, is defined differently.

This federal definition is taken from the Javits Act[3], which provides grants for education programs serving bright children from low-income families:

"The term gifted and talented student means children and youths who give evidence of higher performance capability in such areas as intellectual, creative, artistic, or leadership capacity, or in specific academic fields, and who require services or activities not ordinarily provided by the schools in order to develop such capabilities fully."

We have seen how Carole Martin-Wright's giftedness affected her during her school years, and in the introduction to this book I also referred to my brother.

Growing up he was extraordinarily talented, bright and articulate, yet the challenge for him was which gift to focus on and develop to

---

3   http://www.nagc.org/index.aspx?id=572

become what he was meant to be in the world as an adult. He had the added burden of being the oldest son of a Tuskegee Airman. And he even had the weight of being a "Junior," bearing the same name as his accomplished father. Consequently, he went around in circles trying to satisfy his many different talents. Trying so hard to be "**all things to all people,**" he never developed the one talent that would enable him to step out of the Gifted Trap.

Don't allow that to happen to you.

Giftedness takes many different shapes and forms—some that are common and easy to identify and others that manifest in unlikely situations. The clearest way to define giftedness is to give you examples. I will start with the more blatant ones and then reveal others that are less obvious.

Identifying Gateway Gifts

Gateway gifts are those attributes that allow your individual light to shine the brightest—your individual gifts that are the very bridge and gateway to great opportunities in life. We find instances of talented and very gifted people in almost every arena. To put giftedness in perspective, I've identified some extraordinary examples of gateway gifts.

The Gift of Athleticism

In the world of sports, the most gifted athletes strive to master their athletic ability and compete in world-class events such as the Olympic Games or professional tournaments like the Super Bowl, the Masters, the US Open or Wimbledon, to name a few. As examples I cite Olympians like U.S. gymnasts Jordyn Wieber and Aly Raisman, Victoria Komova (Russian gymnast), Michael Phelps (U.S. swimmer), Bruce Jenner (U.S. decathaloner), Usain Bolt (Jamaican sprinter), Kim Yu-Na (South Korean figure skater), and ground-breaking U.S. tennis phenoms Venus and Serena Williams.

The Gift of Intelligence

Mastering the use of the mind or intellect—having the ability to think, articulate and provide perspective—is indeed a gift. Intellectual gifts are of tremendous value throughout the world. We find outstanding examples of intellectual talent in extraordinary people such, as former U.S. Secretary of State Hillary Clinton, South African social activist Desmond Tutu, television host and entrepreneur Oprah Winfrey, U.S. Supreme Court Justice Sonia Sotomayor, and the world famous spiritual leader Deepak Chopra.

We can expand the intellectual microscope to include the fields of science, medicine and chemistry where we find the great minds of 2012 Nobel Laureates in Physics Serge Haroche and David J, Wineland, the 2012 Nobel Laureates in Chemistry John B. Gordon and Shinya Yamanaka, as well as two African-American pioneers in medicine, the world-renowned nuero surgeon Dr. Ben Carson and my very own uncle, the great endocrinologist Dr. W. Lester Henry, one of my angels to whom I dedicated this book.

My uncle was a quiet, unassuming giant. As a Buffalo Soldier, master physician and mentor to many, he used his gift of extraordinary intelligence to train thousands of doctors who passed through the halls of Howard University Medical School. He epitomized what it means to claim your greatness. He claimed his and left his mark on this world by helping to cultivate other gifted and talented doctors.

The Gift of the Arts and Creativity

The imaginative ability to dream and visualize what is possible and then bring it to life leaves many of us in absolute awe. We can attest to the gift of such creativity in the artistry of motion picture masterminds like Steven Spielberg and James Cameron, and Academy Award winners like Meryl Streep, Julia Roberts, Denzel Washington and Robert De Niro. Additionally, we can mention domestic divas like Martha Stewart. In the architectural world, such geniuses include I.M. Pei and Frank Lloyd Wright.

In the musical arts there are the diverse vocal geniuses of Andrea Bocelli, Audra McDonald, Diane Schuur, Whitney Houston, Celine

Dion, Barbra Streisand, Michael Jackson, Ray Charles, Justin Bieber, and the family of the talented "Dixie Chicks."

Artistry through movement is showcased by the likes of dancers Martha Graham, Judith Jamison, Alvin Ailey, Mikhail Baryshnikov, and the tap-dancing Hines brothers.

The visual arts are represented with the extraordinary talent of painters like Picasso, Claude Monet, Rembrandt, and the famous muralist John Biggers.

Those that used their gifted hands to sculpt include Michelangelo, Donatello, Auguste Rodin, Edmonia Lewis, Alexander Calder, Louise Nevelson, and Isamu Noguchi.

As in each of the previous categories, we have merely scratched the surface of extraordinarily talented people that use their gifts to do extraordinary things.

The Gift of Communication

The ability to communicate messages in ways that allow others to expand and journey to places in their minds requires an adept ability to manipulate, massage, and mold the written and spoken word masterfully. Examples of communication excellence include Mo Yun, the 2012 Nobel Laureate in literature, along with legends such as Ralph Waldo Emerson, Henry James, T.S. Elliot, and poets such as Maya Angelou, David Whyte and the inspiring gay, Cuban immigrant Richard Bianco (chosen as the poet for the U.S. 2013 Inauguration ceremonies).

The Gift of Innovation

To be innovative is to think outside of the box and achieve the previously unthinkable. In the United States innovation is part of the American dream. It is evidenced by the late Steve Jobs' creations at Apple, Walt Disney's vision for movies and theme parks, Microsoft's Bill Gates' technological brilliance, and FedEx founder Frederick W. Smith's fortitude.

Stop for just a minute and absorb the magnitude and impact that the lists of talent in each of the areas highlighted have had on the world.

Simply put, the world is richer as result of their incredible gifts and genius. And yet, giftedness goes beyond even those boundaries…

The Gift of Beauty

Throughout history, physical beauty has been regarded in society as a force that has the power to shape and influence circumstances and relationships between people and even nations.

Present-day examples of beauty include Angelina Jolie, Zoe Saldana, and Veronica Webb.

In history there's Helen of Troy, whose legendary beauty caused a war between the Greeks and the Trojans. We only have to look back a few decades to the Hollywood legends of old with their transcendent beauty, revered through the ages. The beauty of icons such as Princess Grace of Monaco, Jackie Kennedy Onassis, Lena Horne, and Lady Diana are imprinted in our hearts and minds forever.

Marilyn Monroe epitomized the curse of beauty in the depths of the Gifted Trap. The world was enthralled by her ravishing beauty. Yet again, we see a manifestation of negative PB&Js, those perceptions by others that she chose to focus on that led her into a spiral of self-sabotage. Her breathtaking beauty and allure left her susceptible to toxic relationships with the most powerful men in the world. The gift of her beauty gave her legendary status and led to an iconic immortality. Yet in a brutal response, the Gifted Trap ultimately led to her demise.

The Challenge of Giftedness

Those among us who are aesthetically blessed often experience a similar ripple effect in society, albeit on a lesser scale. I'm considered "middle-aged" now, and I dedicate myself to being in peak physical shape on a regular basis, through healthy nutrition and regular exercise. My years spent in the fashion world taught me which clothes flatter my body shape, and I have reached a place in my life where I relish the feeling that comes with looking good and being confident in my appearance.

That confidence presents itself as an aura—a "presence" around me. When I walk into a room for the first time, I often sense a shift in energy from others as a result of the confidence, poise and presence that I exude. That energetic shift from others is sometimes positive, yet it also can be negative, based on other peoples' PB&Js.

For years, I considered my physical appearance to be somewhat of a curse because of the resentment it engendered in others, both male and female. For most of my adult life, from my early 20s to my mid 40s, I perpetually wrestled with my inner self, purely in response to the reactions of others when I walked into a room. All of us have a desire to be accepted and to be liked, to feel we are part of something. I was no different in that regard.

I questioned myself…
How could I adjust me to make other people feel good?

As a runway model early in my adult life I was accustomed to the attention of others, and became sensitized to their reactions as I sashayed along the runway or simply walked down the street. Through the years, I instinctively tuned into the energetic vibes as I entered a room, the intriguing blend of acceptance, rejection, envy or admiration.

For years, I minimized the dramatic effect of my flowing long hair by tying it tautly into a chignon to play my looks down to placate the feelings of others. As a corporate wife, my then-husband was uncomfortable with me wearing clothes that flattered my body. He expressed a preference for a more conservative style of fashion. I assumed the role he wanted me to play, and became someone other than who I was at my core. I altered me, and played the role of corporate wife perfectly.

Perhaps you have experienced something similar, repressing your natural zest for life, embodying a persona that diminishes your light. You may have been playing a role unconsciously for years out of a desire to please others.

This is the essence of the Gifted Trap. It's time to put an end to this habit and simply BE YOU!

Your Unique Gifts

What one special gift were you put on this planet to develop? Are you an artist? Are you a gardener? Do you enjoy singing? Or maybe it's math, science, or sports that lights your fire.

It took me a while to sort through my many talents and figure out that my primary gift is my voice. My ability to use my voice to communicate meaningful messages that inspire transformation is my number one gift. All of my other talents support my voice.

I am blessed. It is easier for people to pay attention to me because I have the external package of beauty. It is easy for people to listen to me because I have the gift of clarity, of being able to articulate my message clearly. It is easy to hear my voice because of the way I habitually move with grace from my years of dancing and athletic training.

My other talents support my voice and my ability to communicate vital messages.

You may be pursuing one gift, yet deep down you are feeling like something within you is awry—because your focus may be on the wrong gift.

Lawyers and doctors who have trained for years developing one particular talent may finally find themselves at the peak of the mountain they have climbed throughout their career to find that it's the wrong mountain. Oh My God (OMG), they've climbed to the peak—to the very top of the wrong mountain!

As part of the process of writing this book, I interviewed several gifted people who have experienced what it means to be caught in the Gifted Trap and have all been through—or in some cases are still working through—the process of emerging. Dike Drummond, MD was one of those people. Dike was encouraged by his family to study to be a doctor but in his own words at the age of 40 he realized that wasn't what he was called to do, Dike explains:

"My story involves three generations. My grandmother and my mother went to college wanting to be doctors. They were diverted into

careers in teaching. They had great careers, both had schools named after them, but that was not what they had dreamed of being. When I was the firstborn male grandchild, according to both my grandmother and my mother… I was going to be a doctor; that was it. I lived up to their expectations and became a doctor, but wanted to quit every year along my journey. I was a very successful small-town family doctor. I delivered over 500 babies and became a medical director. To look at me from the outside I was the 'Marcus Welby' of the 1990s. It was intellectually stimulating; I had a great relationship with my patients. When I reached 40—fourteen years ago—my medical practice had no meaning for me, my mother had died and I just couldn't do it anymore. It lost all sense of purpose for me."

To the outside world, Dike had everything, but he was caught up in his own Gifted Trap and he needed to escape. We will see how he emerged as the book unfolds.

Unconventional Gifts

An unconventional gift is a gift in "unusual wrapping paper." Think about Christmas presents. We love them decorated in sparkling paper or beautiful gift bags with delicate tissue paper, bows and ribbons. Sometimes we may choose to overlook the gifts wrapped in unusual ways like, for example, in old newspaper. Concealed in that unconventional, out-of-the-ordinary exterior, may be a unique gift that can enrich our lives in ways we can't conceive.

Throughout this book are excerpts from interviews with people who have emerged from their own gifted traps to become authentically aligned with themselves. My hope is that you will find much to inspire you in these rich shares. Each person profiled in Appendix A embodies unique gifts and serves as a shining example for this discussion.

One of my interviewees, the inspirational Vasavi Kumar, was diagnosed with bipolar disorder. Most people would consider that a major problem. Vasavi chooses, however, to view her condition as a gift. As Vasavi explains here, sometimes your obstacle *is* your gift:

> *"Sometimes, the thing that you think is your biggest challenge or your obstacle is actually your greatest gift. It is your training ground to become the warrior that you are. A warrior is trained on the battlefield. Your challenge will make you into that warrior. Without challenges, you cannot become a warrior. My bipolar disorder has made me one of the most resilient people I know. It is a gift. Whatever hurdles you face, this is all about a shift of perspective. You are stronger than average because the average person doesn't have to go through that. You are being trained to be a warrior."*

Through working on her own self-imposed—and societally imposed—judgments, Vasavi has now come to accept this as a form of giftedness and is channeling it into a whole new energy. She has refused to accept it as an impediment to her life and instead has reframed the less favorable Perceptions, Beliefs and Judgments about her condition into empowering beliefs. She uses her new beliefs as a fueling station from which she draws creative energy and freedom to move her life forward.

The gifted Carole Martin-Wright, mentioned previously, was adopted as a child and had some physical abnormalities that she sees only as a gift. This is a prime example of what I would call an "unconventional" gift.

> *"That is another kind of gift I've received from the faith, and as it turned out the physical things I have are only cosmetic. Nothing has ever really limited me. I'm living life to its fullest. So, I'm gifted in the technical, academic sense and gifted in the sense that I've been really darn lucky almost all of my life."*

Autism is another such example of a gift that is often held or perceived by others as a problem. There are examples of people born without limbs, yet what they achieve with their lives is an extraordinary example for others. Just examine the stories of the one-legged female Olympic skier Bonnie St. John, and the very successful Russian-born United States Paralympic swimmer Jessica Long. Both their stories are amazing!

Despite having her right leg amputated at age five, St. John became the first African-American ever to win Olympic or Paralympic medals in ski racing, taking home a silver and two bronze medals in downhill events at the 1984 Paralympics in Innsbruck, Austria.

Long, as of the writing of this book, is the current record holder in 13 Paralympic events. She won five Gold Medals, two Silver Medals and one Bronze Medal, making her one of the most celebrated Paralympic swimmers ever.

When reframed, what may be perceived as impediments are actually gifts.

No matter who you are, you have a gift. Your gifts can show up in many different areas of your life and while you may perceive yourself as not fitting into society, or as a "misfit" because of an unconventional gift, if you take a closer look at yourself, you will be able to use that perceived flaw as a gift.

During the course of my work, I encountered a woman who had come to the United States as an immigrant from Colombia in search of the much-sought-after "American dream." Upon arriving here she experienced challenges and was treated with extreme wariness due to her language limitations, yet in her native land, she had been regarded as successful and had achieved much. In America, given her language limitations she was forced to begin again. She was perceived as having little to "bring to the table."

Her example is classic, rife with the PB&Js that can emotionally paralyze you. She began to doubt her own giftedness. Understandably, she felt unworthy and began to doubt that she would ever be accepted here. Finally, she realized that what she was holding in her mind as an obstacle to her being successful was in fact her gift. When she looked at her situation from a different perspective, she saw that her gift was her ability to teach her language to and share her culture with others. Her true skill lay in teaching others to become bi-lingual and multi-lingual—as she had learned to do herself. By shifting and reframing the way she viewed her experience, she was able to totally shift her reality.

To reach that state, however, she had to undergo a period of feeling emotionally trapped and an overwhelming sense of not being "good enough" because of those PB&Js.

Everyone has a gift. This book is here to help you find yours and emerge using it. When my friend came to the United States she was met by a barrage of negativity that threatened to entrap her permanently. Fortunately, she chose to hold on to her beliefs and experiences in empowering ways, reframing them from something negative into a positive. She felt awkward and much like a "misfit," yet when she emerged in authentic alignment with herself, she began to soar.

Just as she was able to make lemonade out of lemons, you, to, have that ability. Follow her example, emerge from that trap, and start enjoying some fresh-squeezed lemonade.

Gilded Golden Gifts

As an inspirational and transformational speaker, I often listen to other great speakers for my inspiration. Recently I was listening to a speech by one of America's greatest speakers, Les Brown.

In his "It's Not Over Till I Win" speech, he shares a story that, exemplifies how we can step away from Perceptions, Beliefs and Judgments into a world of our own making. During his speech, he asked his audience to think about the challenges they faced in their daily lives and how those challenges affected their own perceptions of their lives.

Les then called on a woman to share her response to his query. The woman eagerly responded that no challenges had entered her head.

What makes her response so noteworthy and remarkable is that this incredible woman had *no hands or legs*. She had only one stub that she used to operate a mechanical device that enabled her to move. She simply did not perceive herself as challenged or handicapped.

She didn't have what everyone else took for granted—a pair of arms and a pair of legs. Yet she was able to see beyond those limitations. Therein lay her magnificent gift—her refusal to allow what the rest of the world perceived as a disability to hold her back and her ability to view her life as one of unlimited possibilities. **"Optimism in spite of all odds"** is the unique gift she shares with the world everywhere she goes.

She refused to allow society's limiting Perceptions, Beliefs and Judgments to impact and influence her own perception of who she is and how she shows up in the world. How many of us in that situation would have that level of self-belief?

There's a parable that I love that speaks to the ability to reframe how we view things in life:

"Ages ago in a distant land, a simple sage arrived by foot in a village. His style was simple…unassuming, yet sure. His heart was warm. His smile was gentle. And his voice was clear… like music to villagers' ears. His mere presence seemed to soothe their souls.

"Word spread quickly of his arrival. He became a pied piper of sorts—for everywhere he went, every time he spoke, people hung on his every word. They were inspired—often transformed by the wisdom he shared and truth he spoke.

"Well it didn't take long before the Ruler of the land got wind of this 'silver-tongued sage.' Displeased about the groundswell of enthusiasm about the 'wise old sage,' the ruler decided to confront the sage publicly. He would impress his people with his prowess, and prove that HE, the RULER, was the ONLY source of truth in the land. He would have the last word

"The Ruler devised an infallible plan to embarrass the wise old sage. The ruler would hold a live bird in his hand, hidden from sight. He would confront the sage and demand that without seeing the bird, he must tell the truth about whether the bird was alive or dead. If the sage said the bird was alive, the ruler, with his hand out of sight, would snap the bird's neck in his palm and then reveal a dead bird for all to see. And if the sage said the bird was dead, the Ruler would allow the bird to fly free. Either way…the Ruler would win and all would see the Ruler as the True Truth Teller—and the sage would be exposed as a fraud.

"The Ruler sent his servants to find the sage and summoned him to the grand square for a 'stand off of truth.' Villagers came from far and wide to witness the standoff—not an inch of space to spare in the square.

"The Sage approached the Ruler as summoned, bowing gracefully with respect.

"In front of ALL his people the Ruler boldly blasted, 'So old man, I hear that you present yourself as a teller of absolute truth?'

"The Sage replied calmly, 'Royal Ruler, I speak from my heart what instinctively I feel to be fact, if that is of which you refer to as truth.'

"'Well, if you 'know things instinctively,' the Ruler retorted, 'then tell us the TRUTH about the bird that I hold in my hand behind my back. Is it alive or dead?'

"The sage paused thoughtfully and with a clear, compassionate voice responded...

"Royal Ruler...that which you hold in your hand is what YOU make of it.'"

Your talents are represented by that bird lying in the king's hand, and you have a choice. You have to decide whether you are going to allow your talents to soar or whether they will shrivel and die in your hand because you did not choose to claim them and share them enthusiastically with the world.

It's a parable that has many different meanings and applying it to the context of "the trap" demonstrates how you are all given different gifts in life, though you don't always recognize them at the time or even know how to use them. You have a choice to figure it out and allow yourself to live fully in tune with all you are capable of being, or to allow yourself to stagnate or self-sabotage. You crack the neck of the bird—or in your own terms, you sabotage your own talent by not living in alignment with your talents.

That Which You Hold in Your Hand Is What You Make of It

The girl that Les Brown referred to in his famous speech understood totally what she held in her hand, and she was determined to live in alignment with her God-given destiny. She inspired others, despite the PB&Js that so easily could have hampered her every move.

Vasavi Kumar also recognized the hidden gift in her bi-polar diagnosis:

> *"First of all, for people with this diagnosis I want to say that it is without doubt a gift from God. From a very young age, I was on an accelerated path of spiritual evolution and awareness. I am 30 now, but my wisdom is that of an 80-year-old. I have never been 'of this earth,' and the bipolar disorder heightens the awareness of conversations in your mind. Most people listen to their ego; they believe it's real. For me, I heard a constant conversation between my higher consciousness—God—and my ego. It's a gift because as I listened I started to truly understand the human condition."*

That's truly what this whole process is about, becoming aware of what you possess as your gift and becoming comfortable with what it takes to bring that into the world and make a difference. Only then can you emerge from the Gifted Trap and live in authentic alignment with yourself first, and then as we will explore in later chapters, with the rest of the world.

Being at Peace With Your Gifts

Imagine If You Were Invisible

Before we explore Perceptions, Beliefs and Judgments in greater depth, I want to share one more experience with you that demonstrates how PB&Js gradually, over time as we grow up, pervade our life.

During a visit to Savannah, Georgia, I was relaxing one evening in the hotel lobby and noticed near me a group of women sitting with their daughters in a circle. There were about a dozen and a half of them in total. I later found out that their Girl Scout troop had come to Savannah in celebration of the anniversary of Girl Scouts of America. It was a rainy evening, so they had stayed inside. To entertain themselves for the evening, one of the mothers took out a box of cards to play a game.

One person in the group would randomly pull out a card and then read the question on it. Taking turns, going around in the circle, each person would answer the question in her own way.

One of the questions posed was, "If you were invisible, what would you do?"

To me that sounded like a fun question, and as I eavesdropped, I entered into a realm of possibilities in my own mind.

The responses from the girls varied from answers such as visiting the White House and listening to the conversations between the President and the First Lady at night when no one else was in ear range to hear what they really thought… to going to Disneyworld and jumping on all the rides without having to wait in the long lines for hours.

It was fun and it was enlightening to hear their responses.

As an observer, what I found most interesting was the beauty and creativity of experiences they imagined. These mothers were giving their daughters an opportunity to imagine and to dream about possibilities. **What would they do if…**

What I noticed in the responses of the mothers and daughters is relevant to our conversation about what happens to us and how the PB&Js negatively impact and limit us as we get older.

As a child, the world wants to know what it can do to support you and encourage you to develop your gifts. There are countless programs to cultivate your talent. Yet when you become an adult, the support suddenly diminishes to the point where it no longer exists.

In the case of this game, the answers from the children were unfettered, unencumbered by perceptions, beliefs and judgments—they were free to express themselves.

Yet, for their mothers, on the other hand, there was, I noticed, internal struggle as they confronted their thought processes and fears and answered with "safe" neatly "inside-the-box" answers.

What if… What if…?

It struck me that this was a key part of the whole gifted trap liberation process.

What if You Were at Peace with Yourself and Your Giftedness?

What would you do; how would you live your life? For most people an internal struggle takes place every day.

The purpose of this whole process is to reach a place of being at peace with yourself and your gifts.

The purpose of emerging from the Gifted Trap is to emerge into a place of authentic alignment—into a place where you are truly comfortable with yourself.

I seriously pondered that question. What would I do if I were invisible? In a moment, I knew exactly what I would do.

I'd head straight for the Olympic Games in London and listen in on the exchange between Gabby Douglas and her coach. I'd want to understand, firsthand, what he shares with her to empower her to position herself—mentally, spiritually, emotionally and physically—to be able to focus on delivering world-class excellence under such profound pressure. I would want to know how she manages the PB&Js—how she ignores the negative ones, the endless jibes and comments that might take her off her game. And I would want to know how to use the positive PB&Js as fuel to propel her forward.

I would want to understand just what it is that enables her to stay in that place of authentic alignment, to allow her to do what she was put on this earth to do—to be an Olympian and a champion—to be the best at her sport, while simultaneously allowing the sheer beauty of her spirit and talent to be experienced by the world.

Wouldn't you like to hear that, too? I was especially interested in Gabby's coaching because of the behavior I noticed from the Russian team during the 2012 Summer Olympics. Then, Russian athlete Victoria Komova became frustrated by even the slightest error, to the point that she exuded only anger, rejection and frustration. This particular athlete was unable to deliver at the top of her game when she needed to the most.

On the evening of the gymnastic competitions, I tuned in a little late. As I watched Komova's reaction, not yet knowing the final results, based on the look on her face, I assumed she had failed to achieve any

Olympic medal at all. I later discovered that she had finished second and won an Olympic silver medal. Her outward display of self-denigration and frustration epitomized how we judge ourselves when we fail to reach our preconceived standards.

In contrast, Gabby Douglas was the perfect example of someone who had emerged from the Gifted Trap.

She was at peace with herself for the great achievement of simply being present at the Olympic finals, and in her ease she joyfully achieved her goal of not just one, but two, gold medals. For an Olympic gymnast that is literally a once-in-a-lifetime opportunity.

I had the honor of interviewing Carol Callan, Women's National Team Director for USA Basketball. In our interview, I asked her what distinguishes world-class athletes that allows them to be on their game, despite the PB&Js that are working against them. Her answer was clear:

"First, I go back to a team atmosphere. I think we're fortunate in our women's basketball program, as we have great athletes and great coaches. We've been able to sustain a level of success where we are supposed to win every time we go out. That could create a new pressure, or you could take that and build on it.

"We've had several situations where we've been in games where things aren't going well and our coaches have taken it and broken it down into—rather than the end result being the most important—into simply a possession-by-possession type of scenario. There is a complete understanding of what it is we want to do, and a good amount of preparation for the tremendous talent we have. Our coaches are there not only to provide direction but also to offer complete support."

In summary, reaching a zone of peacefulness with your gifts often requires that two things be in place:

1. An ability to be fully present and take life one day at a time; and
2. An emotional support structure that helps you re-member how gifted you are and re-minds you how best to hold your gifts.

We'll discuss more about how to make certain both of these elements are in place for you. So, keep reading.

THE BAIT THAT LURES
YOU INTO THE TRAP

Early on, I mentioned that getting into the trap is an unconscious process. Therefore, logic would suggest that learning to recognize the bait that lures you in would be of great value in helping you avoid the trap, as well as helping you unleash yourself from the hook once you realize you have bitten on the bait.

Toward that end, this chapter is designed to be a deep dive into the most common gifted trap bait, PB&Js™—perceptions, beliefs and judgments.

In my own case, I was lured into my gifted trap by the perception that I was supposed to be perfect, by the belief that in order to be loved I had to do things the "right" way, and that if I didn't, I would be judged as unworthy. Consequently, I spent most of my life trying to prove myself worthy to the rest of the world. It manifested as a relentless, debilitating **"disease to please."** We'll talk more about this disease a little later. The point now is that I was nibbling on gifted trap bait as a child and wasn't even aware of it.

Bait is everywhere, lurking and looming, looking to impact you unknowingly at every turn. Even as young children we are taught unwittingly to believe things that do not serve us.

Dr. Cherie Clark identifies some of those indelible emotional imprints that become PB&Js that hold you back:

> *"You might get bullied in school. There are so many constant examples... for example, the little kid who comes to school and is criticized by his or her teachers as being stupid. I do muscle tests with people and even if*

the word "stupid" is not said about you, it will reduce your ability to think or even hold your arm up in a strength test. That word has a debilitating effect on people. Our brains interpret it and believe it must be true."

She continues by explaining the impact that PB&Js imposed by society have on particular ethnic cultures. She illustrates how they can traumatize you and unconsciously entrap you:

"If you were born in certain neighborhoods, you got strikes against you going in. For example, in the 1880s, the people who went to prison were the Italian, Irish and Polish. It was rare to see a person of color in pictures of inmates. There were ads in the papers of those times saying, "Irish need not apply" for even the most menial jobs. They were the ethnic cultures who were scorned. So the prisons were full of them.

"It was these types of PB&Js that led to the execution of six million Jews in World War II. They were seen as inferior. In the 1950s, with the advent of the Civil Rights movement, the PB&Js resulted in the prison population escalating to being largely people of color and guess what? The Polish, Italian and Irish were still there, only now they were running the prisons.

"Vietnam resulted in more and more people coming back with terrifying post-traumatic stress disorder. People may say there's no such thing, that it's just an 'excuse', but there is. I personally feel that I have a form of PTSD from far less traumatic situations because I carry around things in my body and mind that I experienced when I was growing up, that are 'triggered' in a situation that brings old events into the present. My years as a therapist and counselor confirmed this, as I saw these similar patterns, repeatedly, in those with whom I worked."

These examples show how you are fed societally-imposed and self-imposed Perceptions, Beliefs and Judgments bait that stifle your ability to embrace what is truly possible in our life. These limiting PB&Js suppress you because it is virtually impossible to hold limiting Perceptions, Beliefs and Judgments in the same mental space with more expansive possibilities, empowering beliefs and joyfulness. Simply put, the two opposing points of view cannot coexist—*where there's limiting, negative judgment, there simply cannot be joy occupying the same space*.

The important distinction to make here is that not all judgment is limiting and negative. For instance, we must have judgment in order to make good decisions. The point is that when you allow the negative and limiting thoughts to take hold, they will hold you back.

So in order to live up to your own giftedness, it is imperative that you not place limits on yourself. The beauty is that you have a choice. Yes, you get to decide what and how you want to think about your experiences and how you want to hold them.

In the previous chapter, we saw two quite different examples of how the PB&Js can impact you in your life. From the contrast between Gabby Douglas and her Russian competitor and the Girl Scout mothers and daughters playing a simple game, I hope you took away the difference in how you can be impacted by PB&Js.

Living up to the expectations and standards of others can be debilitating. Too often you are taught to believe that what other people think of you is more important than your perceptions of yourself.

One of my mentors, Lisa Nichols, a globally-recognized premiere personal growth and development icon, often refers to a philosophy that her grandmother shared with her about how best to handle what you think other people think of you. I share that philosophy with you, with the hope that it will serve you. Lisa's grandmother's golden nugget is…

> ***"What other people think of you…
> ain't none of your business."***

This is so true. What really matters is what *you* think of you and how you choose to hold the Perceptions, Beliefs and Judgments looming around you.

PB&Js – Nourishment or Sewage?

The PB&J sandwich analogy was introduced early on in our discussion. I reference it here in relationship to Perceptions, Beliefs and Judgments that impact you as a way of driving home a very important concept. Whether you treat your PB&Js as "yummy sandwiches" or "yucky sewage" will determine whether or not you fall prey to The Gifted Trap. When I say "sewage," I compare and contrast it to the waste in your home. If waste is left to fester inside rather than being put out by the curb for pickup, it begins to cause a smelly, foul odor. That same smelly, foul odor permeates your mental space, causing it to feel unpleasant, thus the adage of "stinking thinking."

Your response to the PB&Js—positive or negative—is a choice between sandwiches or sewage. You get to choose to either hold it as "stinking thinking" or as clear-headed confidence.

You might be wondering how on earth you can better recognize PB&J garbage, so you can better manage the waste in your mind.

Examining Perceptions, Beliefs and Judgments individually will enable you to better recognize them and understand how they impact your life. Awareness is the first step in any transformative process. So let's heighten your awareness about perceptions, beliefs and judgments.

P – Perceptions

The definition of a perception is a way of looking at things, an observation or an awareness of something. The perception can be yours (how you see yourself) or that of others (how others see you).

To put it in context, think back to those times in your life when maybe you were preparing a presentation for work, for a social group or possibly for an event at your church. This is your opportunity to shine and take your step into the limelight. It's your chance to present yourself the way you want others to see you, not simply in what you have to say, but in terms of your appearance and overall image.

Your thought process is framed by one of two trains of thought. Possibly you know the people you will be presenting to, and you know that perhaps they already accept and respect you for your achievements and expertise.

Conversely, this may be your "inaugural" presentation, your opportunity to prove yourself so that your colleagues or audience will accept you.

It has been established that perceptions can be positive or negative and your own thoughts can have a significant influence on how you feel you are perceived in the world. When you are paralyzed by emotional entrapment, your perceptions often manifest as limiting thoughts. They may show up as you feeling **"not good enough"**—feeling that the way you are perceived by the world is insufficient, that it doesn't measure up. If you believe that others share that view of you, your entrapment deepens. You feel **inadequate** and sink deeper into the quicksand.

Let's return to the preparation for the presentation where it matters to you what your audience thinks. If you are confident that they value you, you will feel secure, exuding natural confidence.

On the other hand, you may feel that it is imperative for you to prove yourself. For example, if you are a new employee presenting to unfamiliar colleagues for the first time, the stakes are raised. You have no way of knowing what their reaction to you will be and as a result, doubt often floods your mind. "Am I up to this task?" "Do I look the part?" "Will I be able to deliver on the expectations?" This is a common—and to a certain extent natural—reaction. However, the big question to ask is: Is this simply a common question mark or a sign of deep-seated debilitating **self-doubt** creeping in?

Later in the book, I will talk about my experience at an eWomen competition that I participated in for North America's Next Greatest Speaker (NANGS). As I walked into the competition hall for the first time, countless thoughts ran through my mind. How would the people in that hall—who might be hearing me for the first time—receive my message?

Perceptions are powerful influences. Your perception
of the expectations that other people have of you is
pressure you place on yourself with far-reaching consequences.
Understanding this is critically important to your emotional
health and well-being, so let's take a closer look.

Internal and External Perceptions

As we have already mentioned, perceptions fall into one of two categories, namely, the perception you have of yourself or the perception that others have of you.

You will hear me reference my esteemed mentor, Arthur Joseph, throughout the course of this book and you will find a link to his website in the Resources section. In his work, the Vocal Awareness Method™, he challenges you to determine how you wish to be perceived in the world. Specifically, he asks, "What is the persona that you wish to present in the world?"

As part of the process of establishing your persona, Arthur recommends taking yourself through an exercise where you respond to two questions. Personally, I found this to be one of the most life-altering exercises I had ever done.

I offer Arthur's two questions to ponder:
1. "How do you perceive yourself?"
2. "How do you think that others perceive you?"

Too often, you are preoccupied either with other people's negative perceptions of you or what you perceive as your own imperfections. That is the experience most of you have in the real world. Let's look at a perfect example of this.

Jennie Hernandez is an incredibly gifted author, motivational speaker and teacher whose life, in her own words, has been one of *"change, possibility and growth"*. During the course of her career, Jennie developed a parenting process based on business principles that eventually became published in a highly successful parenting book. Yet, for a long time, Jennie was held back by the PB&Js:

"One of the biggest traps I had to get out of was my own lack of self-esteem and lack of understanding who I was and what I was capable of. It was one of the biggest hurdles I had to overcome."

Jennie allowed herself to be influenced by both internal and external PB&Js:

"The religion and Mexican culture I grew up in was also very male-dominated, so it took me many years to realize that I was not the least deserving or ugliest person in a room and that no one is less than anyone else. We are all just different. We all have gifts and strengths that we need to develop and share. Coming from that background, with those limiting beliefs, I know I made some choices, such as my marriage, that I had to overcome through the years."

Sometimes, even when all of the evidence is there that you are gifted, special and unique, your self-doubt can deny your truth.

Many gifted and talented people live **"less than lives."** You may have settled for a way of living that doesn't allow your giftedness to express itself. Episcopal priest Susan Purnell describes it this way:

"They are attempting to live someone else's narrative, without realizing that it has everyone else's name on it except their own. Frustrated and fearing that they are failures in life, they blindly push harder to make this projection-based narrative work for them."

For Dike Drummond, as we saw earlier, it was the multi-generational PB&Js, the expectation that he was always going to be a doctor. This point was further emphasized in my interview and case study with a career and relationships coach, Rainbow Chen.

Rainbow is exceptionally gifted, a high achiever who is in the process of emerging from her own Gifted Trap yet is still affected by the multi-generational PB&Js and the expectations that she would attend an Ivy League school:

"I recently went through a box of all of my elementary and high school stuff and I was flabbergasted. I made 100s across the board; I believe my lowest grade in high school was a 92 in tennis. It was one of those known things. It may have been the unspoken pressure from my parents to excel academically. I knew that part of the reason they came to the US was so that we could have more choice in what Ivy League university we went to. My parents pulled me out of the city ballet company because they were concerned it wasn't a school activity that would help me get into an Ivy League school. That was really painful to lose something that, for me, was my escape and my place of bliss."

Part of Rainbow's current process of emerging is learning to express and find harmony with both her artistic and her intellectual talents. The challenge has been honoring her family's cultural priorities and PB&Js that are more societally accepted, without denying her own desire for creative expression.

Rainbow and I are both mentored by Arthur Joseph. Arthur encourages you to put a stop to such mental and emotional conflict. Instead he encourages you to focus on the positive perceptions you want to embody and develop. He challenges you to create a persona statement that aligns with your gifts and then begin to claim that persona.

In my own case, there is absolutely no doubt in my mind that I am blessed. I am fully aware how fortunate I am.

One of my gifts is that of being physically attractive. The positive perception I have of myself, therefore, is that I am beautiful. This perception is a result of a lifetime of people telling me that. My experience has been that my beauty sometimes makes people uncomfortable when they are in my company. For some, my very presence causes them to feel they are lacking in some way.

That is my perception, which is simultaneously a belief, and it is a strongly held limiting belief. As a consequence, for most of my life I felt the need to adjust and alter me in order to be **accepted** and to fit in. This was especially true in my professional life.

Such a perception is often held by people blessed with above average intelligence. Too often the smart person in the class is the one who people tend to exclude, to **isolate** and to make fun of—to sometimes even **bully**. For those of you who are comfortable and at ease with your own intelligence, how you are perceived by others will not be a problem.

However, those of you who are uncomfortable with the unsolicited spotlight and unwarranted negative comments may play your intelligence down in an effort to be accepted and be perceived as "normal."

Many of you that are caught in emotional entrapment are in similar predicaments—you compromise yourself in some way in your quest for **acceptance**. You find yourself in situations where you're perceived as being extraordinary in some capacity. It may be a high intellect that makes you stand out, as we saw earlier with Melissa. It may be athletic prowess that makes the rest of the world feel inadequate as you pursue your gifts to the highest level possible for you.

We tend to forget that professional athletes are human like the rest of us. The only difference is their self-discipline coupled with their commitment to themselves to use their gift and perfect it to a point where they are recognized as "extraordinary." I come back to Gabby Douglas again because it was her incredible work ethic and commitment that enabled her to become the first female African-American gold medalist in the all-around gymnastic competition. She used positive perceptions to fuel her as she achieved her personal and professional best.

In my discussion with Troy Vincent, he shared an interesting perspective on perceptions. I share our exchange with you here to round out this discussion.

Troy: *Often times I am in conversations that are either dispelling myths, or breaking down perceptions. There's a scripture from David that comes to mind that I always share with young men and women. It's probably one we've read and heard a thousand times, but when we really look at it and analyze it, we focus on the first part rather than the latter.*

       In Psalm 23 it reads, 'Yea though I walk through the valley of the shadow of death, I fear no evil, for thou art with me, my rod and thy staff they comfort me.' Most people stop at "Yea

> *though I walk through the valley of the shadow of death." But I*
> *ask what is a shadow?*
>
> Anne: *A reflection of something that is created when light is cast upon it.*
>
> Troy: *Yes, but it's a perception. The shadow is a perception. So most of*
> *us look at the valleys, but Scripture says, "So I walk through the*
> *valley of the shadow of death." It's the shadow of death. It's not*
> *death itself. The perception is not real. But most of us live in it,*
> *and when we hit that ultimate low, we stay there!*
>
> Anne: *Yes, far too many people allow Perceptions, Beliefs and Judgments*
> *to trap them right there.*
>
> Troy: *And we never move from it. It's just a perception. It's false. It's the*
> ***False Evidence Appearing Real (FEAR).*** *It's not even real!*

I invite you to reflect deeply on the perceptions that you are allowing to manage your life. Get clear about whether they are real or based in some False Evidence Appearing Real (FEAR) that you are holding on to.

Every single one of you reading these words now—*without exception*—has the ability to emerge and claim your unique giftedness. But to do so you must be willing to examine and embrace those PB&Js, as Erline Belton explains:

> *"It is those very things you don't want to look at that keep you*
> *trapped. If you don't embrace them, you can't move forward, you'll stay*
> *paralyzed and you'll keep repeating the same pattern over and over*
> *again. There's a high-ranking University official who I work with—and*
> *every time she gets a job the same issues come up. The reason for that is*
> *that she has not looked at the root cause of her behavior. She repeats the*
> *behavior patterns and similar outcomes repeat themselves. If you don't*
> *do the work, you stay emotionally entrapped. The PB&Js that you men-*
> *tion keep you in a dysfunctional state and don't allow you to be your*
> *very best self."*

Don't allow that to be you. You have seen how the perceptions work within you—both good and bad. Reflect on the wisdom shared here about perceptions and begin to put them in a healthy perspective.

Now we'll look at overcoming the beliefs that hold you back and prevent you from being your "very best" self.

B – Beliefs

A belief is a sense of certainty, of knowing something for what it is while eliminating any room for another perspective. It is something you hold within your heart, something unassailable, something you know to be true.

During my transformation out of the trap, I did some deep work to remove many of my limiting beliefs with belief expert Gina Maria Mele, M.S. Gina has chosen to merge the disciplines of traditional medicine, holistic medicine and the study of how we view our reality together to challenge those PB&Js and enable her clients to undergo what she describes as a "Thrivable Transformation"™. So I thought there is no one better to help define beliefs than Gina herself. Below, she explains her definition of belief:

"The way I hold the word 'belief' is the smallest distillable unit that creates what we call our reality. For example, a lot of times you may have heard a phrase like 'what we think we are.' The philosophy of belief that ties into that concept is that the ideas you have in your head not only play an immediate role on how you feel, which impacts how you act, but also over time impact how other people behave around you. So a belief is a thought or an idea that an individual holds to be true. Traditionally, for many people, a belief will be subconscious and you won't know that you are believing it. Yet fundamentally it is dictating your experience."

Remember the goal I mentioned in the introduction…

Either you learn to manage them or they will manage you.

Beliefs On Professional Playing Fields
Beliefs dominate in professional environments.

On a daily basis we see examples of female executives wrestling with the belief that they're not strong enough emotionally to make tough decisions. This is such a well-ingrained belief in the business world that many women adopt masculine characteristics to gain corporate acceptance in the workplace. Whether it's wearing pant suits to work or suppressing the emotional sensitivity that women tend to instinctively possess, these actions reflect ways that many women alter who they are in response to what they "believe" they need to be to succeed.

> *Often women alter who they are in response to what they "believe" they need to be to succeed.*

As a woman, you do not have to pretend to be someone you are not to become an effective leader. You have so much to offer with your intuition and clarity of thought. If that is you, all you need to do is just believe that and claim it!

At the opposite end of the scale is the belief that men cannot show a hint of vulnerability or compassion for fear that it will be perceived as weakness.

> *As a man you may feel you cannot show a hint of vulnerability or compassion, for fear that it will be perceived as weakness.*

Both of these beliefs are stereotypes that the world continues to hold and that are only gradually changing.

We have already heard from high-achieving executive Carole Martin-Wright, who continues here to describe her own experience of how PB&Js operating within her working environment had a profound impact on her career.

"I took a senior role with a company several years ago. When I started I felt starry-eyed about the person who I was working for and blessed to be working for him. He had done so many wonderful things that I had heard about over the years.

As time passed, I began to wonder how my boss had achieved so many successes. I eventually understood that those successes were achieved by taking credit for things that other people had done. It became a very toxic situation for me knowing this.

Interacting with this individual was worse than going through a bad divorce. Emotionally I found this more damaging, but because of my nature, my competitiveness and my determination, I felt I just needed to overlook this one person. I felt it was a fabulous company that I could help to be successful.

I was in that role for six years. There were the normal corporate politics. I had friends in most of the right places and one day, with no prior warning, my boss informed me that they had decided to transfer me into a consultancy role. The whole experience was pretty painful because it was handled badly. I was asked to go into the office and clear my desk in the dead of night. I was promised that the people who worked for me would be informed that I had chosen to take a different position within the organization.

It turned out that my team was actually told that I didn't care enough to say goodbye to them, which left my team wondering what on earth was going on. Fortunately, many of my colleagues reached out to me. Together, we were able to piece together the truth of the situation."

Carole's experience epitomizes how the PB&Js of the people you work for can work against you, especially if you are a successful executive in the corporate arena. Her boss was intimidated by her brilliance—and found a way to extinguish her bright light.

Beliefs in Athletic Arenas – "Just Do It"

You've already seen how beliefs prevail in the sports world among coaches who are always expected to win.

If they achieve what's expected of them, the perceptions and beliefs are in alignment. The same principles apply for those who don't quite make the grade. If they do overcome PB&Js and win despite the odds, it's deemed a fluke or an exception.

Women's National Team Director of USA Basketball Carol Callan recalls the impact of beliefs during the course of her career and the vital role of coaches in reinforcing positive beliefs:

> *"Take any professional sport; in order to stay at the top of your game and on a team you have to work on things daily, and hopefully there are the resources that are available that will help you to fill in those weaknesses. When you have anxiety about your weaknesses and you don't or can't work on them, you tend to hide them and they become a bigger problem.*
>
> *I remember a coach referring to herself as a safety net; you have what it is you want to do and you are a support for those athletes, which means we'll let you make some mistakes but we won't let you fall from a high wire. That is a very supportive and comfortable way for athletes to function during the biggest stage and the biggest games of their lives. We've gone into games that really matter – semifinal and final games of the Olympics—behind on the scoreboard, and the environment in the locker room at halftime is incredible.*
>
> *Being in an environment where you are expected to win and you are behind at halftime can cause even the most confident athletes to question what they are doing. When your coach and your other athletes are very clear about what they need to do, the result is such that you will, at the end, win the game. It's really interesting to watch those dynamics in play; you can't leave anything out, otherwise you're not going to win."*

Gabby Douglas is again a case in point, as the widely held limiting belief was that the Olympic gold medal was beyond her reach, primarily because of her ethnic background. Yet against expectations of a Russian victory, Gabby believed in her own ability and the commitment she'd given to her training to allow herself to be fully present and become all she was destined to be. Clearly her coach reinforced her belief in herself.

We gain great insight and inspiration from Gabby, who rose above those limiting perceptions and beliefs to achieve greatness.

If you're reading this now and making excuses, singling her out as an exception, I want you to stop right now.

Every single one of you, without exception, possesses the ability to use your gifts effectively. You simply need to learn how and as the Nike slogan says…Just Do It!

Putting On and Taking Off Beliefs

As you put those peanut butter and jelly sandwiches in your belly as a kid, you also put on beliefs and coping mechanisms as a result of the Perceptions, Beliefs and Judgments that you were fed from the world around you. During my interview with Gina Maria Mele, she used the metaphor of wearing a red jacket to explain how you put on and take off your beliefs just like you put on and take off a piece of clothing:

Gina: *I've been doing belief work on myself, on thousands of my individual beliefs, for the last seven years. Over that time, the cumulative effect that's happened is I've realized that these beliefs aren't fixed things; they are more like clothes. For example, today I can wear a red jacket because it's cold outside, but I can take it off later. For most of us, we don't know we're wearing that red jacket because those beliefs are fixed. The individual belief work would be to focus on why you're hot because you've been wearing a red jacket in the summertime and you don't need it now because it's not serving you, but you can wear it again in winter if you need it. It creates a sense of flexibility in the way you view yourself in the world and in your relationship to the world.*

Anne: *You are saying that you have gotten to a place where you are able to determine whether a belief is serving you, and if so, when it can serve you best. Using your red jacket analogy, it might serve you in the wintertime, but not on a 100-degree day at the beach.*

Gina: *Yes. If individuals went through the process of removing one single belief at a time, which I call "belief work," when they realize they've been wearing that red jacket and that's why they are so hot, they also realize the only reason they are wearing it is because way back when they were young they were trying to make sense of their world subconsciously and they put on the red jacket to be warm. They didn't realize they'd done that. Yet, they've been wearing it ever since. Another benefit is that they get the idea of the red jacket being an illusion all the time. They can then choose to put it on or take it off at any time.*

As Gina's words show, at times we may find ourselves functioning in the adult world with childhood coping mechanisms. The process of shifting these beliefs is called **"reframing,"** and we will examine it in detail in a later chapter. For now, we'll move on to examining the J in the PB&Js—Judgment.

J – Judgment

As a legal term, judgment is an opinion, a decisive way of holding information that is often shrewd or punitive in some way. If you view a courthouse's definition of a judgment, one side will always win while the other loses. Extending its meaning and putting it in the context of The Gifted Trap, judgment is generally held as punitive.

Let me be clear here. All judgment is not bad. In fact, exercising "good" judgment is an important ability to have in order to live your life in a healthy way. Understanding how being judged by others as a leader or in a positive way motivates, inspires and propels you forward in life. I make the distinction here because when you use healthy, good judgment, the outcome is almost always favorable and you experience an uplifting end result.

Your emotional response in that case is positive and may be joyful because you achieved success. That is a far cry from the state of emotional entrapment that comes with the effects of negative or punitive judgmental experiences that entrap you.

When you judge yourself harshly, you are holding yourself up against unreasonable standards, and you are making a decision about whether you measure up. This can happen on a personal basis (how you judge and punish yourself), or it may affect the perceptions you hold of others too (how you judge or punish others).

Let me go a step further to emphasize and drive solidly home that this is NOT a matter of "good versus bad" either. This entire discussion we are having around perceptions, beliefs and judgment boils down to you simply becoming aware of and attuned to what is going to serve you best. Take away from this exchange what it is you need that allows you to live in authentic alignment with your truth—the truth of who you were designed to be without all the layers of limiting emotional baggage and debris weighing you down, keeping you from living into your greatness.

A wonderful example of how to get in alignment with what you are called to do lies in the story of Dr. Niki Elliott.

Niki Elliott, PhD is Founder and President of Innerlight Sanctuary. The purpose of Innerlight Sanctuary is to create a safe space where families, children and adults can safely discuss the concepts surrounding energy and intuition and how these powerful characteristics of our natural being impact our ability to function, survive and thrive in our daily life.

Dr. Niki's combination of mainstream professional degrees along with her intuitive healing arts energy expertise creates a palatable balance of two extremes of judgment. This allows people who might not otherwise open themselves to her intuitive gift, to accept it and explore the possibility that they have it as well.

Yet initially Dr. Niki struggled to come to terms with the judgments surrounding her unique gift. Dr. Niki discusses how she reframed the PB&Js together with the vital role her inner GPS played throughout the E.M.E.R.G.E. process, with a particular emphasis on self-care. She also shared her gracious daily prayer.

"The challenge came more when I chose to study energy, healing and intuition. When I chose to study it, the trap I found myself in was the perception of 'You're making it up. It's not real.' Yet once I managed to produce objectively verifiable information that I had no way of knowing, that was accurate, there was a fear in people. When people realized I could discern knowledge intuitively, it transformed from judgment to fear. The reaction was 'Now you're making me afraid that you can access more than I want you to know.'

"The trap was trying to show people that my gift is valid, but also to show that it's not always 'turned on.' I don't walk around always probing their deepest darkest secrets. It's reaching that balance that I believe everyone has. It's just the degree to which we choose to tap into it. I believe everyone can tap into it to heal—to heal within their own family structure and guide and enhance their own lives. So the trap or challenge for me was making people feel comfortable around me. But it does shift the dynamics of a conversation when people think you can see things about them."

Dr. Niki learned to reframe her gift so that others held their experience of her differently—in a healthy way. That is not always an easy process, as we will discuss.

We all have beliefs that were formed as a result of the life that we've lived and the experiences that we have personally experienced or been taught. The judgment we make is a result of the standards set by ourselves, our families, by people around us who influence us, or by society at large. Way too often that judgment does not serve you well.

Episcopal priest Susan Purnell shares her view of judgment:

"Judgment has the ability to kill if we let it. That is that judgment can block us from being open to seeing life-giving truth. On the one hand, if we are willing to pay attention to when we are judging ourselves, judging others, or feeling judged by others, we open ourselves to the opportunity for healing. By being open to these healing points we open ourselves to discover and own unmet needs that drive us to judge or be judged."

For those of you stuck in the Gifted Trap, it is unhealthy **judgment** that usually limits you and is one of the most challenging hurdles you must overcome to emerge from the trap. Too often you judge yourself, and others, unfairly. When you do, you limit both their ability and your own to achieve the unthinkable or dare to "dream the impossible dream."

If Gabby Douglas had judged herself by the perceptions and beliefs of others, do you think that she ever would have stepped onto the podium to receive her Olympic medal? The answer is a resounding 'no.'

Victoria Komova, the Russian athlete who competed against Gabby Douglas, presented herself immaculately, without so much as a single hair out of place, yet failed to achieve her goal on the day that mattered most. Gabby, on the other hand, simply showed up and achieved the impossible. On that particular day she embodied the perfect example of emerging, which we will discuss in Chapter VII.

Gabby was authentically aligned with her truth and did not allow, for a fleeting moment, the perceptions and beliefs of others to get in her way.

We can draw a parallel with my own experience in the NANGS competition, which I will explain in detail later. During the competition, on the day of the finals, I didn't allow myself to listen to the speeches of my competitors, refusing to allow any doubts to penetrate my thoughts or to begin to judge myself on whether I would measure up.

It was imperative that I stay within my zone of doing what I knew I was capable of doing and being. I allowed myself to emerge and deliver my personal best and accept that my performance was going to be good enough for me, regardless of the outcome. As I prepared to take the stage, I listened to music on my iPod and only allowed positive affirmations to enter my mind. I was there to deliver my personal best, whatever that was going to be.

One thing was certain. My best was "good enough" for me. I was determined not to judge myself and to just embrace the joy in that moment. I invite you to embrace a new mindset about judgment:

> *"The truth is that where there is limiting judgment,*
> *it is virtually impossible to experience joy."*

In examining work by the great inspirational thought leader Marianne Williamson, I came across a passage about judgment that is incredibly profound. In it she says:

> *"We live in a world that is based on a thought system of fear rather than a thought system of love. Judgment is a cornerstone of the thought system of the world. It becomes your instinct to recognize and focus on what is wrong with a person rather than what is right about them... you judge them."*

Williamson concluded her powerful message with a provocative notion:

> *"A spiritual path involves unlearning the thoughts of the world."*

Destination By Default

We are all susceptible to being lured into the gifted trap in today's world. You may be asking how you can avoid this. How can you prevent becoming trapped? You may feel that you are already trapped and are wondering how you got here.

We have already seen Gina Maria Mele's use of the red jacket metaphor, which explains how you subconsciously acquire beliefs that hold you back. Gina perfectly explained the way that you hold onto those subconscious PB&Js, believing that this is how your life is and not recognizing that you have the option to take them off whenever you choose. Accepting those PB&Js as part of life—not choosing to take off that red jacket because you don't realize that you can—you sink into emotional entrapment.

Like many situations that have the power to suck the very life out of you, entrapment doesn't happen overnight. It is an unconscious process that can begin to take root at a very early age. Dike Drummond describes how his clients slip gradually into the Gifted Trap:

*"As a doctor, we're told to sublimate our emotions. So when some-
one loses a baby, your colleagues run in the other direction rather than
support you. Healthcare mission statements are purely focused on the
patient rather than doctors and staff, so there's a "spirit-sucking-black-
hole" inside the process of becoming a doctor that no one explains to you.
You're programmed to be this way."*

Executive coach and organizational healer Erline Belton works with
executives at the pinnacle of their career success who on the surface have
it all, yet underneath find themselves caught in their own Gifted Trap.
Echoing Gina Maria Mele's sentiments, Erline explains how her clients
fall into their own emotional entrapment:

*"One thing that causes emotional entrapment is that people don't stop
to look at or examine their beliefs and how they carry them. They don't
stop to examine either their beliefs or their values. Most of the time they
don't even know where these beliefs came from. Part of my work with them
is going back and hearing their stories to help them understand where the
beliefs and values were formed, where they have served them, and where
they have been dysfunctional. If you don't find the root cause, you will
never be able to help people move outside of their entrapment. They have
to understand how they got there in the first place. Many times it comes
from childhood, from family, or from what was missing. Sometimes it
comes from what's presently occurring. Either way, those things have to be
examined so they can free themselves from the entrapment."*

As Gina and Erline both confirm, you begin to unconsciously
absorb the Perceptions, Beliefs and Judgments that envelop you and
restrict you over your lifetime, accepting them as truths when they are
in fact far from it. Over time, they become who you believe you are until
you find yourself in that state of emotional paralysis. The internal voices
of doubt and insecurity take hold of you and you are unable to access
your true self. Vasavi Kumar refers to it as her "ego" talking:

> "*The ego voice will keep you miserable, stuck and like you're the victim. You're being attacked and you're powerless...we are so trained to listen to the ego because we live in a society when it's all about 'you,' it's all about 'us' all the time...with the ego it's like being caught up like a hamster on a wheel. There is no peace at all.*"

In Vasavi's wise words,

"Where there is no peace, there is no full expression of joy."

She goes on to say:

> "*It is uncomfortable at first because we truly do think we need to be miserable on the way to being happy, but we don't. Happiness is acceptable the minute you choose it.*"

Before you know it you've stopped living joyfully. All you are doing is going through the motions...simply existing. Each day you wake up asking yourself, "What do I have to do to survive, to make it through today?" Life becomes a mundane and monotonous cycle of 24-hour periods that you string together, making it from one to the next one with little or no regard for your gifts or your passions.

Withering On the Vine

You feel trapped because you deny your own truths and don't acknowledge your gifts. In fact, you suffocate those gifts before they've ever had an opportunity to come fully to life.

Think about the green shoots of young plants. Unless we nurture the delicate signs of life and constantly clear out the weeds that invade the soil around them, these plants will be denied the chance of life. They will wither and die before they've had their chance to bloom and flower. Much like I felt when I was awakened with the realization that I had to change my life, they are suffocating and will die unless something changes dramatically.

The tragedy of the withering blossoms is that no one ever knows they existed; no one will ever be able to see the gift of their beauty.

Much like the neglected plant that slowly withers and dies, that is what happens when you are stuck in the Gifted Trap and choose to stay there.

Your gifts and passions begin to die on the vine.
Do not allow this to happen to you.

Susan Purnell, an ordained Episcopal priest living in Southern California, recalls God speaking to her during her ordination. The words Susan heard are words we should all take into our heart:

"During my ordination, just before the Bishop called my name, I heard inwardly these words: 'Susan, do not give away what I have given you.' To fulfill these words I must continue to seek the unfolding truth of what God has given to me. A central truth that I carry is that I am loved by God. Knowing this and refusing to give away this priceless gift helps me to be true to who I am and to respond to life's challenges in life-giving ways. Knowing what I have been given allows me to see more clearly when others, for reasons of their own, attempt to project onto me something different than my truth."

Through her faith and utter trust in God, Susan is able to reframe the PB&Js that may otherwise have led her into the Gifted Trap.

"Not what we say about our blessings, but how we use them, is the true measure of our thanksgiving." ~W.T. Purkiser

At the Pinnacle of Success

A common perception is that it is easy for high achievers such as world-class athletes and successful celebrities whose images grace our media to use their gifts to attain financial wealth and establish a privileged life for themselves.

However, we often see tragedies among celebrities that beg the question of whether their success was a direct result of a conscious alignment with their gifts. Was their rise to the top a response to them posing the questions "Why was I given this gift?" and "What can I do with it to make a difference?" Or, did they get steered into their success and just rode the wave, simply going through the motions. The abrupt and premature deaths of great music talents like Elvis Presley, Whitney Houston and Michael Jackson leave us wondering, "Why? Didn't they have it all?"

Premature deaths of athletes give rise to the question of whether managing success is a burden for athletes. Look at the great tennis trailblazer Arthur Ashe, who underwent heart bypass surgeries and contracted AIDS from a blood transfusion during one of his heart-related operations. The question is, was his heart condition a by-product of the stress that he endured as an African-American trailblazer in the tennis world?

Another premature loss was the tragic suicide of the 10-time All Pro, 12-time Pro Bowl selection, San Diego linebacker Junior Seau. Both the Seau and Ashe situations beg the question of whether they were suffering from emotional entrapment.

We've heard from Dike Drummond how emotionally burned out he was from living the perfect life as a successful doctor, which was simultaneously a perfect facade. And Erline Belton reflects here on the three common symptoms of the Gifted Trap that she sees regularly in her high-achieving executive clients:

> "*Number One is **loneliness**. There is a feeling of isolation because they feel they have to provide a persona to the world that says 'This is who I am.' In that persona the true person doesn't really have a chance to shine because they feel they have to protect themselves. They feel under pressure to project a certain image because that is what people expect of them and it creates a sense of loneliness.*
>
> "*Secondly, they have to be at the **top of their game all of the time**. They **don't feel they can let down the shield** and allow people to know they are vulnerable. Wearing a mask constantly drains their energy and keeps them in a space that doesn't allow them to consistently give their best because they are so busy perfecting this persona.*
>
> "*Finally, they are trying to stay in that place (at the top), believing that if they cease to project that 'perfect' persona they may lose their 'perch.' There is a **fear that people will find them out** or that they'll lose their position. This paranoia keeps them in a perpetual state of fear that uses up a huge amount of energy.*"

Even when you are at the top of your game—the pinnacle of success—the PB&Js of others can influence your life if you allow them to. The good news is that there is a way for you to overcome those PB&Js and still claim your greatness if you so choose.

We can take the example of the Olympic Games as a clear illustration of this.

Mastering and Managing Excellence

As competitors, Olympic athletes make sacrifices for at least four years prior to the Olympics. They train both body and mind to the extreme, honing their athletic abilities as close to physical perfection as is humanly possible. They leave no stone unturned to reach this pinnacle of excellence.

Carol Callan talks here about the challenges faced by the athletes she coaches:

"While our athletes come into our program as young kids, we set the tone and have a lot of excellent coaches to help them develop their game. The beauty of coming to a basketball trial or being on one of our teams is that it takes you out of your comfort zone. Young kids come to us and they've never been rejected before. We have 35 kids come to a trial and only 12 make a team. And on that 12-member team we have kids that probably don't ever come out of a game unless the team is ahead by 30 points. Which leaves half of the talented 12 on the bench most of the game.

"…. By the time players play for us in the Olympics, they will have been on 3, 4 or 5 championship teams.

"Take any professional sport; in order to stay at the top of your game and on a team you have to work on developing yourself daily and hopefully there are resources available that will help you to fill in those weaknesses."

The responsibility to master and manage your gifts is ultimately yours.

In the case of a gymnast like Gabby Douglas, her fate was in the hands of the Olympic judges. Whether she took her place on the podium or achieved a respectable placing was not her decision to make. The ultimate result rested in the judges' perception of who she was. Her responsibility was to manage her expectations of excellence and to simply be her best self.

Staying with the athletic theme, let's take a look at Venus and Serena Williams. The sisters who dominate the world of women's tennis have demolished the barriers of our perceptions. They weren't going to allow the world's PB&Js to interfere with their natural giftedness. The general perception of the world is that successful tennis players come from elite backgrounds, so two "sisters from the hood" who achieved such extraordinary success are, to all intents and purposes, anomalies.

Gabby Douglas was the first African-American gymnast to win not one but two gold medals at the 2012 Olympics. She won those in the face of the limiting PB&Js that she wasn't capable of competing in that arena because women of her ethnicity simply don't compete at that level in gymnastics—an external limitation that she did not allow to define her.

Women umpires in the national football league face the same external perceptions.

We can even look at United States President Barack Obama to see similar perceptions in action. Whether it is President Obama or previous Presidents, the world's perception is that the Commander-in-Chief is supremely powerful, to the extent of being almost superhuman and he is judged against extraordinarily high criteria—leaving him vulnerable to criticism no matter what he does.

The fact is that these seemingly omnipotent beings are flesh and blood, just like the rest of us. It is their giftedness that leads them to achieve a place of extraordinary leadership. Staying grounded in the truth of who they are meant to be and how they are meant to use their gifts is the key to a successful life for them.

The key to success is in mastering and managing of your gifts.

Unfortunately, ethnic and gender perceptions often taint the way you perceive yourself and the way others perceive you. It is up to you as a gifted individual to master and manage your commitment to excellence, to overcome judgments and escape the Gifted Trap. It is the intent of this book to offer you tools to do that.

Disappointment and Desperation

"The Most Likely To Succeed Syndrome"

During my thirteen seasons as the co-host of a NCAA women's collegiate basketball talk show, I made some interesting observations about coaches. Pat Summit and Geno Auriemma are referred to as two of the "winningest" coaches ever in women's basketball—both with incredible achievements in breaking records. The world's perception of them has been that they were bionic machines, that they had this unique ability to turn any team into winners, under any circumstances and against all odds.

To all intents and purposes, it appears that both the internal and external perceptions of such high achievers were aligned, allowing them to step up and claim their greatness. We can only surmise this, however. What is it within them that enabled them to stay quite literally at the top of their game for consecutive seasons? Did they thrive on the pressure, or did they continually try and figure out what they needed to do to win? What did they need to do to deliver and meet the expectations of others and perceptions that they are winners?

Without doubt, it was simultaneously a motivating factor and a burden, in equal amounts.

We can't all be number one winners in life. We also see those coaches and players who are highly respected for what they have accomplished during their career who don't possess a track record of winning the top trophy. Their self-perception is of someone who is "nearly there" but perhaps not quite able to complete the task set out for him or her. As they allow that limiting perception to take hold of their psyche, they limit themselves emotionally and as a result rarely progress beyond that "also-ran ranking."

Carol Callan reflects on her experience of this through her extensive coaching career:

"God doesn't give you the whole package. Sometimes you have a kid that's the greatest leader—the toughest, most competitive kid—but doesn't have the physical tools. Or you have a kid who has the physical tools but the emotional and mental package isn't there. An Olympian is gifted at maybe nine out of the ten, and a kid that doesn't make it that far is gifted either in other ways or doesn't necessarily have all the gifts necessary to keep progressing.

As a high school athletic director it was sometimes a sad reality that not every young person who tries out for a team is going to advance and play for a Division One university. For some kids it's just OK to be a high school athlete; in college it's OK to be a collegiate athlete. Sometimes it's OK to be a professional athlete, but not everyone's going to be an Olympian.'

Perhaps in the eyes of the world some people will never be winners, but the real question is: "Does that matter?"

The key to self-confidence is that as long as YOU are conscious of yourself and giving your all—your personal best—then second or third place is good enough. Sometimes, it can be a blessing because you don't have that added pressure of being expected to always win.

We heard earlier from Rainbow Chen about the subconscious—and at other times very conscious—pressure placed on her by her family, who expected her to always succeed. Here, she expands on the effect those expectations had on her life:

"… So I grew up with all 'A's in private school, and I was in there until eighth grade, until my parents realized the other pupils

were all going to religious universities. I was pulled out and put in public schools to get the opportunity to go to an Ivy League institution. My class was the most competitive class the guidance counselors said they had ever witnessed. Our GPAs were insane.

My parents came from Taiwan and part of the reason we came to the US was so I could go to the Ivy League school of my choice. I remained at the top of my class through elementary and high school, and when it came down to it, I got into every university I applied to. I chose to attend Stanford University, and graduated with a Bachelors in Human Biology and a Masters in Organizational Behavior.

One of my advertising mentors in New York said that my accolades should be like adornments you are proud of, that you can put on your lapel but they shouldn't weigh you down. *You should be able to take them on and off, depending on the situation you're in. It was one of those things I began to realize when I took ten months off after doing management consulting at a top firm after school and having my body disintegrate from all of the travel, stress and anxiety from consulting to walk away from an accolade that was wearing my body out and weighing my soul down. My mother told me not to tell anyone I quit my job that was in line with my master's degree, but my soul was dying. I had no time for dance and my creative pursuits. The work I was doing was too far removed from what I truly love—which is helping people feel more alive in their bodies."*

For a long time, Rainbow was trapped by the PB&Js that came with the cultural indoctrination that informed her that her path in life should be guided by her intellect and a desire to achieve educationally—not by a desire to express herself creatively or artistically. Only now is she beginning to emerge from the Gifted Trap as she takes control of her emotional reins and allows her artistic expression to thrive in tandem with her intellect.

You too have an opportunity to master and manage your giftedness in a way that will allow you to release the judgment and embrace joy… IF you choose.

If

A Poem By Rudyard Kipling

If you can keep your head when all about you
Are losing theirs and blaming it on you;
If you can trust yourself when all men doubt you,
But make allowance for their doubting too;
If you can wait and not be tired by waiting,
Or, being lied about, don't deal in lies,
Or being hated don't give way to hating,
And yet don't look too good, nor talk too wise:

If you can dream—and not make dreams your master;
If you can think—and not make thoughts your aim;
If you can meet with Triumph and Disaster
And treat those two impostors just the same;
If you can bear to hear the truth you've spoken
Twisted by knaves to make a trap for fools,
Or watch the things you gave your life to, broken,
And stoop and build 'em up with worn-out tools;

If you can make one heap of all your winnings
And risk it on one turn of pitch-and-toss,
And lose, and start again at your beginnings
And never breathe a word about your loss;
If you can force your heart and nerve and sinew
To serve your turn long after they are gone,
And so hold on when there is nothing in you
Except the Will which says to them: "Hold on!"

If you can talk with crowds and keep your virtue,
Or walk with Kings—nor lose the common touch,
If neither foes nor loving friends can hurt you,
If all men count with you, but none too much;
If you can fill the unforgiving minute
With sixty seconds' worth of distance run—
Yours is the Earth and everything that's in it,
And—which is more—you'll be a Man, my son!

THE BURDEN OF GIFTEDNESS

Y OU MAY BE ASKING YOURSELF HOW GIFTEDNESS CAN BE A burden. Doesn't giftedness enable you to shine in the world?

If you live in authentic alignment with yourself, your giftedness does just that. And getting you to that place is the goal of this book.

Being stuck in the Gifted Trap, on the other hand, is like being caught in a spider's web. The more you squirm to break free, the more entrapped you become because you don't understand how delicate the situation is and how you can get out.

I refer again to the story of my brother. He was extraordinarily gifted, an incredibly bright light. He was blessed with enough gifts to make him a star and he measured himself against extraordinarily high expectations—his own Perceptions, Beliefs and Judgments of himself. In conversations we would have, he seemed unfulfilled and overwhelmed at times. He seemed unable to fully live up to, or into, what he felt the world expected of him.

You may well be able to identify with the complex place in which my brother found himself, unable to meet often self-imposed expectations and unsure of which direction to take. When you are caught in the claustrophobic confines of the Gifted Trap, you feel isolated and become further entrenched with no visible means of escape. You feel burdened by your gifts. At this point your emotions go into free-fall and are expressed in ways that don't serve you. Let's explore what burdens look like.

CHARACTERISTICS & SYMPTOMS

High Self-Confidence, Yet Low Self-Esteem

As victims of the Gifted Trap your emotions can shift direction suddenly from extremely high self-confidence (when you feel you are capable of anything and appear to be on top of the world) to times when you plummet to the depths of despair, your self–esteem lower than low because you are questioning yourself. At times like this, your esteem hits an all-time low and you hit rock bottom.

This is a common occurrence among high-achievers who become successful based on their professional performance and talents yet personally doubt themselves.

In my interview with Troy Vincent, we discussed this phenomenon among super athletes. Many of them don't value themselves or they have a question mark about their own self-worth off the field. When something happens and perhaps they don't go as far as they thought they were capable of or their success starts to wane, they struggle. Finding a way to hold the emotional space of being highly visible and self-confident is hard. The super athlete begins to question his or her self-worth. Troy described it as follows:

> *"That's every day, that's who the athlete is. For the athlete typically, in most cases, your ability is what has allowed you to mask your pain—your suffering—and to disconnect from family and environment. It is your athleticism and someone celebrating your ability to perform that allows you to achieve something extraordinary. And then as you go through life and transition in life, you can wear a mask because your performance allows you to literally mask pain. So what happens is, once the performance is gone, there are no more stages to perform on, no more cheering, no more autographs. You are now into what we call your 'new normal.' What is the new normal? You are now being judged from your*

neck up. It's no longer the tackle. It's no longer the interception. It's no longer the performance on Sunday afternoon. It's now all about your gift and your character. Who are you?

Life behind a perfect façade of a gifted high-achiever can often lead to loneliness and depression. There is a constant need to live up to expectations in your personal life that match how you performed professionally.

An excerpt from my interview with Vasavi Kumar shows how that can often manifest itself in depression and can be a symptom of bipolar disorder. Vasavi describes it as:

"… that awareness of having to be 'on.' Most human beings are on auto-pilot, driven by a subconscious flame. I'm very conscious. With that level of consciousness comes a great responsibility. So there is no way I can let myself off the hook. Even if I wanted to, I am ridden with guilt. The lights are always on from the time I wake up until the time I go to sleep—when the lights are always on you can see everything. You can't ignore anything. For me it manifested itself in bipolar disorder, a battle between my ego and my higher consciousness, and it was so much easier to listen to my ego. That was the easy way out. I know better now and to reach the level of success I want to reach, I have to manage my ego and challenge the chatter of the ego in my mind. It's a lot of work and often exhausting! But I am learning how to deal with myself in kinder and more compassionate ways.

"People think it's effortless because of the results I produce, but it doesn't just come. I have to focus, I have to prioritize and choose who I'm hanging out with, and have to choose not to go out and get drunk on the weekends like many young people choose to do as a way of not dealing. I question myself—is that what I really want to do? No, it's not. Most people are on autopilot—I'm not on autopilot."

Alienation and Loneliness

Victims of the Gifted Trap are often paralyzed by a sense of alienation and isolation; they tend to be perfectionists, seeking excellence in everything they do. Though they are outwardly perceived as having high levels of self-confidence, internally they are often plagued by perpetual self-doubt. This low self-esteem inside a person with high self-confidence would shock those on the outside if they only knew.

On the surface you are multi-talented, multi-gifted, and are a highly intelligent person, yet inside you are battling with demons that threaten to destroy you. You feel separated from the world and alienated from reality, with no one to understand you.

Let's take a look at the beautiful soul of Whitney Houston as a prime example. Whitney's life epitomized the debilitating effects of the gifted trap. To the rest of the world she had everything; she was blessed with beauty, intelligence and the awesome, inspirational talent of her sublime voice. Yet those closest to her shared at her memorial service that somewhere within her lay this overriding sense of **not being good enough**.

Throughout her short life she searched for respect, acceptance and validation. She longed to be valued and loved for who she was, to be understood emotionally, and to feel like she belonged, yet somehow she failed to reach a level of acceptance that allowed her gifts and allowed her to be at peace with herself.

Many gifted people are at the top of their game and feel like they can't afford to let their guard down for one moment. You feel you are continually expected to be perfect. You seek a sense of community, acceptance and a place you can call home.

At the same time there are so many gifted people wallowing in frustration because they, on the other hand, can't see how to reach the top. You are trapped in your environment living a "less than" life, allowing yourself to be "less than" you deserve to be. Sometimes you reach the point where in **trying to be all things to all people**, your inner flame, that inner spark that propels you forward, begins to fade. Your emotional equilibrium becomes unbalanced and unstable, and a slide towards depression is extremely common.

Corporate executive Natasha Phoenix explains how after years of unparalleled success she experienced a professional setback that greatly affected her:

> *"I had one major setback with a boss who came in and took me to task for a series of irrational, unethical things he wanted me to do which I wouldn't do. I ended up leaving that job and became involved in an interesting lawsuit that dragged on for five months. During that time I just shut down and I realized that going back to work at that point was going to be really difficult. Everything I'd known and believed about myself had just fallen apart. When you're desperate, you look for a short-term fix.*
>
> *At that point, I went to my doctor. He knew I was in a stressful job—I traveled a lot and had people reporting in to me. He gave me anti-depressants, which I took for two days. In those two days I was in such a drunken stupor because of those tablets that I realized I had to do it the hard way. I went back to my doctor and he pointed me towards this meditation program, it's called Mindful Meditation—I think this is going to be a lifetime in development. The interesting thing was it forced me to deal with a lot of my belief systems. I thought it was a career thing and that my breakdown was a result of losing this one job, but it was a result of all those things that had been pent up inside me since I was a kid.*

As we have seen, often highly intelligent and multi-talented people like Natasha Phoenix and Carole Martin-Wright in Chapter III have feelings of alienation and loneliness as they struggle to balance their giftedness.

Perfectionism – The "Disease to Please"

Another symptom of being in the Gifted Trap is the constant striving for perfectionism, the "disease to please" people. Melissa Evans reflected in Chapter II on her constant attempts to play herself down and make people around her feel better about themselves.

In my interview with Marie Guthrie, she described the disease to please this way:

> *"It feels like you are alone, with a responsibility that if you aren't the best and don't uphold your skills and talents, you are somehow going to fail and let down, not just yourself, but all those who are counting on you. It's time to break this savior/martyr pattern that all talented great people are in and to realize that you can't do it by yourself anymore."*

It is a behavioral pattern that is all too common among Erline Belton's high achieving clients. She explains as follows:

> *"The whole concept of 'not being good enough' is tied to the high-achievers' need to be perfect. But the drive for perfection is an endless pursuit. You can never get there because you always feel you could have done more. In high achievers you find it over and over again. The quest for perfection becomes the driver, so it's never good enough; they can never reach that peak. So that leads to the feelings of 'not good enough.'*
>
> *"The part that's too good is the part that wants to please everybody and 'make nice.' That's an endless pursuit, too, because there are some people you will never please, no matter what you do. Part of the work in that space is finding your voice. Finding your voice is really the critical part of getting out of the Gifted Trap. Until you find your voice and have the courage to speak up—even though it doesn't please people—is when you get in touch with your most powerful self. The finding of your voice is the critical part of moving out of that other place."*

Gifted people continually wrestle with an internal tug-of-war that is symptomatic of this syndrome. Finding out how to exist in the world means you often live with the internal battle of "Are you good enough?" and the external pressure of "You're too good; you're too perfect." This struggle feels like you are walking through life on a proverbial "tight-rope," always afraid of falling.

If you are too good, too perfect, you may well find that people will want to cut you down.

Walking A Tightrope

During the process of emerging into authentic alignment we learn how to walk the tightrope and discern how we wish to show up in the world. Vasavi Kumar personifies this ability. As the following interview extract demonstrates, Vasavi suppressed her natural personality when she sensed resentment towards her from others who were uncomfortable with her giftedness:

Anne: *Have you ever been in a situation where you knew you were just simply being all you are and being true to you, and even in doing just that little bit you found that the rest of the world couldn't handle it? So the rest of the world didn't acknowledge you. Did they ignore you and pass over you for someone else? It's a situation where your brilliance is too much and you were denied something.*

Vasavi: *I know when my brilliance is too much. So, if there is any shred of "haterism," I won't show up in my brilliance because I know where it is I want to play.*

Anne: *That demonstrates a level of awareness when you have emerged from The Gifted Trap and you are very clear that you are authentically aligned and you know how to walk the tightrope and balance. You are very discerning about how you want to show up in the world.*

You epitomize the end result of this project, Vasavi. You are liberated from the trap. This book is all about emerging and surrendering, becoming aware of your internal PB&Js and reframing them so that they serve you rather than limit you. You have what I have defined in the book as a "misfit gift." You've found a way to emerge and be totally aligned as who you are in a way that brings joy to yourself and others.

Living a "Less-Than Capable" Life

Melissa Evans discussed in Chapter II the effect of living a "less than" capable life, having to play small to stay safe and avoid offending the people that she worked with and for. On one hand, she played small to stay safe. Yet internally she wrestled with her constant striving for perfection. The two mindsets were at opposite ends of her emotional high wire, and she was in search of a safe emotional haven.

Turning again to my interview with Vasavi Kumar, she revealed how this phenomenon still affects her from time to time:

> Vasavi: *If I'm around certain people there's a jealousy I feel from them. I immediately become a child. It happened just two weeks ago with someone who was very condescending. I immediately became "less than" and I usually fight with my husband after that because I want him to save me from that "child mode"!*
>
> Anne: *You cause them to experience their own insecurities and dissatisfaction with where they are in their lives in terms of accepting and loving themselves. Yet that child inside you that wants to be loved and held and invited to play on the playground feels in some way that you did something to make them not want to play with you.*

Balancing your emotions as you walk across the high wires in your life requires awareness of what you are facing, and the energy to endure it. Both the challenge and the secret are to manage your PB&Js emotionally so you remain physically healthy.

Determination / Exhaustion / Burnout

Too often high achievers learn the hard way about the high price of staying in perpetual pursuit of perfection. In Chapter III, we saw how a combination of Carole Martin-Wright's own determination and the PB&Js she was resolute about living up to eventually conspired against her.

Carole was caught in classic emotional entrapment. It was taking its toll on her both emotionally and physically:

> *"It was a teeter-totter between exhaustion and determination, and at some point I figured out that I was going to outlast this guy because they had brought someone in to succeed him—which is another interesting story about how that played out—or he was going to have to fire me, and I knew what separation packages they paid."*

Carole still suffers from the consequences of that burnout and is slowly emerging from her own Gifted Trap. Occasionally she is still plagued by doubts about whether the path she has taken is the right one for her, but she is working through it. Her experience is typical of high achievers determined to prove themselves despite the toll it takes on them.

Struggles Inside the Trap

Self-Doubt

Sufferers caught in the gifted trap often find themselves experiencing searing loneliness, isolation, and a lack of self-esteem underscored by overwhelming self-doubt.

My brother's story demonstrates the all-too-real consequences of the burden of giftedness when it is coupled with a sense of self-doubt.

As I mentioned previously, my brother, Gus was multi-talented. He was a great student, an athlete, and a talented musician. As a high school freshman, he was identified as a "highly-gifted African-American high school student." It was the 1960s and Ivy League preparatory schools were looking to integrate their classrooms. Gus was recruited to attend Deerfield Academy in Massachusetts. The chance to attend an Ivy League preparatory school was a rare opportunity that my parents agreed was an honor that he should take advantage of—even though it meant sending him thousands of miles away from Texas, where our family lived. Typical of my brother, he quickly excelled, being selected for the gymnastics team, participating in the choir, and playing on the football team too. On top of that, he was an exceptional scholar in the classroom.

It seemed that nothing was beyond him, and in the world's eyes he had the potential to go far in his life. He was perceived as "most likely to succeed" and was certainly destined for greatness.

Yet there was more to the story. The environment that my brother was thrust into was an alien existence for him. It was a reality filled with Caucasian young men who were born into a world of privilege with expectations of attending Ivy League schools.

The environment was literally and figuratively much colder (think Texas versus Massachusetts). It was a lonely place for a teenager to be on his own thousands of miles away from his family.

Yet my brother never complained. He was aware of the huge opportunity that he had been presented with and the sacrifices that our parents made for him. He felt he had to live up to the expectations placed on him.

At first he succeeded even under the burden of great expectations. He graduated with flying colors from Deerfield. From there he became one of the first black students at Johns Hopkins University in Baltimore, Maryland.

After completing three full years of college—one year shy of graduating from one of the top universities in the country—he hit an emotional wall and dropped out of Johns Hopkins. That was the beginning of my brother's slide into emotional entrapment—the beginning of his spiraling descent into the "Trap."

Fortunately, several years later he returned to Hopkins and finished his education. But at that point, he was already in a place of emotional entrapment, struggling to manage his PB&Js.

His multi-talented giftedness brought with it both great opportunities and great expectations, which for him were both societally- and self-imposed. When he reached a point of feeling he was not living up to and into those expectations adequately, he struggled emotionally and resorted to behavior patterns that took him deeper into the trap.

In our regular brother-sister talks, he would express feelings of frustration and inadequacy. It seemed as though he felt like somewhat of an imposter. Despite his many successful accomplishments, he seemed to feel he presented himself one way on the outside, while he was feeling "less than" on the inside. After all, in his mind, he was the son of a modern-day king of sorts. As his namesake, he felt there was an expectation for him to be a rising prince. They were big shoes to fill.

The internal warfare and burden he lived with is symptomatic of people caught in the gifted trap. For many, it is described as a state of paranoia that paralyzes you. It keeps you stuck just waiting for the world to find out what is really happening behind your perfect façade.

You may have all the accoutrements and accomplishments in the world, yet underneath them remains a void of desperation and an overwhelming sense that you are **"less than."**

As we have seen from the interview with Erline Belton, these emotions apply to people at the top of their game who are fighting hard to stay there and in doing so are living a less than optimal life. Equally, it applies to people who have yet to find their way to a successful perch in their mind, who settle for mediocrity, who are scared to step out because they are afraid of either their own failure or their own success.

The self-doubt we heard about in the previous chapter that plagued Jennie Hernandez meant that her perceptions of herself were at odds with the reality of who she really was:

> *"...I had a tendency to accept what was given to me, those limiting beliefs. I just accepted what I was 'taught' by my mother. As I look back now I see my perceptions of myself were very inaccurate... I realize that I wasn't ugly or bad. I was just different.... I believed what I thought was true, rather than knowing reality. I always had the highest scores and test grades at school. I started playing the piano when I was young. I was smart and talented, a great sibling and kind to people—but it's interesting **how we judge ourselves in spite of reality.**"*

Even when all of the evidence is there that you are gifted and special, that you are unique, your own self-doubt can deny what is actually your truth.

People struggling with acute self-doubt inevitably start to lose their equilibrium. With that, their zest for life diminishes too. Ultimately, you begin to simply go through the motions of life and/or succumb to self-sabotaging behavior and overindulgence (i.e., excessive eating, drugs, alcohol, or even sex).

Sabotaging Behavior – Being a Victim

Self-sabotage is one of the most destructive—and in some cases potentially fatal—aspects of the Gifted Trap. To illustrate this point, allow me to share a story about a beautiful soul called Jennifer.[4]

Jennifer was a gifted young woman with three beautiful children. She had divorced her children's father and was in a new relationship with someone she loved very much. Jennifer expressed to me that although she and her partner were very much in love, his family—in particular, his mother—was reluctant to accept her. This lack of acceptance by his family became a source of tension between Jennifer and her beau and was driving a wedge between them.

Over time, Jennifer lost her emotional footing—she sank deeper and deeper into her own emotional quicksand, which threatened to totally engulf her. One evening after a particularly embittered exchange with her partner about how his family treated her and judged her, the abyss of Jennifer's emotional entrapment became too much for her and she ended her own life.

The tragedy was that Jennifer failed to find a safe place to be inside herself. She was striving for acceptance, acknowledgement and recognition of her greatness. She allowed herself to be defined by the perceptions and

---

4   Name has been changed

judgments of other people. In the midst of wrestling with her emotional entrapment she failed to love herself and allowed the limiting PB&Js of her surrounding world to gain a deep seated hold on her spirit. They recklessly whipped her around until she just couldn't take the pain anymore.

The burden of giftedness, as we have seen with Jennifer, has the potential to lead to extreme self-sabotage when what you expect of yourself doesn't live up to either your own or the world's perceptions. It has the propensity to become an ever-swirling downward spiral. The internal emotional "twister," in its most critical form—without any emergency preparedness or evacuation plan from "the trap"—can whip a person around, leaving mental devastation and physical destruction in its wake.

Both Jennifer and my brother struggled with an overwhelming sense of self-doubt and became victims of their own giftedness.

As you fall deeper into the trap, the dilemma of your giftedness may manifest itself in the form of self-sabotaging behavior patterns that arise out of frustration and desperation.

Self-sabotaging behavior has the propensity to turn into addictive patterns when your day-to-day reality becomes the world you long to escape from. Common unhealthy ways of escaping include alcohol and drug abuse or inappropriate sexual behavior. Seeking solace in a path that isn't healthy all too often leads the emotionally entrapped person into compromising situations and relationships with devastating consequences—sometimes with life-ending outcomes.

It happened to Jennifer. It happened to my brother. Don't let it happen to you!

Searching For Joy In All The Wrong Places

Relief from the trap, when sought through artificial states of joy, yields only fleeting moments of utopia. The temporary relief eventually wears off, reality returns, and in floods the realization that the dank trap is even colder and lonelier. The immediate response becomes a desire to seek that high and douse that discomfort again by indulging even more in unhealthy ways of reaching that utopic state. It becomes a perpetual cycle of searching for joy in all of the wrong places—anything to numb the emotional pain.

I am so grateful to the beautiful Vasavi Kumar for being gutsy and sharing her first-hand experience of self-sabotaging behavior during her period of emotional entrapment:

> *"You name it, I did it. I numbed myself through alcohol, through seeking validation through men, through my drug of choice—cocaine—through marijuana, and so on. Yet I needed more. For me, cocaine made me feel like a demi-goddess; it was a very safe place for me. On a high I felt like I could do anything. When I came down, I needed to get back there. I sabotaged myself through self-medication and being with the wrong people to fill an emotional void.*
>
> *"I was very disconnected; it was like my ego was in one place, my higher God in another, my spirit in another and my body elsewhere, and I was trying to manage all of it. I didn't know what to do. It was all too much, juggling five different personalities in one shell of a body.*
>
> *"For many gifted people it's cigarettes, alcohol, higher drugs, and men. But I have to admit I had to go through that experience to get back to this centeredness because I had to go through that to come back and do a 180-degree turn and remember 'who I truly am.' Even in that chaos I could still hear that higher consciousness telling me 'This is not you'—but who was I? I had to go through that suffering—and it was the worst period of my life—to really learn how to operate from that higher place. I always had it. I just didn't know how to use it."*

When you are caught in the trap, as Vasavi shows, you are vulnerable to this self-sabotaging behavior. It takes an awareness of where you are, and a deep willingness, to reach for lifelines to get out.

The tragedy of this predicament is that there are so many of you who possess incredible gifts and talents that, if you channeled them in a totally different way, would lead to your being extremely successful in your life. The narrow-minded PB&Js that have dominated your life have become deeply ingrained in your mind. You see yourself as simply "not good enough." This is an opportunity for you to use your gifts in a way that you begin to value yourself. That will give you what you need to claw your way out of the trap.

In the unfortunate case of my brother, he abused his body to the point where his body rebelled and yelled at him, finally saying, "I can't do this anymore." In December 2008 he suffered a fatal stroke.

Being Discredited By Others

When threatened by your giftedness, often the people around you will resort to undermining you and take measures to douse your light. This is an all too common occurrence on professional playing fields, can have significant ramifications in your life and calls for you to find a way to cope with attempts to discredit you.

Carole Martin-Wright understands the devastating effects all too well, as she experienced it first hand:

> *"In the middle of this, when you've been emotionally devastated and you're questioning whether you really are a legitimate player in this arena, is the time you have to put on your happy confident face. You are expected to talk to a lot of people who want to know how you are and what's going on. And you really don't want to discuss it. So you expend a lot of energy finding a way to tell the story that is a fair representation of what happened yet doesn't sound like I'm 'falling on the sword.' You go through denial, anger—'I can't believe they did this to me'—and you eventually reach a point of resolution and understand why what happened, happened."*

Melissa Evans explained how her own colleagues attempted to discredit her on a regular basis:

> *"I would be giving a speech for a client and my own colleagues would want to attack me with questions in an attempt to discredit me, while I was serving a client. That happened more than once."*

And for Natasha Phoenix, the resentment and attempts to discredit her led to a personal crisis point:

> *"So that was a jolt to my system because up until then, despite the hurdles in my life, I'd been really successful and on an upward track and that was just a dead stop to me personally and in my career. It was the thing that shut me down."*

As Natasha struggled to cope with what was happening in her professional life, her personal life was challenging her too. Her family witnessed her breakdown and helped her to label it in a healthy way.

> *"There were two things that converged. I lost my job, and my dog of fifteen years died at the same time. I'm a huge animal lover and I ended up falling in love with a puppy that I bought to replace my dog. My family called it my maternity leave, as opposed to 'Natasha lost her job!'"*

I applaud Natasha and her family. She intuitively realized what she needed was something to pour herself into as a healthy distraction from all the loss she was experiencing. And bravo to her family for helping her hold that devastating period of loss and grief in a positive way.

Learning how to reframe being publicly discredited and diminished is a critical component to managing your way through crises in your life. Understanding that you have a choice in how you respond is the first step in the reframing process.

I will share more about this valuable tool in the section on how you E.M.E.R.G.E from your trap. Keep reading.

Play Small Or Be A Target

In the depths of despair and emotional entrapment, it is not surprising that you begin to "play small," to dull your natural talents in order to avoid being a target. Melissa Evans' attempt to "play small" left her feeling increasingly unfulfilled.

"I was contributing my gift to a corporation that thought every-thing was fabulous, but I was living 30-60% on a great day just to make others feel comfortable and I felt stifled."

This is a typical "trapped" experience. You feel in your heart that you have the capacity to produce so much more than you are putting out, yet you know that to exert yourself and "show up" fully will be like wearing a T-shirt with a bull's-eye on it. You are reluctant to step forward for fear that when you do the daggers will start flying at you from every direction. Therefore you decide that it is better to play it safe than to be sorry. The problem is that deep inside you know you are capable of more. That reality causes an internal feeling of discontent.

Can you dare to step out and claim all that you are capable of? It is possible. You are being called to step out and dare to claim all that is possible.

Misunderstood

To have your words or actions inaccurately interpreted can be frustrating, disheartening and the source of great emotional angst that people struggle with. Being misunderstood hits a common chord among many, and reverberates within me as I write this book. Too often throughout my life I struggled with others misinterpreting the intentions behind my actions or words. The dilemma of being misunderstood occurs when the intention behind an act or the communication delivered is not received in alignment with the original intent.

In short, misunderstandings happen when the message that the sender intends to send is not what the receiver receives.

This happens frequently when words or actions are taken out of context and get muddied by the receiver's PB&Js. What often results is an unpleasant exchange that fuels deep-rooted emotional scars and activates internal chatter in your mind.

Ineffective and unclear communications—both verbal and non-verbal—are the root of so many emotional upsets that you face in life. You listen and read communications through emotionally cloudy, murky and muddy PB&J lenses. The lack of clarity, open honest dialogue, and ability to have exchanges rooted in love with others keeps you struggling in the quicksand of life.

Feelings of being misunderstood are a direct result of the lack of clarity on three levels:

- *Lack of clarity of the message itself;*
- *Lack of clarity in the way the message was communicated or delivered; and*
- *Lack of clarity in the way the message was received or interpreted.*

To have greater clarity and more effective communication, five elements, in my opinion are necessary to have your messages understood. They are:

1. **Intention.** The aim or objective of the message being sent must be clear to the sender. Knowing the desired outcome of the communication is always a healthy first step. Taking that a step further and stating the intention out loud to the receiver reduces the margin of error for misunderstanding.

2. **Context.** Establishing surrounding conditions or a framework for the transfer of the data or message is a foundational component. Messages delivered without the proper context almost always are misinterpreted because it is left to the receiver to frame the message within whatever context he or she chooses.

3. **Verbal exchange.** The actual selection of words is important. My mentor, Marcia Wieder, has a slogan that is most appropriate in regard to this concept. Her sage wisdom is to always "Say what you mean and mean what you say." If we could all commit to this honest way of communicating, without manipulation or emotional jousting, there would be far fewer emotional battles being fought in the world.

4. **Congruency**. Vocal tone, inflection and body language can speak volumes. When they are not congruent with the verbal words being spoken, the receiver of the message gets mixed signals and does not trust what is being said. Being clear and having all facets of the message delivery aligned—intention, context, verbal and non-verbal elements—will considerably reduce and minimize misunderstanding.

5. **Listening deeply**. This is likely the most important element to effective communication, as it's clear that listening makes a huge difference. Too often we tune others out and don't hear what is being said. Developing the practice of listening deeply—not only to what others are saying to you, but also to what you are saying out loud and the messages that are going on within you—is a major component of more effective communicating.

   In order to listen, you must be silent. I find it most fascinating that both words—**listen and silent**—have the exact same letters. Reflect on that for a moment. **You must be silent to listen**.

I owe my mentor Arthur Joseph a debt of gratitude for helping me fully grasp the concept of "Deeper Listening." It is a cornerstone of his work called Vocal Awareness™ and has served as a pivotal paradigm shift for me. Once I fully grasped the magnitude of the freedom that was available to me when I focused on living in a place of deeper listening, it became significantly easier for me to eliminate limiting judgment from my communications with others and allowed me to recognize when unfair judgment was being inflicted on me. I then had the opportunity to choose whether to allow the judgment that wasn't serving me to take me on a wild roller-coaster ride or not.

You too have the ability to manage the emotional manipulation that you feel when you are misunderstood. You get to choose. From this moment on, I invite you to be more conscious of how you are communicating AND to choose how you receive the communications that are delivered to you.

The concept of "choice" is so empowering. As Arthur says, "even in the act of not choosing, we are making a choice."

Two Greatest Fears

It is Arthur again whom I thank for raising my awareness of the two greatest fears that most people wrestle with. They are the **Fear of Abandonment** and the **Fear of Claiming Your Greatness.**

Think about it. The one thing that frightens little children more than anything is being left alone with no one to care about them or love them. In that regard we never really grow up. We all want the same thing—to have another person truly care about us. You will go to great lengths to keep from feeling like others are turning their backs on you and leaving you alone. Right?

What I found most interesting is how your psyche works, signaling you that it senses abandonment in the most unusual circumstances and putting up barricades that hold you back from claiming your greatness. In the chapter that follows, we will go into more depth about the voices within you, what they say to you, and how you react based on your fears.

As I searched my emotional memory bank for an example of being misunderstood and fearful, a childhood memory came to mind that speaks not only to being misunderstood, but also to one of the most common and greatest fears—the fear of abandonment. This story illustrates how emotional wounding happens in childhood, takes root in your psyche, begins to hold you hostage in emotional prison, and continues to keep you trapped into adulthood.

It was the summer that I turned thirteen. My family was moving from Houston to Washington, DC. My parents were juggling the massive job of moving a family across country. They made the best decisions they could at the time. One was to send my grandfather and me ahead of the rest of the family to stay with my mother's sister and her family. It so happened that my body was changing that summer. So much was happening inside me. Moving exacerbated an already emotional time. I was struggling to make sense of so many emotions and fears.

Several weeks later, when my family finally arrived in DC, they all stayed with my father's sister and brother-in-law. Instead of being reunited as a family, I stayed where I was and did not get to interact with my family on a daily basis. While my aunt, uncle and cousins that I was staying with were very loving, it was still very hard for me to handle my feelings of being isolated and alienated from my family.

While I never expressed it to anyone, inside I was confused and upset that I had not participated in the going away parties with the rest of my family. Nobody ever bothered to ask how I felt or what was important to me. What I was longing for was attention and a need to know that I mattered. So, I devised a plan to get the attention that I longed for. I decided to run away. Now, I was smart enough to know not to put myself in any real danger. I ran away by climbing a big tree in the back yard at the house where my family was staying.

When my parents realized that I was nowhere around, a massive search for me was initiated. Several hours passed. I had been missing long enough for everyone to take my absence seriously, and I felt that my objective or intention to get attention had been achieved. As my father walked under the tree where I was, I decided to speak out and let him know I was OK. What happened next was totally *not* part of my plan.

My father told me to come down out of the tree right that minute. The anger in his voice was far from the caring, compassionate, love-filled embrace I had imagined would come at the end of my carefully crafted plan. Instead of getting the love I was longing for, I was scolded and reprimanded for how much trouble I had caused. Not once did anyone ask why I had done it or what it was that I was feeling that had made me do it. My action was misunderstood, in my mind, and I was further emotionally abandoned. I felt awful. I felt unloved. I felt like what I needed and wanted just didn't matter.

In hindsight I understand that my parents' decisions and actions were coming from a place of love and concern. But back then it was emotionally painful. In the next chapter, we will revisit the effects that the move to Washington that summer had on me and how voices set up camp inside my emotional trap with me and were determined to protect me from ever feeling that kind of pain again.

What You Long For From Inside the Trap

Above everything, all victims of the Gifted Trap are seeking is that one elusive element in life…LOVE!

Love

Sometimes, when you are gifted, the people around you assume that you do not need their help and that you are self-sufficient, yet at times, nothing could be further from the truth, as Vasavi Kumar explains:

> *"The perception that people have is that I don't need their help, that I have it all together. Unless I ask for support I don't have any help, and I rarely ask for support. A colleague told me she hadn't called me in a few months because she saw from my Facebook page that I was doing well and she remarked, 'What do you need that I can give you?'*
>
> *"I said to her, 'I still need love. I may not need your tangible help, your resources or your money, but I still need love and acknowledgement like everybody else.' The lonely part of being gifted is that people don't think they can contribute in certain ways, but just because you can make things happen and manifest in your life doesn't mean you don't require the basic human needs of being loved."*

With love comes acceptance and feeling respected and valued by other people at last. Later in her interview, Vasavi reveals how it was the love of the man who was to become her husband who helped her to find inner peace:

> *"Honestly, I was saved by my husband. Now that may sound like a fairy tale, but I needed someone who was unshakeable. I needed saving. I got that from my husband. His name is Ashish Patel. My husband was able to be with all of me. He was often confused and bewildered, but he just held me. This went on for four years, but he was that solid person in my life who just wanted to love all of me. It wasn't that easy for me. I had to grow into his love; I found it impossible that he would want to*

love me, but he did. His love was always there. I only had to give myself permission to be loved."

The invitation I offer to you within these pages is to love yourself. It is indeed the greatest love of all.

Acceptance

A **sense of community** is vital to feeling grounded and connected. Finding a network or a community of like-minded people where you are free to celebrate your giftedness is a seemingly insurmountable challenge for many people. You deserve a safe place, a haven to celebrate your gifts rather than find fault with others or find a way to diminish them.

You deserve a safe space to nurture and love yourself so you are able to EMERGE into a healthy frame of mind.

As I explained to Marie Guthrie during my interview with her,

"being in community with others that are emerging from the trap makes the process less scary and more of a fulfilling adventure. It makes it easier to step towards your fear. And when you do…it disappears."

If you, or someone you know, are looking for a community to support you as you emerge from your trap, I invite you to visit www. TheGiftedTrap.com to find out how to engage with other gifted and talented adults who, like you, are committed to claiming their greatness.

Validation

In addition to wanting the blessing of acceptance, you also likely seek validation from others to confirm who you are, that what you are doing is acceptable. Carole Martin-Wright admits she thrives on validation:

"It sounds trite to say that external validation is important for me, but I'm very comfortable with the idea that it's OK for people to tell you when you've helped them, when you've made them laugh or helped them solve a problem. That creates strength for me. It's like 'I did a little bit of good today. Maybe I should try again tomorrow and maybe it will happen again,' and even if it only happens once or twice in a lifetime, that's enough."

In the book **The Five Love Languages**, author Gary Chapman cites "words of affirmation" as one of the five dominant ways people experience feelings of being loved.

Understanding the power you give to being validated and what is possible when you learn to validate yourself and others can make a profound difference in your emotional stability.

Knowing You Are Not Alone

When caught in the Gifted Trap you will remain in the unbearable state of not knowing where to turn. This will not change until you begin to live in alignment with your gifts and identify safe, restorative places to heal and stay healthy.

For Carole Martin-Wright the simple, yet therapeutic, exchange of stories during my interview with her helped her to recognize that she is not alone:

"Thank you for sharing your story with me and giving me the opportunity to share mine, because we always have days when we think we are the only one in the world going through these emotional challenges...so thank you so much for that."

Just like you and everyone else, I long to use my gifts and have them appreciated. I'm writing these words sitting here in my perfect little garden that I crafted with my own little hands. This is one of the safe spaces I created to nurture my soul.

My culinary queen mother passed down to me the gift of cooking with love. I know how to make bread that melts in your mouth and how to cook creole food to tantalize your taste buds. I show up in a "physically fit body," always looking the part—not to prove anything, but just to be me. I was blessed with natural talent and gifts. As I grew up I was fortunate enough to be exposed to experiences that allowed me to become this whole expression of myself.

My desire is no different than that of most people. I simply want a place where I am free to celebrate my giftedness, be loved for it and be accepted for it—just as I am—without having to play it down in any way. We all need validation and a special place that honors our giftedness.

When you can't see a way to "show up" in your giftedness, to live comfortably in your own skin, and to share your unique talents and gifts with the world, you may resort to behavior patterns that excuse you from not having lived up to it. The examples of Jennifer and my brother, Gus, epitomize the physical manifestations of the Gifted Trap that have the propensity to lead to life-threatening and life-ending situations.

In both cases, and in seemingly different ways, they were enmeshed in that trap. In my brother's case, I feel he died with beautiful songs buried in his soul.

How many of you have incredible songs within you that you're afraid to sing?

Waking up in the dark on my own life-changing night made me realize that I had a choice. I could choose to stay where I was and lead a life full of "what-if's," full of regrets…or I could challenge myself to be courageous enough, bold enough, and brave enough to step out and see what was possible.

It would have been easier to remain "comfortably uncomfortable—and that is what it was, painfully comfortable. Many of you reading this book will be in just that place, wrestling with your inner voice, waiting to hear words of encouragement, in search of a lifeline or an affirmation.

Getting clear in your own mind about where along your journey you are is vital. AND—I promise you this—there IS a way out of The Gifted Trap.

Some say they CAN and some say they CAN'T. Both are right. Which do you choose?

As you embrace a new way of being with yourself, it is almost inevitable to feel a sense of loss or grief because you are letting go of an old way of being. This feels much the same as losing a loved one.

After losing my brother and father within a month of each other, and then my uncle two months later, I became aware of a new space in my life that represented the grief I was feeling. I penned a message to describe it. I offer it to you as you leave an old way of being behind and embrace a new attitude...

This Space Called Grief
by Anne Palmer

This space called grief is really a new existence, I believe
One we find when our loved ones are called to leave

Sometimes it comes without warning, a sudden jolt to the heart
Other times a bit more peaceful when from earth they depart

For all who loved them, there is a newly imposed reality
One that calls for us to adjust and find a new center quickly

It requires new thinking, feeling—tolerance to emotional pain
Holes in hearts must heal, and minds must now be re-trained

To hold memories of the good times, the laughter…the love
Remember bodies leave…but souls watch over us from above

We find ourselves asking questions like…where are they, you
think?"
The reply, "right here in our hearts. Close your eyes you'll see them
wink"

Walking with eyes closed—not an option that makes very
good sense
Instead we find other ways to be with them—adapt to this
new existence

When grieving over any type of loss, there is no right or wrong way
Patience, understanding are needed—another choice is to pray

Grief will teach us so much—through this experience we will grow
The goal is to…listen, learn, love…because deep inside we know

While we have waves of emptiness, our lives are richer in
other ways
Gestures of concern, compassion from others fill our days

Friends and family take time to express that they care
To offer heartfelt condolences and reassure us they are there

So we focus on the good stuff, no room for negative energy
at this time
Healthy healing is the mantra to meditate on and hold in
our mind

Wherever you are in the waves of emotion that grief and
sorrow cause
Take time to tell others you love them…take time to pause

That is why I chose to share this poem—what it is meant to do
To inspire you to turn to someone close and say…my dear,
"I Love You"!

THE VOICES WITHIN

D O YOU HAVE A VOICE IN YOUR HEAD? I DO. AND IN fact it's not just one voice; it's many voices. It can be a jarring and unpleasant sound when they are all talking at once—with each one of them expressing its perspective as the one I should listen to and act on. Those voices can be debilitating and paralyze you in a place of not knowing who to listen to or what to do. These voices represent the "parts"—parts of your psyche that are formed as you grow up as a result of the Perceptions, Beliefs and Judgments (PB&Js) we have been discussing.

In your youth, the PB&Js that you are exposed to can hurt you and make you feel emotional pain that you never want to experience again. In an effort to protect you, your subconscious mind and inner emotional security guards come to your rescue and establish defense mechanisms in the form of behavior patterns to warn you and keep you safe from harm and pain. Your security guards seek to communicate with you on a conscious level. So they speak to you as voices in your head, reminding you what you should think and what behavior you should default to.

Different voices are created to protect different aspects or "parts" of your emotional landscape. Each voice had its own unique set of reasons for being formed in response to specific wounding that you experienced in your past. And each voice firmly believes in its mission and the tactics it developed to keep you safe.

On the surface, the concept sounds simple and reasonable. The challenge comes into play when the various voices attempt to speak and exercise influence that runs counter to what you want for you. It is especially challenging when more than one is speaking at the same time, creating an internal tug-of-war. When they all try to speak at once, the sound becomes much like a dissonant choir—each voice wanting to sing a solo rather than sing in harmony with the rest of the choir.

This gets further complicated as you grow into adulthood and find that the advice the voices are giving, and defense tactics (behavior patterns) they have been recommending, are less effective in an adult world. Those behavior patterns formed in childhood simply no longer serve you as an adult.

I first became aware of this logical outlook about the voices in my head during my Dream Coach®Certification training with my esteemed coach Marcia Wieder, who is known worldwide as America's Dream Coach. While therapists and many personal growth experts had shared the perspective of "silencing the voices within," Marcia introduced me to the concept of turning up the volume to hear the voices and listen to them because, using her words, "If they are in you…they are Divine."

What a beautiful way to reframe the cacophony into "chatter that matters." Turn up the volume, listen to what those voices have to say, and respect them each as valued partners in your life.

Marcia introduced me to the concept and then my awareness of these "parts" of my psyche was expanded to a whole new level when I began to study the brilliant work of my mentor Tim Kelley, the creator of the True Purpose®movement. In his book entitled *True Purpose,* Tim outlines these voices as parts of our psyche that are formed as a result of the inevitable wounding that occurs when we are young. In my mind these voices represent the chatter that lures you into the emotional trap.

Through a process of communicating openly and honestly with these voices I was able to establish a healthy dialogue that made it possible to release some of the limiting judgment that was holding me back.

So I submit to you that understanding the various parts that make up your individual psyche is a vital factor in the equation that will allow you to emerge from your trap.

Now it is important to note that not all the voices of the parts are pretty. In fact, some of them are less attractive than others and act downright ugly at times. The secret is to embrace Marcia's perspective that they all represent the divinity within you and each has its own innate value and beauty.

Realizing the value of even the ugliest part of me—that B word that rhymes with itch and acts like a witch—inspired me to write the following poem:

The Beauty In "Miss B"
by Anne Palmer

A look within Soul reveals an energy that is truly fierce
An energy that through dangerous façades has the ability to pierce

Her role in life is to protect and shield from any and all harm
She detects deception or malice and signals an immediate alarm

To stand up, speak out…use whatever she feels that she must
To right a wrong, demand respect, or defend against a broken trust

This "B" within is a part that is important—one we truly need
Equally as valued as the part within that does all good deeds

Yet the "B" part is often misinterpreted and gets a bad rap
Because, to surface, this part must feel threatened and then snap

Most often she lies dormant, waiting patiently for the call
To awaken and respond—bringing attitude and standing tall

When unleashed from the caged place within the heart
"B" emerges in grand style, looms large, ready to start

A masterfully choreographed dance or artful verbal defense
That stirs up emotions and often creates drama and suspense

An ability to disarm those who approach with unhealthy intentions
Is a gift that Miss "B" brings forth with deliberate and focused attention

Her wrath is one others wish not to encounter—one they even fear
For to experience her first-hand may cause volcanic eruptions
and tears

In full force her mere presence causes those around her to
squirm and itch
She rubs people the wrong way and in return they refer to her
as "That Bitch"

From B's perspective, her goal is steadfast…she rarely wavers at all
Her goal is simple—look out for best interest—defend against a fall

Embrace her and acknowledge her for the important role she plays
For her loyalty and commitment serve in many meaningful ways

Light is now shed on this vital part—hope you are able to see
The artistry and majestic beauty within the part called "Miss B"

Again, I wish to express gratitude to both my mentors, Marcia and Tim, for their insight into the "parts" that influence and control our thoughts and behavior patterns. As I mentioned previously, Tim's explanation of some of our psyche's most common parts are outlined in his book *True Purpose*, and in his workshop that I attended entitled "Clearing A Path Through Ego."

In my journey to release restricting judgment and embrace life-enhancing joy, I incorporated Tim's framework about parts into my own process of shifting the chaotic noise from my wayward voices internally, into a melodic choir that allows my heart to sing harmoniously. So I share the concept of getting to know the voices of your parts, along with a touch of Tim's teachings, to help you turn the dissonant choir in your head into "chatter that matters."

The process of building a healthy rapport or truly transforming your relationship with the voices of your parts has the potential to alter your life in a positive way. The importance and magnitude of this work could be a book by itself. So, I will only touch on it here to whet your appetite and to put into perspective what is possible.

For a deeper dive and greater understanding about how the voices of your parts work, I offer you resources at the end of the book to support such exploration. And of course you can always reach out to me personally on the web at www.TheGiftedTrap.com.

So let's explore these voices and what they might be saying in *your* head...

The Most Common Voices

As I've previously highlighted through some examples, the word judgment is generally, and all too often considered by its very nature to be, punitive.

While that is one form of judgment, I want to be clear and state again emphatically that **judgment is not all bad**. To live your life emotionally well-adjusted, it is necessary to exercise and maintain an openness to healthy judgment as a means of making healthy decisions and empowering yourself to step into your greatness. I reiterate and drive home this point to provide you with a balanced perspective on judgment as you embark on the next phase of embracing a new way of being emotionally aware.

When limiting, unhealthy judgment rears its head, you likely begin to experience an emotional tug-of-war while you ponder whether to accept it as true or reject it. Endless questions run through your mind: What makes you think you can do that? Who do you think you are to even consider doing that? Is that the right dress or suit to wear? Is it really safe for you to put yourself under that kind of scrutiny? You get my drift.

My questions to you are:

Do you believe and accept the voices of your parts that are judging and ruling you as your truth, and allow them to be the basis of your decisions and actions?

Or,

Do you dismiss them because you just don't like what they are saying and make decisions that run counter to what they tell you to do or how to act?

An exercise I recommend is to write down your honest answers to those two questions. First answer yes or no, and then explain your position in detail. This will help you to get clear on how the voices within you are manipulating or controlling how you feel about yourself. Remember, awareness is the first step in any meaningful transformation.

If your voices are using the old paradigms and practices that they formed during your childhood as defense mechanisms against circumstances and situations that they deemed harmful or bad, then defaulting to either (1) believing them or (2) dismissing them is not going to get you where you want to go.

Listening to the old replays of your voices keeps you stuck in childhood paradigms. While that course of action may please the voices, it limits you.

Not listening or ignoring the voices—as many therapists, counselors, and even some coaches recommend—gets you into deep doo-doo with the voices. Basically you upset them because...who likes to be ignored? I don't. Do you? Well, neither do the voices of your parts.

In order to triumph over the less favorable judgments that entrap you, you must collaborate with the voices and enlist their support in living the life you want as a gifted adult.

As you might guess, this requires change. And most people vehemently resist change. Parts can be rebellious also, especially if they think they are being forced to do something against their will. When they feel threatened, they will often sabotage your attempts to live your life in what you consider to be a purposeful and peaceful way.

Let me be clear, this form of rebellion isn't for malicious reasons. It is simply based on the voices' previous experiences and life-long ways of existing in your psyche on your behalf. Look at it from the perspective of the voices themselves: "Just who do you think you are to turn against me after I have served you so well for so long? Why are you changing the rules, especially when my intent has been so pure—only to protect you from exposure to emotional or psychological danger?"

Interesting way of looking at that voice now, isn't it?

Seeking buy-in and collaboration from the voices of your parts is a much more respectful way to successfully create a peaceful internal emotional landscape. After all, these parts have been serving you most of your life.

Let's take a closer look at real-life examples of this new way of listening to the voices in your head.

Dike Drummond discussed his experiences with his voices in my interview with him. I share his shift in awareness and the ultimate shift in the attitude of his voices below:

> *"It's a big piece of what I do with a lot of my clients too. Parts were things that would speak to me in voices. One core part would say 'Is everything OK?'... and then later... 'Is everything OK now?' It would drive me to perform. What I realized is that that part was driving me my whole life. 'I've got two kids. Is everything OK now?' It ran through my life and drove me in a way that wasn't particularly healthy. I realized that these parts developed when I was a small child and that that particular part didn't need to be stuck on that question. I said to it, 'That's worked so far, but it's a hassle now. What's the real question?' And the part said, 'What's perfect right now?' And that changed everything. It used to be called The Question; now I call it The Gift because 90% of the time I have perfection in my field of vision when it asks that question now."*

As I have discovered, and keep reinforcing for you, awareness is always the critical first step in any kind of meaningful transformation. Toward that end, let's explore some of the most common voices and what they might be saying, so that you can identify them the next time you hear them in your head.

After the description of each voice, I invite you to note whether you have a voice similar to it that speaks to you and to write down what position it takes or what it tells you to do.

The Voice of Doubt: "No Way...You Can't!"

The voice of doubt wants to figure out a way for you to resist that negative judgment and to prevent emotional pain. While you're in the Gifted Trap, that may not be impossible. Sometimes the only way you can cope is by shutting down. This is probably the part that all of us relate to the most. Think about it. The minute an opportunity presents itself, the voice of doubt is the first to appear to tell you the reasons you can't do something or why you shouldn't do it.

In my case, I consider myself blessed to have achieved success at most things I put my mind to. Yet, in the midst of my success—of what was seemingly a perfect life—I was plagued by an inner voice that began first as a whisper and eventually built to a crescendo. That voice of doubt was always lurking in the shadows of my mind, questioning my every move. As a result, I often found myself holding back, playing small to prevent myself from going all the way and achieving as much as I was capable of.

My reasoning was simple; "holding back" enabled me to cling to excuses for not being truly accepted or not having achieved the greatness I knew in my heart that I was capable of.

In retrospect, now that I am out of the trap and see clearly the value of the voices within, I understand that the Voice of Doubt's motivation is noble—it merely wants to keep you safe.

The Voice of Doubt is usually the part of you that talks you out of your greatness.

In this case, shifting how this part views your gifts and your capacity to use them effectively is vital. It's the voice of doubt that you have to establish a new relationship with if you want to claim your greatness and live into it joyfully.

What is your Voice of Doubt saying to you?

The Voice of Perfection: "You'd Better Do It Perfectly!"

Most gifted and talented adults have a voice of perfection as a dominant part of their psyche. For me, I thought the P in Palmer stood for perfection. I grew up hearing the mantra "Do it right, or don't do it at all." Consequently, I spent inordinate amounts of energy in pursuit of perfection. I believed that if I did things perfectly, then the people who mattered in my life (i.e., family, friends and, later, significant others) would love me more. I equated perfection with love.

The voice of perfection is persistent. It is determined to prove the whole world wrong in order to help you overcome the limiting judgments of the world.

Gabby Douglas did just that when she won her two gold medals. If we were to imagine that she had voices working in her head during the Olympics, her voice of perfection was likely cheering her on to strive to do her personal best in hopes that it would be a global best as well. There was no room for the voice of doubt to play a role. It had to be impossible for her to allow doubts to enter her mind. She believed in herself and got her internal voices to believe in her abilities, despite any external societal judgments. It appeared that Gabby was able to reconcile any conflict among her voices and get them to all agree to work with her to achieve that "global best—an Olympic Gold medal."

For people caught in the Gifted Trap, that is not always the case. At times, it seems like judgment and the voice of Perfection comes in and takes over, knocking you completely off your game.

What is your Voice of Perfection saying to you?

The Voice of Skepticism: "Better Not...That's Not Possible!"

The voice of skepticism within you seeks evidence for unsupported claims. Strong voices of skepticism may find it difficult to believe anything, and they often suffer from a lack of faith. Their view of people may be quite critical and they often assume the worst. Extreme voices of skepticism are often unfulfilled. On the other hand, the lack of an effective voice of skepticism may lead to becoming gullible and vulnerable to extortions and scams. I stress that you be aware of this voice because it is important to honor its role and to negotiate a new way for it to serve in your life in a healthy way.

In my case study interview with Rainbow Chen, it became clear that her voice of skepticism plays a significant role in her thought processes:

> Anne: *It sounds to me like your intellect is expressing itself as the voice of your internal Skeptic and is questioning everything you have known to be true intuitively and spiritually.*
>
> Rainbow: *Yes, and I don't want to deny that Skeptic. My pattern is to trust very quickly. I feel that I need that Skeptic because I seem to have an 'openness' about how I show up in the world. I have a great heart for life. I have no fear. I just trust that all people are good. But sometimes I wonder if I should pay attention to my Skeptic more because some people may not be as trustworthy. So, should I follow my gut that knows I am spiritually connected, or pay more attention to my intellect? It's hard because part of me wishes I didn't ask so many questions so that I could have blind faith, and bliss. I wish I could follow the rules and have that kind of spiritual communion, but I can't seem to do it! My intellectual parts and my spiritual parts are in conflict inside me.*

For Rainbow, it is her voice of skepticism that holds her back and keeps her from believing what is possible for her to achieve fully. Is that true for you?

What is the Voice of your internal Skeptic saying to you?

The Voice of the Protector: "Be Careful!"

The Protector is defined as a safety observer. It's the Protector's role to prevent you from stepping in front of buses or gambling all of your cash away. Most of us will have a version of this part that varies in visibility and, according to Tim Kelley, typically those of you with a strong Protector will appear to be "less emotional and more logical." Risk taking is done on a closely calculated basis, if allowed at all. Tim goes on to explain that where the Protector's presence is weaker, people generally "take part in riskier activities and are more spontaneous and fun loving. You will still have a Protector, but its presence will not be sufficient to prevent excessive risk taking."

As Rainbow questions her internal "GPS" (Guidance Protection System), which we will explain in the E.M.E.R.G.E. section, she is confused by the voices of the various parts within her. The voice of her Protector is speaking through a megaphone to protect her from taking risks that it feels may not serve her. Rainbow is unsure which voice to listen to as she longingly looks for a way to emerge from the Gifted Trap:

Rainbow: *How do you work out which voice is the one you really should listen to? How do you know if it is just that part of the ego trying to protect me, or if it is the one telling me the truth that I should pay attention to?*

Anne: *When you say "protect you," that Protector voice has been doing it a certain way for a very long time. That's the way it did it when you were younger to keep you from taking risks that were not in alignment with the PB&Js that have been running your life. The question is: Is that a healthy behavior for where you are right now?*

For you to "realize with your real eyes—the eyes of your soul"™ the truth about the voice of your protector and begin to adjust how the two of you relate to each other within your psyche is like going to the gym to reshape your body. You start to do workouts to tone your muscles. As a result of using muscles you haven't used in a while, you begin to ache. The question is, are you going to keep exercising that muscle so it will get stronger and support your body, or will you stop because it's uncomfortable and allow it to atrophy? Your belief system functions much the same way. Either you build up that muscle to be strong enough to rely on it to hold you up when you're floundering, or you allow the muscle to atrophy by not developing it and you suffer the confusion of not having a strong faith in your internal GPS. Having a healthy relationship with the voice of your protector—where it respects your spiritual connection as a strong muscle that helps you make wise choices—requires that you trust your internal GPS and strengthen that muscle. As you do, the voice of your protector will adjust and align with the stronger, new and more aligned version of you.

What is the Voice of your Protector saying to you?
What is it protecting you from?

The Voice of Criticism: "You Aren't All That!"

Internally limiting judgment emanates from your voice of criticism, who in "parts" language is referred to as your Inner Critic. It will constantly inform you what is wrong with you and what you are undeserving of—suggesting that you are ugly, stupid or fat, and that you don't deserve love and happiness. Can you relate to having this part? People with a prominent and loud voice of criticism may be excessively critical of others as well as themselves.

Interestingly, as I learned from Tim Kelley, this voice is often strong in most successful people because it instills high standards and ambitions in them and can actually serve as the spark that fuels your ambition or a motivating force to push you beyond perceived limitations. However, when it is a weaker voice, it will manifest itself in a corresponding lack of motivation or ambition.

In working with Tim, I came to understand that my drive for perfection, high-standards and disciplined work ethic are driven and governed by my inner Critic. This part of my psyche was formed as a direct result of being a daughter of a Tuskegee Airman who drilled into me to "Do it right…or don't do it at all." Therefore I embraced a strong determination and discipline to get things done. Not a bad trait to have…unless it drives you to be compulsive, as it too often did to me.

**What is the Voice of your Inner Critic saying to you?
How is it serving you and how is it holding you back?**

The Voice of the Guard at the Gates: "Why Are You Here? And What Do You Want?"

While Tim doesn't specifically address the voice at the gate, or Gatekeeper as I call it, among his most common parts, I feel it's important to mention this part because it often stands guard at "the Gifted Trap gates." The Gatekeeper decides whom you allow in and out of your world and your life. Simply put, it does not want to open the gates to anyone, or for anything, that it feels will harm you or isn't in your best interest.

For most of my adult life, my gatekeepers would evaluate every opportunity that came my way and would quickly point out why it would not be a good idea to pursue possibilities.

Have you ever had an opportunity come into your life and you felt that there was a part of you that was not allowing you to consider it as a viable option? Something inside you kept you from taking advantage of the option, only to leave you wondering later, "What would have happened if I had taken advantage of that opportunity?"

Take Note: What are the Voices of Gatekeepers saying to you? Who or what are they limiting your access to?

The Voice of the Image Consultant: "Is That Appropriate?"

Having a strong Image Consultant means you are the kind of person who constantly worries about what others think of you. The Image Consultant studies the reactions others have to you and encourages you to adjust your behavior accordingly. Remember how I used to adjust and play down my physical attributes to make other people feel more comfortable around me? That was the voice of my Image Consultant at work.

While there are advantages to having this voice coach you, it can also be so unwaveringly judgmental of you that it can shut you down. Its voice can be so commanding that it will prevent you from even uttering what it feels are inappropriate words. In short, it can rob you of your voice—like having a throttle in your throat, it will downshift and limit your ability to speak your truth.

The best Image Consultant will assist you in preparing for important meetings, such as the examples we discussed in the section on Perceptions. An overly dominant Image Consultant may be so adept at changing to suit your audience that you lose touch with your own identity, as I did. People with weak Image Consultants experience difficulties with presentations and events such as job interviews.

The Gabby Douglas story serves here again as a prime example. She performed flawlessly by all athletic standards, yet the focus of attention from the outside world was on her hair. During the Olympics, a disproportionate amount of reporters' ink was used to reference her ponytail as being "unkempt," rather than keeping the focus on her extraordinary, world-class competitive performance. Here, the PB&Js of others that surfaced. Editorial comments from reporters implied that her performances were "less than perfect" because of how her hair looked—even after she had achieved the ultimate accolade of becoming the first African-American woman to win a gold medal in the all-around gymnastics competition.

In her case, I suspect that she had to reconcile with the voice of her Image Consultant and decide whether she was going to listen to the negative judgments of everyone else about her hair. She most likely made a very conscious choice not to let that take her off her game. It seems she reached a place where she reconciled with her internal Image Consultant enough to be able to perform at the top of her game.

Take Note: What is the Voice of your Image Consultant saying to you? How are you altering how you show up in the world as a result?

The Voice of the Wounded Child: "Is it Safe to Come Out to Play?"

For me, this voice was the most tender, fragile and weak voice in my internal choir. For many people, the Wounded Child is best described as "the voice of innocence within" that all of the other parts are trying to protect. Visualize all the internal parts we have discussed so far forming a protective circle around the innocent child within you. They are all determined to keep that child from ever experiencing more emotional pain. Once I clearly understood how the voices in my head were working to protect this part of me, I felt a deep sense of appreciation, compassion and gratitude for their collective mission.

The Wounded Child concept can be challenging to comprehend. So I yield to my mentor, who so eloquently and thoroughly explained it in terms that allowed me to "get it." To provide you with great clarity, and give you a framework for connecting with your wounded child, I offer the following excerpt from Tim Kelley's "True Purpose" and "Clearing a Path Through Ego" work:

> *"When we are babies, we naturally accept everything that comes our way. We reject none of our experiences. At some point we encounter an experience that is too much for us, that is too painful to feel and our psyche makes an executive decision to prevent it from happening again. This may be a baby boy whose mother has fallen asleep and doesn't hear her son crying. When she finally reaches him he is terrified and doesn't want her to leave him again so he makes noises to engage her and keep her there.*

*"Years later, as a teenage boy, he struggles to end relationships even with people he doesn't like very much, learns to defuse conflicts within groups and learns to identify what others like and want to keep them happy. He develops the common 'disease to please' syndrome. As a result relationship challenges and psychological problems in the future are rooted in this early wound. **The wounding is deemed neither 'good' nor 'bad' but is central to creating all of our gifts and all of our problems.***

"Somewhere in your past there most probably exists a key event or circumstance that you experienced which you responded to and adopted a strategy to deal with in your life. It was essential to your development. Without it you would never have gained a reason to control your environment. The theory goes that if people were successful at creating a world where no child ever experienced emotional pain the generation would be unmotivated to the point of barely being functional."

Your Wounded Child is the key to the structure of your psyche, as all other parts are constructed around it to protect that child.

During my transformative process I was reintroduced to my wounded child, ironically named Joy. Parts of me had metaphorically buried her in a hidden cave under a banyan tree near a bayou during my childhood. My parts wanted so desperately to shelter her from experiencing emotional pain that they thought it best to hide her in a safe haven. Unfortunately, by hiding her, they had emotionally confined her from feeling the warmth of the sunshine or the freedom to play openly in life.

Discovering her again was one of the greatest revelations of my transformation. When I understood how my parts had been so dedicated to her safety and well-being, I felt a deep sense of love and compassion for how they had served her and me. I suddenly understood why as an adult when I would visit my parents' house, some voice was rearing itself inside me. No matter how hard I tried, I felt like a child inside. My adult body was defaulting to childhood behaviors.

Reclaiming my wounded child, Joy, nurturing her and allowing her to be a fully expressive part of who I am was life altering for me. It was liberating to be aware of that part of me and to have a healthy way to give it a way to express itself. I now listen to what she needs and make sure that I honor her need for ice cream, time on the swings in the park, jumping rope, dancing with free abandon, riding waves at the ocean's edge, blowing bubbles with other children and simply having FUN!

The secret to creating melodic music with your inner choir is not to silence those voices in your head. As explained, they are put there as a result of the perceptions and beliefs that wound us. The secret is to build rapport with your internal voices and encourage them to sing in harmony.

I invite you to think back to your childhood and relive the things that brought you happiness. Go out and allow that child inside you to express himself or herself freely. After you do...

Take Note: What is the Voice of your Wounded Child saying to you? What is it asking you to do with him or her that is FUN?

We each have countless internal parts, and they represent the hurdles that you face in your search for a purpose. They seek to protect your Wounded Child, who is the key to your ability to successfully claim a purposeful and joyful life.

Discovering my core wound and the experience that precipitated the formation of my Wounded Child was a major step in my developing healthy relationships with my inner voices and parts. This extract from my interview with Gina Maria Mele demonstrates how in my Belief Relief process with her, she worked with me to get in touch with and reframe the belief that created my core wound:

Anne: *I recall standing at the side of my crib at the age of around 14 months old crying for my parents' attention. No one was responding. I felt scared and alone, and I had the sense of being abandoned. When you took me through the process, I understood I had formed an opinion that wasn't necessarily true. My parents probably thought I was safe and very well cared for and simply didn't hear me. So here I was acting from a place of abandonment whereas I was actually in a very safe environment. Shifting from that place allowed me to step away from those closely held beliefs that I had been carrying as a shield of armor that told me I wasn't wanted and didn't matter. My core wound for most of my life had been "I don't matter."*

Gina: *We were aiming to find out why "I don't matter" was a belief that was limiting you.*

We took you back to the time when little infant Anne is in the crib and wants her mom. Most infants would only be happy with both parents holding them for 24 hours a day. You simply wanted something that was natural for a child. But you didn't get it and you had to make sense of that. When we're small, we can't think bad of our parents—it would be a perceived threat to our survival, so we make it about us.

Did anyone ever tell you that you didn't matter? No. You had loving parents who did the best they could, but still you put a meaning on this scene that made the most sense for you because you only had limited experience to make sense of it. You formed the belief that "You didn't matter." From that day on, that belief was your red jacket that you wore constantly and never took off. You weren't even aware you were wearing it until our conversation. You didn't know that "I don't matter" was one of the challenging beliefs you were facing.

So in addressing that, you had to look at experiences in your childhood and then determine what they could have meant. You realized that "I don't matter" was just one conclusion that you came up with back then which simply couldn't be the truth because all of the other interpretations were just as valid. So when you went through those processes, "I don't matter" didn't have a hold over you anymore.

So Anne, would you now share how you feel about the belief that you don't matter?

Anne: *"I don't matter." Those are just three words now. Before it was an*

> *emotional relationship, but now it's just three words. I no longer*
> *hold that as a truth anymore.*
>
> Gina: *The stronger you hold the belief, the greater the intensity of your*
> *need to prove it.*
>
> Anne: *That is an important point to emphasize.* The stronger you hold
> the belief, the greater the intensity of your need to prove it.
>
> Gina: *Yes, and because you matter, you want to change the lives of oth-*
> *ers. Look what's going on for you now. You consciously shifted*
> *your life personally and professionally because there's this new*
> *purpose you have to serve others, which you can do because you*
> *inherently know that you matter.*

These inner voices have been part of you for all of your life. They manifest in your life as behavior patterns that you brought into your adult life.

We're like toddlers in adult bodies. We've grown up physically but not emotionally, because we're allowing these parts of our psyche to determine how we respond in the world.

Know Your Voices

The process of creating a healthy internal emotional environment for me came as a result of a "peace treaty" with all of my internal parts. To have such a healthy and harmonious emotional psyche required that I establish healthy relationships with my internal parts that had been at odds—each feeling that its way of protecting my Wounded Child was the answer to my emotional happiness and well-being. For me, that process was like moving to a new town and having to make new friends.

It is only through developing a relationship (much as you would with a new friend) that you are able to create an environment of trust with your parts that will enable you to negotiate new, healthier behavior patterns.

You will need to invest time and energy to get to know each of your individual voices, understanding how they came into being in your life—what experience caused them to form themselves; what their intentions are for playing an active "part" in how you live your life—wanting you to be safe and protected, to be happy and loved; and understanding how they each show up in your life—what behavior patterns they formed to protect you.

Let's explore how this is done:

Getting to Know All of You: Identifying the Voices

It is essential to identify the voices that are most prevalent in your head and fully understand how they came into being in your life. Fully understanding their desire and what they want to do for you, as my interview with Gina Maria Mele shows, is like meeting a new person, yet that person is "part" of you!

You need to go in and meet those Parts of your psyche. The voices of your parts are talking to you every day and in effect are running your life. But have you taken the time to get to know them? Most of us allow them to run our lives but never take the time or opportunity to introduce ourselves to them. That's really important if we are going to shift our emotional state of being.

Thanks to my Dad having made me account for every penny when I was growing up, I have an accountant part that keeps me fiscally responsible. (That is both a good and bad thing.) On the one hand, I am a good financial manager. On the other hand, it sees everything as either black or white and is always telling me what I am not able to do. It is a challenge to get that part to consider creative, colorful options. This is just one example. There are many more voices inside of me—my athletic drill sergeant, my architectural interior designer, and my head of housekeeping, to name a few. In fact, there are so many that I call them my COP Squad. COP stands for Council of Parts. Together, collaboratively, we run my life and we have regular board meetings.

Just as I have many parts, I suspect there are many inside of you too. Before you go any further, stop and reflect upon this concept. You already started the process of getting in touch with some of your parts by taking note of what some of your voices within you are saying. Take a few minutes now and take an internal inventory of any other parts of you that show up as voices.

PARTS INVENTORY EXERCISE: What other Voices are in your head and what part of your psyche do they represent?

_____

_____

_____

_____

_____

_____

_____

_____

_____

_____

_____

_____

_____

_____

_____

_____

_____

Getting to know your parts is important preparation for liberating yourself from the trap. Identifying your parts is the first step in getting to know them. The next step is to build rapport with the voices of your parts.

There are two techniques that were recommended to me and that worked best for building rapport with my parts. They are Active Imagination and Voice Dialogue. The one I found easiest to master and that I suggest for you is Active Imagination."

Active Imagination Example

The technique known as Active Imagination often strikes people initially as an awkward concept to embrace because it feels like you are simply talking to yourself.

If you've ever read the book *Conversations with God*, you'll understand what I mean.

If you meet someone on the street and form an acquaintance, you gradually get to know them by having a conversation that is an exchange between the two of you.

What sort of questions would you ask him or her?

Who are you? How did you get here? What excites you?

I want you to try it now. Choose one of your voices you listed on your inventory list that you hear from most often, ask it a question, and listen to its reply. Try it right now.

Example:

A (for Anne): Hello, part that is my accountant. Are you here with me?

Accountant: Yes, I am always watching your money.

A: What would you like me to call you?

Accountant: You can call me Ada.

A: Wow, that is my father's sister's name.

Ada: I know. All of your father's sisters knew how to count money really well.

A: So when did you first come into my life?

Ada: The summer that you got your first job, when your father made you account for every penny you made. You wanted to make your father proud of you and you put yourself under a lot of pressure to keep track of every penny you spent. I wanted to help you out because you were nervous that you would mess up and that your father wouldn't think you were doing a good job.

This gives you an idea of how this works. Now you try:

As I said, it may feel strange at first because you are talking to yourself, but you are getting to know your important parts of your psyche. At first, you may feel a bit schizophrenic because you've never tried this before. I encourage you to bear with the process, relax, and get to know the inner you.

Once you understand how each of your parts came into being and begin to establish an open dialogue and exchange with your voices within, you have the opportunity to build trust between you and them. Once there is rapport and, most importantly, trust established between you and your voices, you will have an opportunity to negotiate new mature roles with them that are in alignment with your adult self.

My loudest voice was the voice of my Protector. I shared earlier how when I was young being told "NO" frequently and having decisions made for me without explanation or dialogue about what I wanted had impacted me. My Protector took over in my psyche and convinced me that I didn't need to ask for anything. Furthermore, my Inner Critic made me believe that I didn't deserve to have my desires considered. Remember, my core wound was "I don't matter."

I also shared with you my story about the summer of my 13th birthday when my family moved from Houston, Texas to Washington, D.C. and my parents' decision to send me ahead with my grandfather. That decision was emotionally very difficult for me then and was a source of great pain.

However, as the song says…"I can see clearly now the rain is gone." Through my lens as a parent myself, I now understand that their rationale was to make the transition for my grandfather and me as smooth as possible. My grandfather was to be with his other daughter, and I was to be with my cousin who was my age.

Good parents, like mine, do the best they can to make decisions with the best information they have, and in the best interest of their child. No doubt my parents believed they were doing the right thing by sending me ahead with my grandfather.

Just as my parents had made the decision for my brother to be sent to a private preparatory school for what seemed on the surface to be a "once-in-a-lifetime opportunity," they also made the decision to send me ahead of the "family move." Both seemed like great ideas at the time. In reality, though, their decision and that experience added more fuel to my core wound: "I don't matter." What I wanted and needed did not seem to matter.

While my family enjoyed farewell parties and celebrations in Houston, what formed in my head were thoughts that I didn't deserve to be with them to celebrate. This thought pattern was reinforcing the narrow-minded perceptions of my wounded child that I explained earlier.

Little did they know that their well-intentioned decision actually reignited a limiting belief that I had put on like the red jacket concept that Gina Maria Mele enlightened us about. I was wearing the red jacket called "I don't matter" in my subconscious as a child. That red jacket belief was being put back on periodically each time there was another innocent incident. The more often I put it on, the more comfortable it became—until I started to wear it unconsciously all the time.

For example, at the age of seven I was somehow accidentally left at a gas station when we were on a family trip. There were lots of us to keep track of and heads somehow didn't get counted before the family pulled off in the Ford Country Squire station-wagon. While they didn't get far down the road before they realized it and came back for me, it was far enough for me to come out of the bathroom, find them gone, and feel scared that I had been left. Cold, lonely and scared, I unconsciously put on my "I don't matter" red jacket to help me feel safe at the gas station.

So, here I was at age thirteen with that core wound and belief being reaffirmed by what appeared to be a really great idea—to everyone but the person being separated from her family...me. The incident of me running away up a tree for attention—and instead encountering alienation and more pain—made bad matters worse.

My wound deepened even further during my early teenage years when I would ask to visit the homes of new friends and my parents would say "NO" because they didn't know the parents. This is how "I don't matter" became deeply ingrained in my psyche and how I became really comfortable wearing my "I don't matter" red jacket.

As a result, parts of my psyche that were determined to protect me from this emotional pain rallied and set up defense mechanisms to keep me safe. My Protector voice, determined to keep me from feeling pain ever again, said to me, "Just don't ask anymore. If you don't ask, no one will say no. You will avoid rejection."

So what did I do? I stopped asking for what was important to me. In fact, I stopped even considering what I really wanted. Instead I did what I thought others expected of me and wanted me to do. That behavior pattern was formed and reinforced over and over by my Protector voice and Inner Critic to keep me safe. The problem was, it crippled me.

What was originally formed as a protection mechanism in my childhood paralyzed me as an adult inside of an emotional trap. It wasn't until I began my E.M.E.R.G.E process that I learned to recognize the limiting behavior patterns. I began to understand that it is possible to renegotiate how the voices of your parts serve you. I now have chatter that truly matters going on within me.

Chatter that Matters: Negotiate and Co-create with Your Voices

As an adult emerging into a healthier emotional state of being, I became aware of Tim Kelley's work and learned to dialogue with the voices of the parts of my psyche. When I began to dialogue with my Protector part, I understood that it had established specific behavior patterns as well-formed defense mechanisms that in some ways had definitely protected me.

Understanding that enabled me to say, "Thank you." My parts had really tried to protect me and keep me safe. However, the defense mechanism no longer served me. As a grown woman, not asking for what I wanted was keeping me stuck. So, I had to go in and have an internal dialogue with my parts.

My parts and I had to come to a new agreement about what we all wanted and then negotiate new ways of coexisting. I had to learn to ask for little things that I could in fact get in order to build trust with my parts.

Over time, I showed them that it's OK to ask for what we want. I began to shift to a new belief that I *could* get what I want. Together my parts and I negotiated new terms and behavior patterns. We collaborated and co-created a new paradigm and way of behaving that allowed me—all of me—to thrive joyfully.

When you begin this process, be prepared for the parts you are negotiating with to protest as a way of protecting themselves. If you ask a part to change, it might initially feel that you want to get rid of it. It's natural for that feeling to occur. After all, you don't like it when you don't feel valued. Well, neither do your parts. It's essential to show respect, appreciation and express gratitude before you attempt to negotiate a new relationship and ask that part to work proactively with you towards a new way of being. If you don't, it will work against you because you have disrespected it.

Erline Belton, in her interview with me, agreed:

> *"That's absolutely true. You have to embrace it and not just deny it because sometimes you need a judge and a critic, and you want them to be available to you at the times you need them. You don't want to get rid of them completely because sometimes you need to exercise good, sound judgment. Those are important things to have, but if they are there all the time that's when the paralysis sets in and they consume you and prohibit healthy forward momentum."*

This dialogue with yourself is a key part of the emerging process and the reframing that needs to occur within your inner psyche.

Two of the classic wounds from your inner child might be "I'm not good enough" or "What I want doesn't matter." It is important that you identify which of your parts are responsible for those emotions and negotiate with those voices.

We saw earlier the struggle—the *"teeter-totter"* Carole Martin-Wright had to negotiate to reconcile the differing voices within her mind. It may be no different for you.

"One shoulder was saying, 'The healthy thing to do would be to take your stuff and get out of here,' and the other voice said "You have never quit anything in your life. You're going to see this through."

The voices inside you often play an important role in helping you make decisions that impact your life. Developing the ability to rely on your voices can be a powerful tool when you need to make a choice.

The Voice and Choice

When you are emotionally entrapped, you have a tendency not to value all of your gifts. Too often you may settle or adjust your game to accommodate other people. The story I share with you here is an example of a time when I "realized with my real eyes" the direct correlation between the voice and choice.

I was blessed to take tennis lessons from the family that taught Arthur Ashe, and for years I considered my ability to play tennis well as one of my greatest gifts. When I learned to play tennis, it wasn't yet fashionable for women to play sports. I grew up just as Title IX legislation was being enacted, opening doors for women in athletics. Therefore, I was never encouraged to develop my game seriously.

Consequently, I felt my athletic ability as a tennis player was never something that was valued. However, it was a game I loved. I was passionate about it, and I was good at it. I continued to play into my adult life. I often played as much as three times per week. I played with a friend of mine who also played very well, and was very competitive. She had a tennis court in her backyard, so we either played on her court or at the tennis club to which we both belonged.

As I mentioned, we were both very competitive, but we both played different styles of tennis. Her game was a baseline game. She loved to stroke backhand or forehand, from baseline to baseline, all day long. She felt very comfortable just hanging out on the baseline and stroking back and forth. I, too was good playing from the baseline—really good—but

I also had a powerful net game. My friend on the other hand, was very reluctant to come to the net. The net requires you to react much more quickly and to be more aggressive. Because I often played on her court, my tendency was to be nice, hold back, and play her game.

Until one day we were scheduled to play and my daughter who was seven years old at the time, happened to be home from school. I told her she could come with me to my tennis game, and be the ball girl for us. Excited to watch us play, she came with me, sat on the sideline, chased down our balls and observed. We played several games that day. While I didn't lose every game, I ended up losing the match that day. On the ride home my daughter said to me, "Mom, you're a really good tennis player."

Smiling, I looked at her and said, "Thank you." It made me feel good that she recognized how good I was at a game I loved to play.

And then came the kicker. She turned to me and said, "You play better than she does, so why did you let her beat you?"

In that moment, I went "Wow!" I had never even thought about what she had just brought to my attention. In that moment, I "realized with my real eyes"™ that I was playing somebody else's game instead of my own. What an awakening that was for me.

Later that night, and actually for the next few days until my next match, I heard the voice in my head. Repeatedly, it was asking me, "Are you going to let this gift you have go unrecognized, or are you going to start to use your gift and play your game?"

From that moment on, I consciously became aware that I had a choice. I could choose to own my gift and play my game, or I could choose to continue to play my friend's game and continue to lose. I listened to my voice within and made the choice to play my game. Rarely after that point, did she ever beat me.

It was a conscious shift I made about the choice that I had before me—and my ability to listen to that voice and claim my greatness.

I share this example with you because so many times in my life I didn't recognize or value my gifts, or myself. I sold myself short and played other people's games. The ability to really listen to the voices inside of you is important. Not all of the voices try to limit you. There are voices inside of you that are there to inspire, encourage, and uplift you. The question is: "Are you going to turn up the volume on those voices and start to live your life in alignment with all of the gifts and all of the power that you have available to you to make the choice to claim your greatness?"

In the free downloadable Lifeline Guide available at www. TheGiftedTrap.com/LifelineGuide, there are exercises that help you recognize your gifts and turn up the volume on the voice that is calling you to make a choice. I strongly urge you to answer the following questions:

Where in your life are you not recognizing the gifts that you have been given and not owning them fully?

Is there a voice inside you that you turned the volume down on that is calling you to make a choice and fully own your gifts? If so, what choice is it calling you to make?

Initiating Healthy Chatter

Most of the time, the voices of your various parts simply want you to be healthy, protected and loved. After all, isn't that what you want for yourself? The problem—as I began to understand during my work with Jeffrey Van Dyk, Tim Kelley and Gina Maria Mele—is that the techniques they use to protect you are rooted in your childhood, so rarely will the way they are manifesting in your life reflect what you want for yourself as an adult.

After you enter into a gentle, trusting relationship with your parts where both you and they feel safe, from there you can begin to negotiate with the parts, showing them new possibilities from a place of mutual respect and a desire for a shared outcome. You come to know that both you and your parts ultimately want the same thing.

I echo the words of my mentor Marcia Wieder as a very important reminder:

> **"We don't want you to silence or disregard your parts because they are inside you and if they are inside you they are divine. Nor do we want you to ignore them. After all, you wouldn't like it if someone ignored you."**

Through Active Imagination you often begin to recognize and understand defense mechanisms or behaviors that no longer serve you and then negotiate with your parts to reframe them. You can respect those parts, engage with them in a healthy way, and collaborate with them as part of a team to co-create a new way of being in your world.

This process is vital if you wish to create the internal harmony you're striving for.

Recording the Chatter – Journaling

As you will see in Chapter VIII, journaling is a vital part of the whole process in your quest to emerge into authentic alignment.

To do this you must achieve an understanding of being "in this together" with the voices of your Parts, rather than having them vie for a position that is counter to what you desire for yourself. To figure out what is going to be the best way to co-exist and to co-create healthy ways of handling the challenges in life, there must be a joint willingness to sing from the same sheets of music and work together.

When the relationship reaches a point of understanding where mutual trust exists between you and your Parts, then—and only then—will you live in a new harmonious state within yourself. At that point your existence will begin to flow and become effortless.

My voices come through clearly in my dreams and when I meditate. I then found that Active Imagination and journaling allowed for clarity and compromise. I adopted a daily practice of connecting at dawn and capturing the messages from my voices.

The point I hope you are taking away from this section of the book is an awareness of your voices, and the valuable role they play in helping you realize your greatness. Getting every part of you on board with your vision of who you were designed to be and are capable of being is foundational to getting out of the trap.

I strongly encourage you to take time to know all the parts of you and transform your internal relationship with yourself. There are resources to support you listed in the Resource section at the back, OR request support by going to www.The GiftedTrap.com.

Following is a poem I penned about the transformation I had with my Voice of Fear…

Fear, Too, Has A Purpose
by Anne Palmer

Fear, oh Fear, why are you stirring up soup this night?
A mélange of feelings that are mucky—what a brew!
A mixture of ingredients designed to cause questions
Bringing forth doubt that this dream might not come true

Well Fear lets sit down, let's converse about theses thoughts
The thoughts smelling up the air and wafting all around
It is time to reconcile any remaining limiting beliefs
The residual chains that are binding us to the ground

I say "us" because there are many pieces that must fit
Multiple parts inside that make up an intricate "whole"
And in order for the collective to move forward as one
There must first be agreement about each part's new role

Reaching consensus is a process that must take place first
With each part coming forth to speak truth and be heard
Satisfying their needs to reveal the "why" of their being
Heartfelt truth that allows flight to previously bound birds

Once released and upgraded to their newly transformed state
The parts fly in formation toward a mutually agreed destination
Soaring with grace and ease replaces the trapped feeling held before
Leaving you—Fear—with confused feelings and consternation

Clearing up the confusion for you, and inviting you too along
Is a strange thought that is unusual—considered rarely—if ever
Let's explore if there is any creative way for this to work out
For you too to transform—for ALL of us to fly together

Listening and considering possibilities that might be options
Ways that you, Fear, can be of value and you too can have worth
Is an uncommon experiment that takes a willingness to explore
To step toward you, dissolve illusions and give new ideas birth

What an Ah Hah! Your rumbling soup pot provoked this morn
A revelation of massive importance that this disturbance brought
Into awareness of monumental proportion—a revolutionary concept
That Fear too has a purpose… Wow, what a life-altering thought!

YOUR GIFT,
YOUR LIGHT

Are You Too Good For Your Own Britches?

Growing up you may have heard the colloquialism "*too big for your own britches.*" It means to be overconfident, cocky or conceited. It also can mean to be **too** smart **for your own good**. For purposes of our discussion about your giftedness, we simply say you are too good at whatever your gift is.

The idea that anyone can be "too good" may sound like an enigma to you. After all, how can anyone be too good? To be gifted means you will, by implication, be better than good; you will excel naturally in your given area of giftedness.

Yet an essential part of identifying whether you are enmeshed in your own gifted trap is the answer to this very question: Are you too good?

One of the biggest challenges that gifted people struggle with is living comfortably with your talent in a world that often seeks to diminish it. It comes back to how you choose to hold the Perceptions, Beliefs and Judgments that we explored in depth throughout this book so far.

Often people who encounter you who are not blessed with your particular gift—or possibly are unable to recognize their own giftedness yet—might well be threatened by the power of your essence. Your essence is your purest and most powerful feature. Your talent, your gift and your perfection in the eyes of some people will actually evoke and stir up reactions in them that threaten their own emotional security and status in the world. As a consequence, you might begin to adjust how you show up in the world in an effort to not upset "balance" around others.

Melissa Evans outlines her personal experience of being "overqualified" and being "too good" during her career in corporate America:

"I'm the first Jamaican born here in the US in our family—and our assumption is we're going to be the best. We've had the education. We are so driven to collect all the tools to be the best, but we focus on how to be driven and be that machine rather than on the relationship part. What happens is that after you have all of those tools you become overqualified…you may have gotten in as a manager with your resume and your accolades, and they can't deny it. One thing that drives you is that in my experience people would say there aren't enough qualified black women and we would love to hire them. That gave me the enthusiasm to get all of the tools so when I came to the table no one could say "no"—they would have to challenge themselves to say I wasn't qualified for the job. So I get the opportunity but have to fit within the thread of the company culture, which would sometimes be 'Do enough, don't do too much because that raises the bar and we're comfortable."

For many people the adjustment process begins as children, particularly when you are intelligent. Natural intelligence, as we've seen, can contribute to feelings of being emotionally entrapped.

As a child I was a "straight-A" student, perceived by my classmates as the one "most likely to succeed" in all situations, and that wasn't always easy. Sometimes it was hard, yet I stepped back, feeling compassion in my heart for others. I could see them trying hard to succeed in areas that may have seemed effortless for me—areas in which I was excelling because of my natural talents and abilities.

One of my gifts is that of clarity. I see a problematic situation and intuitively understand what needs to be done to modify it or to improve it. My natural reaction, when I clearly see a way to make something work better, is to step up and begin to make things happen to correct the situation at hand.

As an adult I've come to realize that other people don't always share my vision and ability to see possibilities as clearly as I do.

Since becoming more aware, I admit that at times I was oblivious to the fact that others didn't share my vision. While there were things

I saw and that came as second nature to me, others struggled to understand or see things as I did. Their gifts were in other areas. I began to understand that rather than proceeding like a bull in a china shop, it would be much more effective to articulate my vision to them and paint a picture that would inspire them to collaborate with me on a journey to transform something than it would to have them jump ship at the first port of call because I seemed overzealous and they didn't share my enthusiasm.

Along my professional journey, I was appointed to the position of vice president for an aging services company. With me having been recruited from another industry, some colleagues were reserved and seemingly judgmental about my qualifications for the position. This company cared for elderly people in the final stages of their lives. Now, admittedly I had no previous professional experience in assisted living or nursing homes, but in this case the gift I did possess—that was not on my professional resume—was invaluable.

You see, I had lived the very situation that so many people with elderly parents find themselves in. As a young girl, my grandfather lived with us and as he became frail, he needed care and assistance with his activities of daily living. As the oldest girl in my family, I had been given responsibility to help take care of him. I loved my grandfather and even at my young age, I instinctively cared for him with a tenderness and love that he deserved. Living that experience equipped me with empathy and understanding for the clients and families of the company I worked for. Caring for the elderly and infirmed was second nature to me.

The professional difference was I had hands-on experience caring for an elderly person throughout my childhood, which meant I was able to intuitively see and sense things. Several of my colleagues in the company were qualified executives with track records in the industry. Yet they hadn't necessarily lived the experience the way I had, and consequently may not have been intuitively able to see some of what I could see.

While I was perceived by some of my colleagues to be a rookie, appointed to the role of vice president in an industry that on paper I did not have experience in, I was in fact a seasoned veteran.

At the point that I took the position, we as a nation were on the front end of experiencing a generational shift. The "baby boomer" generation was beginning to reach retirement. Life expectancy in the developed world was increasing year over year. It seemed clear to me that this shift would impact our economy in ways that we could only guess at that point. It seemed clear to me that we needed to understand and prepare for consequences of this new reality.

At that time, from 2006 to 2007, there was very little dialogue taking place about how we were going to respond to this challenge as a nation, or in my organization's case, as a region.

In my role as vice president I intuitively saw, and seized what was a glaring opportunity to bring people together to discuss the impending shift in our society that had not yet been addressed. The golden opportunity I seized was to convene stakeholders in the region for a regional summit to discuss the economic implications of our aging population. I shared the vision with, and invited the President of the American Association of Homes and Services (AAHSA) to be the keynote speaker at the summit. It was a vision that to me seemed obvious, yet had not been considered prior to that point. It was a no brainer! In fact, the AAHSA president referred to it as "an important dialogue that should take place in communities across the nation."

In hindsight, however, I realized that in my drive and enthusiasm to manifest this vision, I was facing alienation from my more established colleagues. My quest to produce the regional summit as a way for our organization to step forward as a leader around this important issue was on the one hand being admired as groundbreaking and revolutionary. Yet on the other hand, there was seemingly a lack of cooperation and push back from those who had been in the industry for many more years than I had, who believed perhaps that this should have been their idea. There seemed to be resentment toward me as an "upstart with new ideas" who had entered their professional territory—an arena where they had long-standing seniority and credibility, but in which they had not ever thought to pull together such a forum.

From my vantage point, the idea seemed to be a common sense first-step toward a region coming together to solve a problem. And who better to do it than an organization whose mission was care for the aging population? It wasn't about me putting a feather in my cap. It was about what was in the best interest of the organization and the region.

As gifted people, it is important to acknowledge that your fervent pursuit of your goals and visions might well stir up resentment in others who are responding to you from within the framework of their own PB&Js. As a result, they might very well look for ways to resist or sabotage the very thing you are working to create. Their resentment is born out of their own self-doubt and insecurity.

As gifted and talented people, it is a dynamic that is very real. You must acknowledge and find ways to handle and hold these situations. As a dear friend often says to me, *"As a leader, you wear a bull's-eye on your front and on your back."*

How Do You Know If You Are "Too Good"?

Think back in your life. How many times have you heard people share that during a job interview they were told, "You're overqualified?" How many times did you get passed over for opportunities for that very reason? The truth is that in those cases, your abilities so far surpass everybody else that you represent a threat to the people who are making the decisions and may well be your boss.

Tiger Woods is a perfect example of the point being made here. The distance between his level of ability and that of the runners-up for years was so great that the word "competition" became obsolete when he was in the mix. In reality, the true competition was taking place between the second and third place competitors.

I have referred several times in this book to my experience in a competition run by eWomen Network for North America's Next Greatest Speaker (NANGS), which I will share with you now.

NANGS is an international contest designed to identify outstanding speakers. I entered the competition with the full intention of being the best I could possibly be throughout the competition. I'm proud to say I achieved "personal best."

Sharpening everything that may possibly be perceived as a "rough edge," I adopted the attitude of a winner. I delivered my message from my heart—having an authentic conversation with the audience. I looked like, dressed like, and embodied the attitude of a winner—in short, "I showed up fully."

The atmosphere as I appeared on stage to around three thousand people was electric. I delivered my message to a hushed audience hanging on my every word. Their energy invigorated me. That wave of appreciation validated the hours and months of preparation. The audience accepted me for who I was, and I felt it. You know in your gut when you have hit a home run.

Three thousand people responded positively, yet my fate lay in the hands of a panel of four judges.

I was critiqued by the judges as being "too polished."

In my quest to be and do my best—100% "on" with all my gifts and talents—and to live up to my father's mantra of *"Do it right or don't do it at all,"* I overshot the mark. The judges' comments suggested that my perfect delivery might make it hard for audiences to see themselves in the message.

The judges measured the three finalists against criteria that was subjective—by what they believed would make a speaker easiest for a listener to relate to. My quest to be my absolute best and be "good enough" had been perceived, believed, and in fact, judged as a bit "too good"—their words were "too polished" (translated to mean not as easy to relate to as the winner).

That situation took me back to when I was a runway model nearly three decades ago. At that time, because of my mixed heritage of African-American, Native American, and probably a lot of other things mixed in too, I was an enigma to many people in the modeling and fashion world. In that world, it is fashionable to label things and people. Often when someone couldn't quite figure out what I was ethnically, and as a way of rationalizing not booking me, they labeled me as "too exotic."

If I had a meeting with the designer who wanted blue-eyed blondes that season, there was no way I could be that. For me to take that "no" as a personal rejection would have caused me tremendous emotional pain. The fact is that I simply am not a blue-eyed blond—never have been, never will be—and there was nothing about that rejection that is personal. It just is what it is.

That frame of reference helped me to process and hold the NANGS experience in a healthy way. The fact that I wasn't selected as "the winner" at NANGS had less to do with my gifts and talents or my actual performance, and more to do with the perceptions of what the judges had determined they were looking for in "the winner"—that unanticipated criteria that they used as part of their "decision-making" formula. That, I could live with.

Sometimes we find ourselves in situations in life where, regardless of whether we "show up" as our best self, other factors that we may not even be aware of come into play to influence the situation—factors that are totally out of our control. These influences, which often stem from the PB&Js of others, result in an outcome that leaves us feeling like we are "not good enough," or perhaps we are "too good."

Being informed that you're overqualified during an interview means you are simply too good, but not in a negative way. On that particular day what you brought to the table was different from what they were looking for or needed.

Being able to handle that experience is the challenge.

How do you walk away from that experience knowing that you showed up as your best, yet you still didn't win? Be able to say in your heart that you *did* win because you showed up as the best you could be. What we have to ask ourselves is 'What can you learn from this situation? How can you grow from this experience?" keeping in mind that every experience is preparation for your next challenge in life.

Remember the parable of the sage: "That which you hold in your hand is what you make of it."

When you have an experience where you stumble and fall, you have a choice—stay down or get back up, dust yourself off and keep moving forward.

My experience at NANGS epitomizes the balancing act, the tight-rope that you walk on, caught between "Are you good enough?" and "Are you too good?"

How do you stay on that tightrope and balance between those two extremes? The challenge is to strike a delicate balance between giving the impression that you are too confident and being able to bring compassion into play.

Balancing Compassion and Confidence

Balancing compassion and confidence is essential to finding that balance between "Am I Too Good?" and "Am I Good Enough?" that allows you to walk that tightrope. It is confidence in your gifts and abilities that allows you to bring your gifts fully to light in the world. When you are managing how to balance the two extremes of "not good enough" and "too good," it is compassion for how others are wrestling with and handling their own Perceptions, Beliefs and Judgments that will allow you to emerge into an emotionally safe space.

With that awareness and compassion you understand that any perceived or real rejection is usually a direct result of the outside world's narrow-minded PB&Js that are their issues. They must reconcile those issues...their issues are not ours to take on.

Your responsibility is to simply show compassion. If that sounds difficult when you find yourself on the receiving end of unhealthy judgment, let me offer a clearer explanation.

It is helpful to understand that others look at your perfection and judge themselves against it. It has nothing to do with what you are doing *to* them. It is their issue. But when you are coming from a place of compassion and love, you can work with that. Everyone has a degree of perfection in his or her imperfection.

On that day at NANGS I wasn't "good enough" to be named the winner of the contest—I was perfectly imperfect. However, the absolute gift to me, and beauty of the experience, was that on the day of the finals, I knew that I brought my best game. My intention from the beginning was to courageously step out on faith and speak truth from my heart as my authentic self. I did just that. So I did win. I may not have won the title, but what I got was worth just as much, if not more. Within myself was a sense of knowing that I'd achieved what I'd gone there for—to claim my voice on an international stage as a world-class speaker.

I found my Voice and I did it with courage, compassion and humility.

I channeled a poem called *Claiming Voice* the next day during my morning meditation in response to my experience. You will find it on the following page.

The poem was my way of reconciling within my own heart what had happened at NANGS. I may not have won the competition, but I claimed my new way of being in the world and a new way of responding to situations where I may be perceived, believed or judged to be "too good."

I learned to balance on that tightrope and artfully get to the other side.

> *So, in response to that question, "Are you too good?" my answer is plain and simple: "Allow yourself to be whoever it is that you are and that is indeed 'Good Enough.'"*

Claiming Voice

by Anne Palmer

∞

Yesterday I stepped out on a world-class stage
Began writing my next chapter on a fresh page

I learned exactly what the word "surrender" truly means
Even when the outcome of doing it hurts a bit so it seems

I learned what it feels like to willingly let go and let God
To step up to the plate and hit a Grand Slam like A-Rod

Stepping out onto center stage and claiming my voice
Was my only option...for me, there simply was no other choice

Had the absolute perfect audience to let go and just speak
As I pulled back my iron-clad curtain and gave them a peak

Of what it looks like to have to carry a burden all the time
Of how striving for perfection should be labeled a crime

Because it robs you of a sense of freedom in your heart
Always "ON" in your role—always playing the "PERFECT" part

Yesterday I cast caution aside, released it into the wind
As I introduced my angels, my spirit guides, my revered next of kin

They assembled in the balconies around the periphery of the room
One-by-one were introduced allowing their spirits to vibrate and loom

That ballroom, that space, was transformed into a sacred holy ground
It became a sacred space where my Divine birthright voice was found

I will forever remember the extra special fourteenth day of July
As the memorable day that I let my old way of being die

And embraced my new way of speaking and embodying truth
Realizing that the World is my new personal sound booth

Where allowing conscious loving breaths becomes my new norm
As I surrender to Source to reveal my life's new form

So, God I "get it" that there is another door you have yet to reveal
Behind which I KNOW it will be safe to allow my "Self" to feel

Alive and accepted for ALL the beauty and gifts you blessed me with
Where my true essence will know its value as truth and not as myth.

Thank you God for challenging me to step up to the proverbial "plate"
And for giving me the boost…the courage to claim my new fate.

Thank you for loving me and for allowing me to emerge and see
That this is only the tip of the iceberg…that you will
ALWAYS watch over me.

How Bright Is Your Light?

Is Your Light Too Bright?

You may be reading the stories I've shared and thinking one of two things. Either you feel I am over-reacting and possibly imagining these reactions, or you are nodding in agreement. Those of you who recognize the symptoms of the Gifted Trap will be in the latter category.

My experience at NANGS provided great clarity on the concept of "being a bright light." There was no doubting the judges' reactions. The verdict on my performance was that I was "a bit too polished." (These were their words, not mine.) Perhaps they sought someone with flaws. Possibly my performance was perceived as inauthentic based on some preconceived perceptions and beliefs that they brought in with them.

Perhaps they were simply seeking someone who to them was more relatable for the average person—the girl next door. That, I am not... and never will be. Not bragging or boasting...that is just the truth, much the same as I will never be a blue-eyed blond.

In retrospect, I interpreted their decision as evidence that my polished presentation made me unapproachable, making it difficult for others to relate to me. It's a dilemma that women face in the corporate world far too often.

In the case of my son being passed over for the baseball team, that too was real.

As a mother, our instincts urge us to protect our children from the world's more unscrupulous influences. When I questioned the coach responsible for the All Star team selection, he explained that he thought my son was over the age limit requirement for the team. His decision was based solely on his assumption. Checking the facts had simply never entered his mind in making the final selection...or did it?

Did the coach's own limiting judgments play a role in his decision?

As you recall, his perception of my son being too old because of his height is what he used as his rationale for denying my son a position on the All-Star team. The consequences of that factually unfounded act still linger today.

In the case of prominent people like President Barack Obama, or Olympic champion and the fastest man in the world Usain Bolt, speculative judgments and prejudicial perceptions are hurled at them thoughtlessly. In the President's case, the evidence of this reality is there for all to see in the media on a nearly daily basis. For Jamaican sprinter Usain Bolt, according to Wikipedia the fastest man ever and regarded by some as the greatest athlete ever, instead of being acknowledged unilaterally for his athletic excellence, his perceived arrogance generated as many column inches as his world-record achievements during the Olympics.

In my early modeling career, rejection was a fact of life. It is prevalent throughout the fashion world, unfortunately leading to self-sabotaging behavior for some of the world's most beautiful women. In their quest to mold themselves into their most perfect self and be accepted, self-sabotage leads to drug abuse and eating disorders such as bulimia and anorexia.

In schools, often the brightest, most talented students are overlooked to give someone else with lesser abilities the opportunity to excel. Everyone should be given an opportunity to shine; that is absolutely vital. Yet the most gifted people will often be overlooked or disregarded due to an assumption: **they have it all together and don't need to be recognized. The real truth is that everyone longs to be recognized.**

When I was a vice president in the aging services industry, my position was eliminated due ostensibly to "financial constraints." In my heart and internal "knowing" (a.k.a. emotional intelligence), I felt there was a different truth. My sense was that a completely different dynamic was at work—PB&Js in their full glory.

Could it have been that the senior executives who sat alongside me in the boardroom brought unfounded perceptions, limiting beliefs and personal judgments about who I was and what I contributed to the organization's success into the equation? Did they not appreciate the commitment and vision that I had brought to the company—not to mention the considerable value that I added with my outreach in the community? Every performance evaluation was stellar, and I was recognized nationally in the industry as a leader. It is therefore logical to question what the reason for the elimination of my position really was.

Was my light too bright? Was I too good?

Sharing the Spotlight

Giftedness sometimes requires you to take a compassionate step backwards. Sometimes you have to realize that other people don't share your point of view, step back a bit, and allow them the opportunity to shine as well—to share the spotlight.

Stepping aside to give others the spotlight is a sacrifice you may occasionally choose to make in order to maintain a healthy equilibrium within your relationships. Here is a simple analogy to illustrate this point. Imagine allowing your young child to sweep the living room. His or her attention to detail won't match yours. He or she most likely won't have the same standards you have as an adult. The child will most likely fail to notice the cracks and crevices that require that extra effort to achieve the "Mr Clean" result that is the standard you measure yourself against.

Living comfortably with extraordinary giftedness is a continual balancing act. How do you maintain your commitment to your own excellence and simultaneously live in a world where the standards of others are markedly different than—and often lower than—yours?

What others see in you as perfection, is simply the manifestation of your God-given talent and gifts. Because it appears effortless, they underestimate the energy you have to exert for that gift to manifest—they may not understand the amount of fuel it takes for your light to shine.

Sometimes, for the world at large, your gift is simply too much for others to handle. And that is their problem to solve, not yours. You should stand in your power and shine.

Broadcasting Your Brilliance

Telling the world about your gifts—shining the spotlight on yourself—is often perceived as arrogance. However, if you don't promote yourself, where will the recognition come from? As we considered in the case of Usain Bolt, his blatant self-promotion was what created the media attention. Achieving something that no other person on the planet has ever done seems something justifiably worth being proud of. What do you think?

Here again, we see an example of that emotional tightrope—the struggle to give your best without alienating others. It is at times an impossible task. You either self-promote on one end of the spectrum, or you refrain from self-promotion at all.

My daughter prefers to live in the zone of no self-promotion at all. By the world's standards she seems "perfect," achieving excellence in everything she attempts. She is an exemplary scholar (Phi Beta Kappa graduate of Stanford University, now a joint Masters/PhD candidate at Princeton University), an accomplished athlete (former All-American on the U.S. National Rugby Team), and breathtakingly beautiful to boot—all of it achieved seemingly effortlessly. Does that sound familiar?

Let me tell you, her secret is sheer hard work and dedication to excellence… with a dose of genetic giftedness added in. Every day she puts her all into everything she does. She seeks no praise. In fact, she literally avoids the spotlight. I'll likely be reprimanded for including even this small acknowledgment of her brilliance. She simply wants to live quietly through every day, just being the humble human being that she is, and be accepted for that. In her case, her brilliance is so bright that it shouts with a whisper.

For all of you that are caught in emotional entrapment the questions are:

> **How do you exist in the world both honoring your level of excellence and celebrating your giftedness, without being alienated?**

How will the world accept you as your authentic self without judging you as something other than who you are?

I return again to the saying of Lisa Nichols' grandmother:

"What other people say about you ain't none of your business."

How do you as a living, breathing, sensitive human beings reach the point of being at peace with your giftedness?

In the following chapters I will share solutions and show you how you can step into your greatness and let your light shine unapologetically for who you are.

Permission to Let Your Light Shine

Part of the process of emerging is finding that place of emotional equilibrium where you can surrender and become your authentic self.

My speech at NANGS represented a point in my life where I demonstrated to myself, and the world, that I have fully emerged from the Gifted Trap into my own authentic alignment. I am totally comfortable in my own skin, perfectly imperfect and willing to be fully transparent. This book is even further evidence of my state of surrender.

In spite of the comments I received from the judges, I totally surrendered, claimed my voice and allowed my gifts to shine. I was authentically me, and at peace with whatever the outcome of the competition was. I achieved first place in my heart for my own personal acceptance of my truth and willingness to "be me" unapologetically.

Lisa Nichols is one of the greatest transformational speakers I have ever met. She was one of the NANGS judges, and I now consider her a mentor. I share with you a quote of hers that I strongly urge you to contemplate and adopt. Her saying is (and I paraphrase):

When you truly connect with the essence of your gift and allow that light within you to shine, it may dazzle others like bright sunshine on a hot summer day. Don't diminish that light to placate others. Let the sunshine in, shine your light—and if it is too bright for others, Lisa's recommendation—and mine too—is to simply *"offer them sunglasses"*!

Vasavi Kumar echoed a similar point worth punctuating here:

"... don't apologize for your existence, never apologize for the creation that you are, whatever it looks like."

For most of my life I attempted to make others feel comfortable by adjusting who I was. I chose to dim my light.

At NANGS, I chose to let my bright light shine.

We see examples of unapologetic great talent across all sections of society. Look at the likes of Billie Jean King, Michael Phelps, and Nelson Mandela. As they each remained true to their authentic self and used their gifts in the way they were intended to be utilized, they faced a barrage of criticism from sections of society whose own self-imposed PB&Js were threatened. As they followed their calling and reached to achieve their greatness, others chose to find fault with them. In return, they each chose to let their light shine even brighter.

Melissa Evans talks of the challenges of her light being too bright for her colleagues and how she chose to respond:

"...I had to come to the table with solutions and evidence to support everything I said. I was forced to be highly prepared. Then I'd come to the meeting, state my position, and no one could see it my way. When I first started out they would say 'I don't know about that' and the guy at the table with me would say the same thing and they would think he had a great idea! Through their perception of me, they didn't see me in an acceptable light. They created a glass ceiling. It didn't make them comfortable if I was in a management job because people I managed were much older than I was. I had to win them over. I had situations where they intentionally kept things from me. It made me so much stronger. I realized I had to have people on the team I could trust but I had to learn it the hard way.

> *"They don't want you to have too much information,*
> *because if you do, you'll shine too much."*

It is yet another manifestation of the delicate tightrope gifted people have to walk across throughout their lives. Even on the tightrope, you need to allow your light to shine so you can see where you are going.

Out of the Trap and Into the Light

If the stories shared so far resonate with you, stay with me. You are on the right path, making the right choices.

Are you feeling "goosebumps" as you read these words? If you are, it's your inner wisdom connecting with these words. Your decision to read this book isn't an accident.

> *You are here because it is time for you to make a difference*
> *in your life, to make the choices that will allow you*
> *to fulfill your destiny and step into your greatness. It is*
> *time for you to step out of the trap and into the light.*

Stepping Out of the Trap
by Anne Palmer

Soul has the desire to understand every part of its unique being
It provides opportunities—clearer lenses to fine-tune my seeing

One lesson is to explore the extreme energies that make up the whole
Opposites that balance energy—much like the North and South Poles

As truth emerges from the exploration of the two distant ends
Awareness comes forth that transforms enemies into friends

The very things that were once perceived to be terrible or bad
That made me feel wronged and sometimes even made me mad

All of a sudden seem necessary parts of the growth that I seek
They have drawn back the curtains and allowed me to peek

At the wisdom and divinity that exists in each and every extreme
That within each space on life's spectrum there appears
a different theme

Be it Victim or Perpetrator, Stage Star or the Critical Judge
Each serves a purpose—designed to stimulate action by giving a nudge

To the Ego to react—step forward and address a specific need
While the Soul provides the chance—it is up to me to take heed

Will the response to the opportunity be outreach with arms—
a healthy embrace
Or will it be dysfunctional unwillingness—the resistance to face

The truth that will free me from repeating the same old story
The truth that allows the full breadth of my gift to reveal its glory

An important choice lies before me—what will it be that I decide
To step out on pure faith or behind the perfect façade to still hide

For me it is a no-brainer, I must take advantage of this chance
The status quo is not an option—my life longs to be enhanced

So the clarity I longed for is staring me right in my eyes
My Trusted Sources have responded to my prayers as well as my cries

Shine light from above to move me forward with grace, I ask for
this please
To step from the boundaries of my gifts' trapped existence with ease

Part Two:

Emerging
The Dawn Of
A New Day –
A New Way

The Dawn of a New Day

by Anne Palmer

With each sunrise a brand new cycle begins
A fresh start is possible…emerging as an old one ends

A chance to "wake up," a chance to open your eyes
To stretch and flex your muscles and to reach for the skies

The sun eases up gently—over the horizon it appears
Breaking through the dark of night, casting light on shadows & fears

As light bursts through and shines bright on the scene
Eyes struggle to open as we ponder—what life that day will mean

In that moment birds are chirping, celebrating each new dawn
Joyfully embracing daybreak, birds tweet, as humans we yawn

In that moment upon arising—the start of each new day
Lies a golden opportunity—an option to embrace a new way

Of being, of choosing what to do with the gifts that you possess
Voluntarily sharing your talent—not acting under duress

Selecting the pathway of giving and serving from the heart
Allows for a rhythmic cadence—the Universe joins in to do its part

This perspective on daybreak…the Dawn of a New Day
Like the sunrise is a reminder…it's the Dawn of a New Way

You have a chance to do things differently.
This is your dawn of a new day.

E.M.E.R.G.E.™

Embracing the E.M.E.R.G.E. Process

To emerge from the Gifted Trap is one of the most challenging and life-altering commitments you will ever make to yourself. The transformation awaiting you will enable you to live in authentic alignment with yourself and become who you were meant to be.

The acronym "E.M.E.R.G.E." represents a proprietary six-step process to liberate you from your entrapped existence that I lived through myself and now coach others through. Each letter of the acronym stands for a verb because the process requires that you take action to shift from where you are, to where you want to be.

E – Examine – Your purpose, passions and possibilities

M – Maximize – Your Talent

E – Engage – Your internal GPS (Guidance Protection System)

R – Reframe – Your PB&Js (Perceptions, Beliefs and Judgments)

G – Gain – The confidence and courage to soar

E – Emerge – With clarity

Finding Your Freedom

Before I explain and we explore the EMERGE™ process, I am compelled to be fully transparent and honest with you. This process is not for the faint of heart. It requires effort…and isn't that the case with anything that is truly worthwhile in life? This is no exception.

You must be willing to persevere when it gets painful—and in no uncertain terms this process will be excruciating at times. There simply is no magic pill you can take to transform YOU from a place of emotional entrapment to a life of joyfulness. However, as I write to you from the joyful side of the abyss—authentically aligned and grateful that I found the courage to take that leap—I guarantee you that it is worth it. I highly recommend that you take the leap too!

There are two commitments required of you in this process.

They are:

1. **A willingness to confront yourself.**
2. **A determination to remain steadfast in the process of self-exploration and self-excavation.**

To be successful, you must allow yourself to peel back the layers that prevent you from truly feeling what is in your heart while in the trap. Then the commitment to "stay the course" is critically important because as you are drawn deeper into the Gifted Trap, you build up shields of armor around your heart. This armor prevents you from becoming who you are meant to be, and from living in authentic alignment with your purpose.

To begin to emerge, you must possess a willingness to explore unchartered territory inside yourself. You must want to free yourself so badly that you are willing to endure whatever it is that confronts you along the way. It's scary at times. It calls for huge amounts of courage, self-discipline, self-exploration and self-excavation.

You know in your heart that there has to be a different way and it's non-negotiable—you MUST find a way out of the trap—and claim that "other" more peaceful, harmonious, fulfilling existence. The EMERGE process is the way out that worked for me.

Again, from a place of full transparency, I say that there are a number of ways to approach freeing yourself from emotional entrapment. Depending upon how severe your situation is, it may require a combination of more than one approach. Basically there are a few common pathways to consider based on the severity of your entrapment:

1. Conventional Psychological/Medical Pathway.

This pathway involves the more traditional "therapist" approach, where you engage with a psychologist or behavioral therapist to diagnose what is causing you to be emotionally impaired. The doctor usually helps you determine how and why you are emotionally out of balance. Then the trained doctor prescribes regular office visits, and in some cases medication as forms of treatment, either getting you out of your curled-up immobile state into a standing position with "emotional crutches," or throwing you a "therapeutic lifeline" as you are sinking into your emotional quicksand. He or she determines whatever treatment method is appropriate to get you back to terra firma (emotionally solid ground).

This can be a very effective process if you identify a professional practitioner with whom you can connect and develop an honest, trusting relationship. Trust and honesty are critical components to achieving successful outcomes in any transformative process. It is even more important that you have those components when working with a skilled professional with whom you entrust with your emotional well-being.

In cases where severe depression or medical/neurological imbalances are in play, this is absolutely a recommended pathway.

In fact, in the early phase of my process, I knew enough to recognize that I was in a state of mild depression and also knew I needed professional support to help me if I was to emerge from where I was in a healthy way. So I sought out, and found an extraordinary behavioral therapist, Dr. Robert Filewich, whom I came to refer to affectionately as Dr. Bob. He threw me my first life preserver and began pulling me gently out of my emotional quicksand. I will be forever indebted to him for handling and nurturing me with such tender loving care.

My final comment about the conventional approach is to honor your gut instincts. If you do not feel you are getting what you need from the professional you are seeing, if the chemistry is not there and you do not trust the person or feel safe revealing what is your truth, CUT THE CORD and look for another lifeline that serves you. That one may simply be a buoy that will keep you afloat, but never get you to solid ground. You could spend a disproportionate part of your life emotionally at sea with total dependency on the buoy to keep you afloat.

These words of caution come from experience. I attempted therapy early in my adult life with a therapist that I didn't connect with and didn't feel safe revealing my truth with. As a result, I probably spent a decade or more inside a trapped emotional state that didn't have to be.

2. Holistic, Spiritual Pathway.

While the conventional approach above is one option, a more holistic and spiritually pragmatic pathway can work equally as well, if not better. Again, determining which pathway is best depends on your unique set of circumstances and the degree of your emotional impairment.

For me, once I crawled to land using the behavioral therapy lifeline, I was determined to stand up and walk without crutches. It was my firm belief that with my strong spiritual foundation and connection to a divine internal knowing, I could get to a joyful and healthy place.

Believing in this possibility, I allowed myself to use my gift of intuitive knowing to guide me to the right mentors, teachers, coaches and tools to emerge in as healthy a way as possible. It is from that experiential wisdom that the E.M.E.R.G.E. process was birthed.

For me, the E.M.E.R.G.E. process was that "other" way. It got me from my place of emotional entrapment to the other side of the abyss— a peaceful, joyful state of being. So with your permission, please allow me the privilege of being your guide as you embark on YOUR journey. It's my intention to honor you and encourage you to Take Loving Care of yourself every step of the way.

I encourage you to download your free Lifeline Guide available at www.TheGiftedTrap.com/LifelineGuide. The exercises in it will guide you on your journey to E.M.E.R.G.E.

Plugging Into Source

It is imperative that I reiterate what I just shared with you about the importance of faith and a connection with a higher knowing outside of, or rather, deeper inside of yourself—that inner knowledge that there is a "force" of divine wisdom within you that is all knowing.

It is by going to that place, connecting with that energy, that you will find the well of strength, the fuel to ignite the flame of courage that you will need to take this leap of faith, so that you emerge from your emotional entrapment.

I share this with you because I found this to be the most vital part of this entire process of emerging. As I evolved through each phase, my "FAITH" never wavered. Emerging into authentic alignment with yourself requires a connection to an energy that is larger than you that will toss you the spiritual lifeline to help you to emerge. You cannot manage your PB&Js or begin to truly claim who you are called to be, who you are meant to be, until you surrender to that Source, that higher force that knows why you are here.

> *You see, alone we can do nothing, but with faith everything is possible.*

This is especially true for high achievers that are expected to be "on all the time" and live under a lot of scrutiny and judgment. When I spoke with Troy Vincent, he shared his perspective on how he managed constant scrutiny.

> *"I believe it was my faith, my belief in a higher power, not relying on man or looking for confirmation or affirmation in man, but a constant reminder that 'Greater is He that is in me, than he that is in the world.' So it's always being able to stand on God's word and what God called me to do."*

As a super-athlete, Troy was always in the spotlight and was expected to always be his best, and for him that was made possible by relying on his faith. He had to be plugged into his source of strength at all times.

Father Rob Rhodes, a self-confessed introvert, explained the importance of faith in his life when he was first called to the priesthood:

> *"I think it's something to do with where I find my confidence. I realized early on this was not about my own power, but God called me into a place of vulnerability and then gave me what I needed in order to do it. That gives me my strongest faith. **I couldn't do it on my own.** God is here holding me up every day and in every way…'If God is with me, who is against me?'"*

The Reverend Susan Purnell describes her way of plugging into Source as:

> *"It's intentionally being very still with one agenda—to know that God **is** God. It's in this deep stillness within myself, while silently watching, waiting and actively listening, that I experience God's presence and know God is God."*

During a certification program that I attended, my mentor, Arthur Joseph, shared a valuable message from a letter from Martha Graham to Agnes de Mille that illustrates this truth so eloquently. The letter has a line in it that I feel is appropriate to share with you as you embark on this journey. That quote that I want you to focus on here is:

> **"It is not whether we believe in ourselves…**
> **we must keep the channel open."**

And that's what I compel you to do here at this point in the journey, to open the door within yourself to that all-knowing force within. That is what I had to do in order to emerge from my own Gifted Trap.

---

5   The letter can be seen in the final section on Resources.

Acknowledging Your Greatness

Once you are plugged into Source, great insights are revealed to you. Your next step is to acknowledge the truth being revealed to you. I share with you an intimate conversation that I experienced in my journaling with my Source within—with my Godly energy that came through loud and clear while I was embracing how best to share with you this process in this crucial section of this book.

It is my sincere hope that through my sharing this intimate conversation you will truly understand where I was in my emotional entrapment before I began this process to emerge to a joyful state of being. My desire is that you draw strength from knowing that I too have been where you are and have actually traveled this journey, taking in every single step of this E.M.E.R.G.E. process that you are now facing.

Without further ado, these are the words I heard directly from my Source. He called for me to "wake up":

"Go inside the trap and think how terrifying it is, how it feels to be in that space with limited light, that feeling of claustrophobia, of a space that's too tight. Remember that awkwardness you feel, contorted in the emotional knots that are tied up within your soul. Experience the cramping that occurs from being in that state for far too long. In order to emerge to a fluid, elongated and liberated place of existence, you have to live through the process of awakening and aligning to enable you to emerge.

"My child, you examined yourself by recognizing that you were in a state of entrapment. I had to help you by shaking you out of that comatose state of existence. You were living on a life support system and didn't even realize it. You were going through the motions on a daily basis— simply existing, like so many others in this world.

"The saddest part was that you were only using a minute fraction of the splendid gifts you were blessed with. I could not bear to watch you let so much talent wither away in an untended garden, so I shook you in the hope that you would choose to awaken and see the new possibilities for your life.

At first when I shook you, you were confused. The second gentle nudge brought you into a slightly clearer state of consciousness, yet you still had a question: 'What was the message?' Finally, on the third attempt to shake you at your core, you woke up fully to hear the message:

"'Choose another way or you will suffocate, wither and die on the vine.'

"You chose to listen and were willing to take the action necessary to change your life. You acknowledged where you were. You recognized you were in a state of entrapment.

"You awakened finally to your own truth. You were neglecting to use your gifts fully.

"By meditating, journaling and spending time in solitude you were able to listen, hear, and awaken to your own truths. Once you received the message, the challenge was to accept that truth. This is often the hardest part of all to accept. That act of coming to terms with your reality requires tremendous courage.

"For you, it took tremendous courage to admit to yourself that you had actually played a major part in creating this awkward reality.

"It was at the point of acceptance that you:

"1. Took a look and decided how high or low you would set the bar for yourself.

"2. How you were exhausted, over-functioning in an attempt to please everyone, doing and being all things for all people.

"3. How you had been putting yourself and your needs last...giving little consideration to your giftedness and your true passions."

That was my conversation with God—my Source. It was another wake-up call of many I have received from Source. I had to acknowledge that I had actually played a role in my own emotional entrapment. I also must confess to you with full transparency that emerging was painful, not only for me, but for the people around me who were directly affected by my decision to emerge from my emotional entrapment.

You may want to take a few moments here to reflect on your own divine Source or that energy—whatever you choose to call it—that force that you know lies within you, that is bigger than you, that is outside of you, that has the wisdom to lead you and guide you on this journey. I advise you to take time and connect with that Source, that "force" within you. As you do, I offer you a quote from my mentor Arthur Joseph again. Arthur so eloquently shares that:

> *"To acknowledge my truth is not arrogant.*
> *To not acknowledge it is."*

Arthur goes on to say,

> *"For who am I to think that I can do anything without Source?*
>
> *A sense of autonomy without being anonymous. It is in the "talking myself into it phase"—that phase where it was too disquieting—that we must listen and connect. If to the best of my ability I can always be connected to Source, then I can be more than the human part of me, but the humanity of me too."*

For the purpose of this book, I have expanded on Arthur's quote and reframed it to state the truth as…

> *"To acknowledge your greatness is not arrogant. To not acknowledge it is.*
>
> *"For who are you to think that you can do anything without Source? A sense of autonomy without being anonymous. It is in the "talking yourself into it phase"—that phase where it is too disquieting—that you must listen and connect. If to the best of your ability you can always be connected to Source, then you can be more than the human part of you, but the humanity of you too. You can claim your greatness."*

Motivational speaker and author Jennie Hernandez shares her own story of when she realized that she had simply had enough and that things had to change. It is a story that Arthur Joseph specifically asked her to share. Once I heard it, I felt called to ask Jennie to share it with you:

"At the end of my first marriage, my children, husband and I had been having difficulties. We'd separated for a while and gotten back together again. During the last couple of years of the marriage, we had a big van that had been repossessed and taken as a result of bankruptcy. Someone lent us a Datsun B-210 two-door hatchback, a very small car.

"I had six kids, was trying to get my marriage to work, and was pregnant with my seventh child. This vehicle had no starter on it. If we allowed it to coast down the hill, we could jump-start the car and it would start. We were going on a trip one day with our six children, and my husband decided to bring our 90-pound dog along too!

"So we were going down the hill, attempting to jumpstart the car, and it suddenly died. At that point, I had had it! I was already upset about the van being repossessed. Now we were stuck on Main Street, with the dog and all of these kids and right then, what came into my mind was the movie Gone With the Wind, *when Scarlett reaches down and picks up the dirt and says, 'If I have to lie, kill, cheat or steal, I will NEVER go hungry again.' I didn't actually use those words, but at that very moment I decided I would do whatever I needed to. I would NEVER drive a car like that again. That gave me the motivation to set the divorce in motion, to go to the welfare office, and to go back to school because I realized that things weren't happening in the situation I was in."*

Plugging into your Source of strength is a prerequisite for your successfully going through the EMERGE process. With that said, I invite you to stop here and take time to reflect on the following questions:

- *Who and/or what is your Source of strength?*
- *Are you connected to that Source?*
- *If so, how can you strengthen your connection?*
- *If not, how might you establish a connection?*

Strengthening the connection to source for me came in several forms. I offer you a few suggestions:

1. Prayer
2. Meditation
3. Journaling
4. Yoga

I will expand on these further and offer other options as we move through the E.M.E.R.G.E. process.

Martyr Wisdom

by Anne Palmer

Martyr within me please come forth and speak
To understand why you exist—that—yes that, it is truth I now seek

Your role has been one I have played for most of my life
In doing so, this behavior has caused alienation and strife

So I am crying and begging now for the truth to be revealed
Of why you are in me? Why must I suffer, and how I can be healed?

From the inevitable pain that comes with your divine presence
Cast away this pain…allow me to excavate my true essence

My essence of a shining bright light and heartfelt pure love
Deliver the message to me, I pray, on the white wings of a dove

Please be gentle with my heart—it has been bleeding a lot lately
Making it a challenge, for me—all parts of me—to stand regal and stately

So this is my plea, as I wait anxiously to hear your reply
I wallow in sadness searching to understand and comprehend, Why?
(SILENCE)

Let there be silence for a moment—quiet space before I,
your Martyr, speak
For together we have journeyed and arrived at the top of this peak
It was necessary my dear to have martyr energy within your soul
It is an extreme energy that not many are able to deliver and hold

It is a fierce form of loving—of taking care of others that is maternal
No matter what the circumstances, your commitment is eternal

That, in itself, is a massive order to deliver and even harder to persist
Especially when others misunderstand the motives and vehemently resist

This pure expression of love that seems righteous and overbearing
When actually, what it really is—is the purest form of caring

That my dear is the divinity within the role of the Martyr
Not everyone has the capacity to handle such a charter

Because with this special privilege often comes ridicule and resentment
The challenge—to embrace this truth so you find peace and contentment

In the knowledge and knowing that Martyr energywithin you is only
one part
Of your breadth and breath—your gifted, sensitive, and loving purple
heart

It is purple because you have had to withstand harsh wounding in your life
As daggers of resentment, jealousy, and envy pierced you like a jagged knife

But rest in the knowing that all that you do is donefrom that place of
pure love
This is the message about your essence that I, your Martyr-self, deliver
from above

The E.M.E.R.G.E. Process

To E.M.E.R.G.E. is a six-step proprietary process that allows you to navigate from emotional entrapment to a liberated state of joyfulness. Let's explore in detail what each of the six letters of the acronym represent in the process:

E – Examine your purpose, your passions and the possibilities available to you. By being inquisitive about what lies beyond your comfort zone, you become the archaeologist of your life and begin to reveal what is possible.

M – Maximize your talent. Look at how you can bring the gifts you have been blessed with into full expression.

E – Engage your internal GPS (Guidance Protection System), by connecting to your inner knowing—that Source or force higher than you with the wisdom to guide you.

R – Reframe the way you hold the PB&Js, the narrow-minded perceptions, limiting beliefs and unhealthy judgments that led you to become emotionally entrapped. Identify and distinguish the difference between the PB&Js that serve you and those that hold you back. Then embrace the process of shifting those that do not serve you into much healthier PB&Js of possibilities, empowering beliefs and joyfulness.

G – Gain the confidence and courage you are capable of when you become fully conscious of Self and begin to soar.

E – Emerge with a newfound sense of clarity of who you are in the world and how you wish to show up. With an open and expanded heart, you claim or re-claim your unique essence, embody it and in so doing EMERGE with a Powerful Presence.

To embark on this process, you must first have a desire to shift from where you are to a healthier, more vibrant way of being—a desire to expand your heart and experience purposeful joy…

Expanding Your Heart

by Anne Palmer

What does it mean to expand your heart?
To allow creativity to flow and reveal truth through art
The art of knowing love that lies deep within
And with each breath blows away barriers or sin

And what does it mean to make room for expansion?
Spirit's process of "spacious awareness" the size of a mansion
Doorways to emotions, stored in rooms yet to be explored,
Rooms that for far too long have been denied access and ignored

As excavation begins that awakens all Parts of Soul,
Light beams bright and illuminates the scary dark hole.
That tunnel of darkness you've been afraid to traverse,
Fear of unknown…unwillingness to face what you
imagine might be worse.

Suddenly the breath that has opened valves of your heart,
Allows for a new beginning and a brand new start.
So, that my dear, is what it means for your heart to expand…
Opportunity to stretch—put down new stakes and
take a grand stand.

Step 1 – Examine

We have already seen how Jennie Hernandez eventually reached a crisis point in her life that forced her to examine new possibilities and reflect on her position as she realized she had to leave her marriage. As she examined her situation she plugged into her Source for strength:

"At the time my youngest child was one year old, and my eldest was fifteen. We had just filed bankruptcy. I had never had a full-time job in my life. I had dropped out of college to have my family and believed I was going to be a full-time mother and stay married all of my life. Yet, in my deeper listening and asking God for directions, I knew I needed to leave. The option at the time was to go on welfare. I didn't have a car. I had to walk to the welfare office and embark on a new life alone. Just prior to that, I had left the religion I had been brought up in and known all of my life, and had no support from my family either. I'd lost my network of friends and family at that time. I had to go through a journey that was very much against everything I rationally knew would support me. At the same time as the months and years went by, I knew it was the right thing to do. It was a gift to have Spirit guide me to a higher place and reveal possibilities in my life."

Dike Drummond, on the other hand, was inquisitive about what was possible for him:

"I knew I couldn't stay on the path I was on. It took me a while to figure out what to do. I believed I could do anything I wanted with my skill sets. I just needed to focus my doctor-style attention in a different direction. I discovered I could do lots of things really well with my doctor's way of looking at things."

To jumpstart your own self-examination process, you may wish to reread the words I shared from my conversation with God again in the section a few pages back under Plugging Into Source. Perhaps you too have experienced a "wake-up" call of your own.

I woke up when I was shaken by my Divine guide and chose to embark on an archaeological dig inside of myself. My mission was to find out the truth of who I was. In the initial phase of self-examination there were three essential passages I traveled through. They are much the same in any transformative process. They are to:

- Awaken
- Acknowledge
- Accept

Awaken

My awakening actually came in the dark of night as I was shaken by Source. You may wish to reread it in the chapter "Waking Up In The Dark," at the beginning of this book, before you continue. When you awaken you open your eyes. It is at that very moment that you have the opportunity to *"realize with your real eyes—the eyes of your soul,"*™ exactly where you are. It is a space where rays of sunshine seem to be streaming in to illuminate a new path. It is at that point that you understand how you have been either conscious or unconscious about your giftedness. You become aware that the power to change is in your hands. During this time, it is essential that you participate in activities that will allow you to achieve clarity of mind.

My recommendation is that you spend time in solitude and self-reflection. The stillness—the quiet—will allow you to get in touch with your inner self. I find it fascinating that the words **silent** and **listen** have exactly the same letters. That is no coincidence. In order to truly listen and hear the wisdom within, you must be silent.

Turn to your own divine Source within, whatever form that takes for you in your life. Learn to meditate and spend time journaling, to truly understand who you are. I found that cleansing my body was essential, so that my channels to receive wisdom from Source were clear and unobstructed. Then I was able to be the chalice that I was born to be and hear new ideas and see new visions.

Most people remain so busy that they don't have time to tune into that inner voice. Your priorities are paying the bills and keeping a roof over your head and food on the table. And yes those are important; however, it is too often easier to remain "comfortably uncomfortable" than to accept the truth of your life. Once you accept your real truths, your resources of courage and abundance appear. They surface to support you because it is at that point that you again *"realize with your real eyes—the eyes of your soul"* that you absolutely MUST do something about it. It's at that point that the flow begins and suddenly you find a way to meet all your needs.

In the free downloadable Lifeline Guide available at www.

TheGiftedTrap.com/LifelineGuide, there are exercises that guide you through each step of the E.M.E.R.G.E. process. I strongly suggest that you take advantage of the one that helps you **Be Silent, Listen & Awaken to Your Truth.**

Acknowledge

Now that you are awake, it is time to look around the landscape of your life and examine the truth about where you are. Take this "Acknowledging Your Truth" quick self-assessment to get an idea about what is true for you:

- YES___ NO___ Do you deny yourself—never considering or being conscious of who and where you really are?
- YES___ NO___ Do you exist in a fantasy bubble, engaging in mind games with yourself and refusing to accept the truth about your life, pretending that it's not as bad as it really is?
- YES___ NO___ Do you procrastinate and put off doing things that you know will help you move forward?
- YES___ NO___ Do you make excuses to justify not doing difficult things?
- YES___ NO___ Do you numb yourself from the pain of your reality by altering your state of consciousness any way that you can?

Quite a revelation when you take time to tell yourself the truth, isn't it? It is important to acknowledge your propensity to resort to limiting behavior patterns that have allowed you to "cop out" and deny yourself a fully engaged life.

This phase of the E.M.E.R.G.E. process is where you start being truthful with yourself. Unfortunately, for far too many people it takes a crisis to jolt them into an awakened state. Once a crisis hits, it forces you to take stock and acknowledge the truth of where you are...wherever that is. It is a common occurrence. The thing is you can start today to acknowledge your truth. There is an entire part of your brain that you are not accessing that is available to you when you simply decide to acknowledge it.

In her professional role as a business strategist, Marie Guthrie works with many clients when they get to the point of acknowledging that there is another truth available to them and that a shift needs to occur. Hear what she has to say about it:

"One of the things to ask a person is, 'Why are they feeling stuck?' They just know that there's got to be a better way and something is starting to really fall apart; usually it's a relationship, either personal or business. It's normally something that's been fundamental to their identity that is starting to fall apart. What I see in this new world of business is that we used to live in this linear world, but now it's coming at us randomly in a circuitous form and we're still using all that left-brain stuff in a right-brain world. The cornerstone for leaders and especially high achievers is to really tap into their consciousness and bring to awareness an entire part of their brain they don't know how to use and have never been taught to use."

Accept

The point of acceptance, in my opinion, is the hardest part of the process. Once you accept that you have not been fully considering your gifts and passions, the most difficult step has been taken. Now you must ask yourself the soul-searching questions below. Be mindful of the voices that are likely to creep in to redirect you from your truth. Ask your inner voices for permission to allow you the space to explore possibilities. Reassure them that you will involve them in the process before you take any major actions.

I share the questions with you here and invite you again to download your free Lifeline Guide at www.TheGiftedTrap.com/LifelineGuide. Use the guide as a tool and answer the questions that we offer to assist you as you learn to accept responsibility for your life AND your transformation.

Here are the questions:
- **What have I been unwilling to accept that I'm now willing to consider?**
- **What am I truly passionate about that I have been denying myself?**
- **What are the possibilities that exist for me that I have been resisting taking advantage of?**
- **Am I willing to do whatever it takes to honor myself, and the gifts I've been given? If so, who else will my decision impact and how?**
- **Am I willing to put a stake in the ground and claim what I know to be my divine birthright in alignment with my gifts? If yes, decide what your first action step will be and when you will take it.**

Your willingness to confront tough questions that you have resisted even asking yourself before is a major breakthrough and break from your old pattern of behavior. It may cause you sadness when you realize how you have not been truthful with yourself. The good news is that inside this painful new reality is an opportunity to take a more truthful stance with yourself from this day forward.

A Truthful Stance

by Anne Palmer

What is the truth hidden within this breakup—this very sad story
The truth that was diminished by untruths in all their glory
Those little ways of bending what was real and made to look "OK"
In an effort to camouflage truth and keep things the same way

Unfortunately, the problem with not quite telling <u>all</u> the truth
Is that it creates small scars that fester like an aching tooth
Just a little painful, perhaps a small cavity—not a very big deal
Until it forms an abscess requiring major surgery in order to heal

At that point the damage is done and the small scar has become large
With enough scar tissue developed that it is carried on a barge
That is like a heavy weight being towed wherever you are
No matter where you go, it is there…always near…never far

Yet the truth is healthy when spoken in a compassionate, caring way
It can be like rays of sunshine on a bright beautiful day
However, when it is silent and kept locked up deep inside
It masterfully whips you around like a wild roller-coaster ride

Twisting and turning the emotions get harder to reveal
Until what erupts is the hurt and anger that you feel
It causes actions and behavior of which we are not proud
What else can you expect to come from under such a dark dismal cloud

Stormy nights and rainfall—fitful dreams and tears
Is what arises after suppressing truth for way too many years
It is a vicious cycle if it goes unaddressed without becoming aware
That there is only one true option…that Soul calls you to bear

The only way to heal from the damage that was caused
Is to get in touch with real truth, take time and pause
To gather all the inner knowing from each of your internal parts
Allow them to align and speak the truth that lives only in their hearts

In breakups the tendency is to paint the other as the one who is wrong
When it is "honest self-reflection" that yields a much more mature song
The lyrics and music that emerge from the less comfortable reflective route
Help to soothe the Soul and handle the inevitable self-doubt

Going forth from here my intention is to live a totally different way
To live each day, saying what I mean and meaning what I say
For in that way of being I honestly believe there is a chance
To find the truthful love I long for—if I embrace this honest new stance

Examine Summary

Self-examination is the essential first step you must take to emerge from emotional entrapment. As you become more adept at recognizing the disempowering PB&Js and negotiating with your internal voices, you will access greater awareness and acknowledge more profound truths that allow you to accept where you are, and how you can create a healthy shift for yourself. It is at this point that you begin to understand and awaken to the possibilities available to you for your life.

As I mentioned, be mindful of falling prey to the limiting PB&Js that were responsible for luring you into this state of emotional entrapment in the first place. I will equip you with some strategies to help you manage them later in this chapter. The deeper you delve into your inner knowing and truth, the more you begin to grasp and dust off the possibilities that are available to you. This is an exciting archaeological adventure for you. Have fun with it!

My mentor, Jeffrey Van Dyk, is a sage who shared this profound truth that I now offer to you with the hope that it will serve you as you go through your self-examination process. Jeffrey's wisdom is this:

"There are no more problems to solve...
just more truth to be revealed."

As you search your soul and get to know yourself, accept the notion that there is nothing "wrong" with you. You are perfectly imperfect just as you are. Allow the truth of who you are to introduce itself to you.

Step 2 – Maximize

Earlier I mentioned how meditation and journaling serve as valuable tools to help you excavate and become aware of your gifts and passions. Other outlets such as dialoguing with friends, family members, therapists and life coaches are vital resources as well. In sharing your story, choose others who are able to understand and validate who you are. Select positive people to share with who have traveled your path with you, and/or have themselves emerged from a similar place of entrapment. They may be able to help you see ways to maximize your gifts.

I caution you to choose wisely who you select as confidants. Look for signs that they have emerged in a healthy way and are enlightened about a more conscious existence themselves. Coaches and mentors served that role quite well for me. Now, I serve in that role—coaching and inspiring transformation by holding the mirror up for others— offering them the opportunity to become aware of and embrace the incredible light within them.

When you do the exercises that I offer you in the free Lifeline Guide (www.TheGiftedTrap.com/LifelineGuide), you begin to see your own unique talent in a whole different way... whatever that talent may be. Be prepared for life-altering, liberating, transformative experiences as you reflect and understand that you've been denying yourself for a long time.

I did a similar exercise with my yoga master when I worked with her on developing her persona statement—how she wants to show up in the world.

First, I must share with you that she is a born teacher. She lights up, comes alive and creates an amazing experience for all who attend her classes. When she drafted her persona statement, she shared it with me.

I immediately noticed that she had left off that she was a teacher. When I brought this significant omission to her attention and shared with her how I, and so many others, experience her, she couldn't believe she had left it off. Tears welled up in her because she knew she was born to teach.

That was a pivotal moment for her, when she realized that in order to live more joyfully, she simply needed to be more intentional about how she would teach more people, and impact more lives. Through my calling her out, she experienced a shift in how she saw herself. She is now fully aware and knows, honors and embraces her gift with even more gusto and enthusiasm.

It can be an enlightening experience as you truly see yourself for the first time. You begin to understand what it is that makes you unique—what you possess—your special gifts and talents. You see the things that you can do that no one else can. As you get to **know your gifts**, you begin to leverage and **maximize** your talent.

Natasha Phoenix agreed with me on this point in our interview and explained:

> *"I know what I'm good at now. I know I have a distinct set of skills that benefit a number of people out there. So I treat myself as a business now. It's 'ME Incorporated.' When I mentor people and train my staff, I try to instill in them that in today's economy you can't depend on a company, a boss or even a friend to look after you.* ***You have to know what you're good at, what you like and how you can sell that—and if you know those things the rest will fall into place."***

I share with you now my own experience of maximizing my talent in an environment that led to an extraordinary Emmy-Award winning outcome.

In the mid 1990s, I was primarily focused on being the best wife and mother I could be. I had put my professional dreams mostly on hold for the sake of catering to the needs of my family. In fact, my story about that is featured in a book entitled *And What Do You Do?* that features women who choose to back-burner their careers for the sake of their families rather than choose Sheryl Sandberg's currently popular challenge to *"Lean In."* (That's a whole other story for a later book—much too complex to address here.)

However, to illustrate the point effectively and put this in the proper context, I must share with you some of my professional experience prior to this story unfolding. I had extensive experience doing on-camera work, having done major national commercials for L'Oreal Hair, Domino's Pizza and Ban Solid Deodorant. Additionally, I had appeared as a dancer in Francis Ford Coppola's movie *The Cotton Club,* as well as having been a spokesperson for major corporations and organizations like PNC Bank, US Airways and the Kettering Foundation's National Issues Forums.

While those were all extraordinary accomplishments, I had done little to leverage them. I generally limited myself to whatever projects arose and came to me, reluctant to place myself in the spotlight or to actually promote my talent.

The limiting PB&J that I believed at that time was that because my husband's career required a 24/7 commitment, if I really stepped out and reached for the stars, it would disrupt my family in a big way. Essentially, I chose to **play small to stay safe** for the sake of my family.

Out of the blue, a dear friend and mentor who recognized my talent offered me an opportunity to be a part of an ambitious—in fact, revolutionary—television concept. It was an opportunity to host one of the first-ever NCAA Division I-A women's collegiate basketball talk shows in the nation.

I confess that my instant reaction was typical of my PB&Js and my parts that had stepped up to limit me. Instantly, a voice in my head spoke up to keep me from embarrassing myself and said, "You can't do this. You're no expert; you've never even played the sport, except in the backyard with your brothers." Yes, that was that Doubter part of my psyche rearing its ugly head. The PB&Js of my family didn't help either. They were saying, "What does she know about basketball?"

In this situation it was the positive perception that others had of me that allowed me to step out of my own way and acknowledge that I was ideally equipped for this role. It was my mentors—Mimi Barash, the first female chair of the board at Penn State University, Bruce Dunn, the producer for the show, and Coach Rene Portland—who were all reflecting back to me the brilliance and talent that they saw in me. They provided the infrastructure and support I needed to succeed.

That point in time—1995, to be exact—was still one year before the 1996 Olympics, when women's sports would become fashionable. Before then, women's basketball was below the radar. It had never been presented to the public using the medium of television. Our show was revolutionary.

What better place to come from than that place of not knowing the game at all? The ultimate gift I could bring was the perspective that allowed me to ask just the right questions that would be in the minds of novice viewers. In addition, my gift of vision—of being able to see things clearly, ask pertinent questions and articulate what I observed— turned out to be an ideal formula for success.

It was fertile ground for me to step out—at least a little bit—from those limiting PB&Js into the empowering possibilities, beliefs and joyfulness using my gifts. What resulted was a thirteen-season multi-Emmy-award winning professional platform. Yes, for thirteen seasons I was in my element, hosting and bringing to viewers an insider's perspective on the world of women's collegiate basketball. I was in service to young women, making a difference and living my life in alignment with my gifts. In short…I was maximizing my talents.

In my case, I was blessed with:

- A captivating presence on camera.
- A knack for asking penetrating questions.
- An ability to listen deeply to others and, in a comfortable conversational exchange, draw out of them nuggets of wisdom

- The artful ability to use my voice and articulate to viewers and listeners what I had observed and heard in a way that would evoke a visceral experience in them—leaving them informed, inspired and/or transformed.

I instinctively knew when to step back and enable people to nod in agreement because they finally "got it." It required that I artfully mix the right degrees of confidence and compassion to emit a charismatic presence.

Again, I use my personal mantra to explain my awakening during that period of my life. *"I realized with my real eyes—the eyes of my soul."* Yes, I realized how to maximize my talents in service to others.

Having support systems that believe in you is an example of PB&J's being positive, powerful and in your favor. When you have such an infrastructure in place, you are able to maximize your gifts and talents. Troy Vincent and I discussed this very concept as it relates to athletes during my interview with him.

Troy was lucky to have a family and infrastructure that believed in him. They saw his gifts and encouraged him to cultivate them. That's not always the case. Without that support, gifts can go unrecognized and uncultivated.

Arthur Joseph, who works with a lot of super-athletes, shared his perspective on the importance of having a support system to cultivate your gifts. He said, "You came here with talent, but somebody had to cultivate the talent that is in you. Somebody had to teach you how to make the most of what you have."

For a lot of superstars, whether they are athletes, entertainers, politicians, or executives, their coaches are their support systems from which they get the belief in themselves. As long as they have that in place, they feel "well held" and are able to meet the demands and withstand the scrutiny that they are constantly under. But what happens when that goes away? What happens when there is a talent that maybe doesn't make it to the next level? I posed these questions to Troy Vincent, who answered them from the perspective of his role to help guide NFL football players on and off the field.

Anne: *Troy, having an infrastructure in place is important, but what happens when that goes away? What happens when there is a talent that maybe doesn't make it to the next level? Often we see many young NFL draft picks two or three years into their career, they don't quite make the cut and meet what is expected of them. What happens when that infrastructure goes away for them?*

Troy: *I believe the infrastructure is always there. It's the athlete not taking the responsibility, or seeking out that infrastructure from which he or she has departed. Let me elaborate on that. Colleges have an infrastructure or a structure in place to support you. Most of the time as athletes we take what we think we need or what we believe we need and then we depart, never to look back. But the infrastructure is always in place.*

    Most of the time when athletes transition, they keep around 'yes' folks. Most are not keeping around a circle-of-influence that holds them accountable. The athlete tends to surround himself or herself with folks that tell him or her just what he or she wants to hear. When the rubber meets the road, and in times of trials and tribulations the athlete falls, who is there to pick us up? The folks who were never really there for us. And sometimes we are either too prideful or too bashful to go back to where we departed from—that infrastructure that believed in us—because of the disconnect created because of how we left."

Troy spoke specifically about support for the gifted athlete, but I maintain that there are support systems available for gifted adults in other professional arenas. For instance, if you went to college, do you use your alumni resources to the fullest? Maximizing your talent may require you to stop and "realize with your real eyes" what is available to you.

Questions to help you to maximize your talent

Again, I invite you to do the exercises in the Lifeline Guide (www. TheGiftedTrap.com/LifelineGuide) to help you to identify and maximize your talents. The following questions are a great place to begin.

First answer the questions for yourself and then ask someone who knows you well the set of questions that follow the ones for you:

What are the things that bring you joy?

What do you do that you do well, is effortless, and seems like second nature to you?

What were you doing when you felt most joyful, alive and felt unstoppable—capable of achieving anything you truly wanted?

Who has supported you in the past? Is that support still available to you now? If not, what other resources are available that could possibly support your talent?

Now ask a confidant, friend or someone who knows you well that you trust to give you honest feedback and answer these questions:

What qualities about me do you feel make me unique?

What do I do better than most people?

Could you share examples of times that you felt I was really passionate about something?

What other resources do you think are available that could possibly support my talent?

Identifying your gifts helps you build greater confidence in yourself. Cultivating a delicate, healthy balance between confidence and compassion for others, which we discussed earlier, helps you maximize your gifts.

Vasavi Kumar expressed this beautifully in this excerpt from her interview below:

Vasavi: *The delicate balance is complete ownership and responsibility for my gifts and the deep knowing and on the other side of that is humility. When I'm angry it shows up as arrogance; when I'm calm, I am just who I am. It's me knowing who I am, but I don't need to compare myself. It just is what it is. The balance for me is being who I am, but also being humble. I have to strike a balance between being calm and confident, but not being overly humble. I view you as my equal, Anne; we are on the same plain, I don't have to dumb myself down because you get it. You're on the same level.*

Anne: *I'll celebrate it with you. You're beautiful, you're sexy, you go girl. You go for it 195%!*

Vasavi: *Yes, when I'm around people who know who they are, I can step into who I am too. When I'm with people who are down on themselves, I can't be me because it intimidates them.*

Anne: *You have just described that delicate balance of 'confidence co-existing with compassion,' that place you can be fully aware of your own brilliance and still be consciously compassionate towards others and come from a place of humility and being humble.*

Once you recognize your unique talents, the next step is to Engage with them in a whole new way.

Step 3 – Engage

My mentor Arthur reminds me often that…

"The real journey is never outward…only deeper inward."

To engage is the act of going inward, into your heart or that place deep in your gut that feels like the essence of who you are. I encourage you to go inward and locate the right gear—like the gear on the dashboard of your car—where you are able to access your internal wisdom. Lock into it. Engage with the truth that is available to you there. It is the fueling station that will propel you and provide what you need to live into your greatness.

Erline Belton explains how critical this part of emerging is to everyone caught in the Gifted Trap:

"...[G]etting in touch with whatever you want to call it, Allah, God, Buddha—that process is a critical process and it's an internal process where you quiet yourself to hear an internal wisdom that is already inside of you. It's a piece of you. You own it. Part of the process is beginning to allow yourself to stay quiet so that you can hear what you need to hear in a different way. Some people think of it as prayer. Some think of it as intuition...some as meditation. There are all kinds of ways to get in touch with the higher power, but the one thing I do know is that you can't get in touch with that higher power when there is noise all around you."

Marie Guthrie encourages her clients to begin by taking <u>just fifteen minutes each day to connect with their inner GPS</u>, preferably at the start of the day.

"...When you do, you are connecting with your inner self. You are connecting with larger forces, whatever you want to call them—Inner Wisdom or Source, or God or Guides or intuition or success. How you bring that into your day starts there. With that comes the emotional scaffolding you're talking about because it clears the deck of any other emotion you are taking on from those other entities. You [otherwise] take on the other emotions of other entities and react to everyone else's emotions and never get grounded in your own. It's just so important.

"When everyone is in the super-doing mode, the level of the negative emotions, of fear and doubt especially have never been greater, so if that's the world you're living in and you're getting a 100% dose of that every day without spending fifteen minutes to erase it, the cumulative effect of that on business decisions, coupled with the feeling you are running with the herd, [makes you unable to] figure out what you want to do or what your value is. It becomes a perpetual downward spiral that takes its toll physically and on your closest relationships for certain. It CAN be interrupted and of course corrected. That's the magic of those fifteen minutes."

As she continues to emerge, Carole Martin-Wright also identifies her internal GPS—her sense of knowing what matters—as crucial to her progress:

"I wouldn't say I'm a religious person, but I do have a strong sense of spirituality in terms of there being something bigger and stronger supporting all of this. Somehow it's very clear when you're on the right path or you're not. Then there's the strength that comes from the responses from the people around you where you know that you've done the right thing for that person and they are better off for that and that matters a lot to me.

During my basketball TV hosting phase and my own process of emerging, my internal system was urging me to "learn the game," and I took that literally. When the basketball team had practices at 5 a.m., I arrived at 4:45 a.m. I became a student of the game. In fact, I immersed myself in it every way possible as I sought to comprehend even the emotions of both the players and the coaches. In an effort to connect with and to communicate effectively with my viewers, I knew I had to live what I wanted to share with them—visually and verbally through the camera.

To do this I had to rely on that wisdom from within. I used that innate sixth sense to truly know what mattered and allow it to guide me.

The irony was that as I sought to engage with my new possibilities, unfortunately there were others around me holding onto the old PB&Js. They were unwittingly trying to lure me back into that Gifted Trap. After all, what exactly did I know about basketball? As I mentioned previously, even my own family questioned my adequacy and didn't take the incredible work I was doing seriously.

By engaging with my inner Guidance Protection System (GPS), I connected with my own inner knowing. It may appear in different forms for you when you begin to engage, but you will know it when it appears. It may be an answer to a prayer, a song in your heart, a voice in your head or just a simple knowingness that is so deep within you that you know it is the right thing to listen to. When you feel it, trust it and engage with it.

Step 4 – Reframe

Full Engagement—being in solitude to listen deeply—can bring a sense of feeling alone which at times is intimidating, a bit unnerving, or downright scary. As you confront yourself in solitude, the accumulation of possibly decades of PB&Js will likely surface. Only you know for sure what you are feeling and whether it is real. At times, the voices of those old parts we discussed earlier in the book will be in direct conflict with the "new you" as you emerge. This confrontation with the voices of the parts of your psyche is an integral part of reframing.

Your whole way of thinking as you engage with your internal GPS and connect with that inner knowing, calls for you to shift how you hold your beliefs. They must shift from limiting you to empowering you. Like reframing a picture, it looks totally different in the new frame.

Sometimes the only way to break free and liberate yourself is by reframing your whole view on life. Imagine taking an old picture that you've kept for a long time and literally reframing it with a brand new frame. Some of the fundamental elements remain the same, but other elements undergo a transformation, and take on a new look—a new way of being.

Shifting the way she was viewing her gifts played a crucial role in Dr. Niki Elliott's ability to emerge from her Gifted Trap and fully accept her giftedness in a new light from God.

> *"That was my own process in terms of your E.M.E.R.G.E. framework. I had previously held, and was just emerging from, the limiting perception that God had given me gifts that I had to hide from the world and that they and I would be rejected. The thing that helped me most was to reframe that limiting perception. Learning how to do that may help people to step out into unique areas, whose gift requires them to blaze new trails."*

In his coaching work Dike Drummond describes how he works with his clients to encourage them to reframe their PB&Js:

*"I work with my clients to switch them from focusing on their dark-ness—their awareness of avoiding the <u>things they don't want</u>—to focus on the light, that rainbow after the storm that illuminates a way to get more of the <u>things that they do want.</u> Many people think if they avoid the things they don't want they'll get the things they do, and that is abso-lutely not true. If you give yourself permission to dream of something you wanted, what would that be? **Because when you know what THAT is we can start taking steps in that direction.**"*

One of the most significant reframing stories I ever heard was one that Dr. Cherie Clark shared with me about her work with the prison sys-tem. Her pioneering Total Learning Environments™ focused on helping men and women in prison to reframe their lives. In my interview with her she explained the program and the amazing results the program achieved.

*"One of the things I'm most proud of is the academic scores that were achieved by participants in the Shock Incarceration Program (NYS). The program was based on the **Quantum Learning™ methodology** designed by a friend of mine, **Bobbi DePorter.** In the Shock program, research demonstrated consistently that in less than one quarter of the time in the academic program, participants took and passed the GED (High School Equvalency test) at twice the rate of comparison groups in other prisons, and throughout the rest of the country."*

"Reframing" in the context of the TLE™ meant **"teaching people <u>how to think, not <u>what</u> to think,</u>"** and transforming prisons into **"places of learning, growth and intention."**

It is also worth noting that during Dr. Clark's tenure as Director of *Shock Incarceration*, more than 42,500 prisoners graduated from the program and remained successful post-release at an unprecedented rate, saving the state of New York more than $1.375 billion in cost of care and capital construction. It was truly a quantum reframing that lead to quantum positive results.

There is no doubt that reframing the methodology was a massive undertaking. The outcomes were well worth the undertaking. It also called for reframing society's Perceptions, Beliefs and Judgments into the new idea that incarcerated men and women are capable of learning from their mistakes, positive growth and success. And it called for participants to reframe their own Perceptions, Beliefs and Judgments that they were "less than"—beliefs that they had come to accept as a result of the PB&Js they formed about themselves because of the environment they grew up in. They were called on to believe that they had an option to make something of themselves through practicing the principles they were learning. As the numbers reflect…most of them embraced a new more empowering paradigm.

One shining example of how the program reframed lives is the story of a young woman, Yolanda Johnson (now Johnson-Peterkin). Yolanda was one of many who made giant leaps in the program. Once incarcerated herself, Yolanda reframed her life. The Shock program was the launching pad for her changing her life. She got her GED while in the program, and went on to get an undergraduate degree, and then later a master's degree in social work. Yolanda is now the Director of Operations and Re-entry Services for the Women's Prison Association in New York City. Her story is riveting and compelling. I share an excerpt from her interview to highlight the power of reframing.

Anne: *My understanding is that while you were incarcerated, you participated in the Shock Incarceration Program designed and directed by Dr Cherie Clark. Would you share the circumstances that got you into prison that you are willing to reveal in the book? Share why you were there and what were your first impressions of the Shock program?*

Yolanda: *I was sentenced to 2.5 to 5 years in prison for the direct sale of a controlled substance to an undercover officer. I was given the opportunity to go to a military style "boot camp" — the Shock Incarceration Program in New York (a six-month, intensive substance abuse treatment and life skills TLE™).*

When I got to Shock I thought, "What is this nonsense? They want you to structure your life and do push-ups and stand outside in the sun." I'll be honest, one of the things I learned very early in life was about racism. My thought was, 'This is some kind of racism' because it was a bunch of people of non-color yelling and pushing—not physically pushing—mentally pushing you to change. To be honest with you, it took me nearly three months to realize that this might be something a little different—to realize that the focus in the program Cherie created was the part where you worked on yourself. It was the part where you learned that you were going back to an environment and you can change people, places and things, but unfortunately you don't have the money to do that. Most people come out of prison and have to go right back to where [they] came from.

You had to develop an opportunity and it kept giving you these positive messages. To be clear, Cherie designed the program so you could start to delve into yourself. So I was hearing things like "People who care don't let you off the hook." If you want to pull out your cup of negativity up in the woods where we were cutting trees, you could pull it out and fill it full of the positive reinforcement we were being taught in the camp. It wasn't something my mom hadn't taught me. It was just something that I now saw differently.

Anne: *Thank you for that beautiful overview of where you were in terms of your mental and emotional state of being. You just were "closed" and not willing to see the possibilities that the program offered you initially.*

In the book, Yolanda, we talk about a concept called "reframing." What you're describing is that you were given an opportunity to put a different frame on an existing situation, so that you saw it differently. Would that be an accurate description?

Yolanda: *Yes. …Again, I didn't think I was closed. I just wanted to do what I wanted to do. In Shock, I learned how to think about myself and my life.*

Anne: *You had been reluctant and you decided to open up at three months in. At that point you made the decision to embrace this program. How did that show up in your life?*

Yolanda: *It was a constant push. You couldn't just speak as a person; you had to ask permission to speak. You couldn't look at a person. (Looking around in Formations was distracting to you and others.) You had to ask permission to look at the officers. When they said "eyeballs," you could look at them. There was a lot of the program that I didn't necessarily agree with which is also in parity with the military, which I never experienced prior to Shock. I just thought they made this up and I was like, "So we can't speak to people? What kind of oppression is that?"*

After a while there was a sergeant who used to constantly call me out because I was looking at him all the time. He used to say, "Johnson, are you looking at me?" and I'd say, "No, sir. I'm not looking at you," and he'd say, "Johnson, I think you are looking at me." I had to practice not looking at this man. It was something so simple, because when I looked at him, he had beady little eyes behind his glasses. I was there with team members and peers and I had to practice that ... form of discipline. I had to practice and discipline myself not to look at this sergeant because he would make me stop and do push-ups. Sometimes the rest of my peers would have to do push-ups because I was looking at him.

So after I got that, I knew that if I really focused I'd get this. Much later, I realized they were teaching us to think before we acted, in every way. Each month new people would come into the program because they were all trying to get out (of prison early). He would call me to do push-ups. He would shout, "Johnson, Thomas is looking at me. Johnson, come and show her what happens when you look at me." I started to get angry at first. I'd finally got it together and here he was trying to push me even harder. I didn't get it at first, but after a while it became a joke. He'd say, "Johnson, guess what? Ford is looking at me,"

*and I would go and take Ford and do push-ups with her and
say, "Don't look at him because he'll make you do this."*

*When he was retiring, we had a ceremony for him. We
were singing songs that go along with the marching. I requested
permission to speak, and he said, "Speak, Johnson," and I said,
"Sir, this inmate thinks you're eyeballing her, Sir." And everybody laughed.*

*When he was leaving he whispered in my ear and said, "I
pushed you the hardest." I used to sing in church all the time. I
didn't know he was a minister, because you couldn't tell he was
a minister, but he used to be in the church and hear me sing.
He kept saying, "You have a gift to give other people, so I pushed
you the hardest to prepare you for society." So from that day I got
it. My mindset had changed—I finally understood that some of
these people really cared. It wasn't a game. They weren't playing
jokes. If you didn't do what you were supposed to, you would go
back to prison and the time you spent in Shock didn't count. I felt
that "Wow, maybe they really do care." I didn't know until after
it was over that they go through a process of breaking you down,
so they can build you back up—like in the military.*

Anne: *So that sergeant pushed you the hardest because he saw the promise in you. That's beautiful. You saw an opportunity to reframe
and you took advantage of it because the people around you were
providing you with that extra incentive and believed in you. You
were able to go from a place where environmentally there wasn't
much opportunity or promise. And now all of a sudden there
were people in your life telling you,"I believe in you. There's
another way." And so you took advantage of that and you chose
to make something of your life.*

As the story of Yolanda Johnson Peterkin and the Shock Incarceration
Program illustrates, reframing anything is conscious, challenging work
because you are reprogramming thought processes that have been in
place for most of your life. While what you are experiencing may not

be nearly as challenging as what Yolanda faced behind prison bars, from your entrapped place—whatever that may look like—reframing is possible for you too.

To jump start your process, do the reframing exercise in the Lifeline Guide (www.TheGiftedTrap.com/LifelineGuide). It will help you take a limiting belief you have been telling yourself that is holding you back and reframe it in a more positive way that will empower you.

I guarantee you, when you do the work of reframing the PB&Js that are not serving you, it is definitely worth the effort! That was certainly the case for me when I did my belief relief work with Gina Maria Mele and my dream manifestation work with Marcia Wieder.

I was able to take the belief that "I don't matter" and reframe it into "I DO matter and I am using my gifts to make a difference."

I encourage you to get started reframing your life!

Step 5 – Gain

Gain The Courage and Clarity You Need to Soar

By this point, as the saying goes… "You've come a long way baby!" With each tentative step forward you are gaining more courage and confidence. You begin to push through those rusty, outdated barriers and limitations that have been holding you chained in a place of not believing in yourself for so long, and for the first time the shackles of entrapment are releasing and dissolving away—no longer do you feel tethered to a limited existence. You feel as though you have wings and can soar.

In my own example, I stepped confidently in front of the camera, posing questions that revealed the truth about the incredible opportunities for women to use their talents. As my confidence grew, I began to soar and as I soared, we all soared, winning Emmys and collectively emerging in the process. During that incredible period, I emerged with a greater clarity about the contribution I could make by collaborating with others who possess great talents to make a difference in the world.

In fact my waking up in the dark experience actually occurred one weekend when I was off taping my show. Reframing your beliefs about who you are and what you are capable of is a powerful process.

Often high achievers face difficult transitions where they are challenged to create new realities for themselves. During my interview with Troy Vincent we spoke about an innovative program that he had a hand in developing at the Wharton School of the University of Pennsylvania's Aresty Institute of Executive Education to support athletes as they transition from the game <u>on</u> the field, to the game of life <u>off</u> the field. Troy explained his vision for the program to me:

> *"The vision that was given to me came as a question: How do we support the athlete in transition? Transition happens throughout your lifetime. The Wharton Program was developed and is geared to assist— not help…assist—the athlete in transitioning into his next career path.*
>
> *"'I know what I can be by what I see, not what I hear.' I use that phrase with my children all the time.*
>
> *"In the program, athletes take part in a three-day workshop with different speakers and they go through exercises on finance, real estate, franchising, whatever it may be, branding. Having an athlete see who he can be, who he will be, gives him a better chance of a smooth transition because the transition will take place no matter what. The physical body has an expiration date. Giving them the opportunity to 'see what is possible' is what the program is designed to do."*

For the athlete in transition it is more critical than ever that you possess not just a passion for sports, but consistent, applicable management and leadership skills and relevant business acumen. Toward this end, the Athlete Development Professional Certification Program was developed. It is described on the Wharton Executive Education website as being a joint venture between Wharton Executive Education and the National Football League in conjunction with the Wharton Sports Business Initiative. The program provides athletes with important business skills, allowing them to become as respected and valued off the field as they are on the field.

Congratulations to Troy for being a catalyst in creating this model program that supports athletes and assists them in gaining the clarity they need to soar.

The revolutionary work that Dr. Cherie Clark carried out within the prison systems created life-altering opportunities for prisoners who would otherwise be unable to see possibilities from within their trapped existence. Those inmates fortunate enough to be exposed to the Shock Incarceration Program gained an opportunity they had never before dreamed of—tools to emerge from incarceration into a new life with wings to soar.

As you read in the previous section on reframing, by implementing the Shock Program, as it was called at the time, the lives of the inmates who were able to participate were transformed forever. The shining example was Yolanda Johnson-Peterkin, who went on to become the Director of Operations for the Women's Prison Association in New York City. She found her wings and her ability to soar.

> **You, too, have the potential within you to soar. When you commit to doing the work being outlined for you in these pages, and in the Lifeline Guide (www.TheGiftedTrap.com/ LifelineGuide), you will uncover your incredible talents, believe in your own giftedness, release your limiting judgments, and gain a new kind of inner peace and confidence that allow you to emerge and make a difference.**

An Exclamation Mark About PB&Js

Our PB&Js never totally disappear. We take steps to reframe and realign them while never forgetting where we have come from. My father always urged me to "Do it right, or don't do it at all"—in other words to be the best I could be.

Once I "*realized with my real eyes*" how to reframe that statement to empower me rather than limit and stop me, I was liberated from it. I began to use it as a source of inspiration rather than limitation.

Rubbing up against your limitations as you go through the process of shifting old patterns can feel abrasive. Creating discomfort for you is often the only method that your soul has of getting your attention to clearly grasp your gifts and talents.

The great Lisa Nichols talks about "gifts wrapped in sandpaper," and as you reframe your life, the voices of your parts that we discussed earlier may resist you initially because they are being tested and called to expand. When you are respectful of them and engage them effectively, they will actually be the very elements that allow you to expand—as long as you reframe how they exist within you in a healthy way.

It will be gritty and feel uncomfortable at times. It may feel awkward and even ugly. You may even feel like what Carole Martin Wright experienced and described in her interview with me as *"like putting lipstick on a pig"*—trying to make something unattractive look pretty.

Believe me when I say that the successful reframing of limiting PB&Js into empowering PB&Js is the most important work you can do for living a joyful, purposeful life.

You either learn to reframe and manage your PB&Js or they will continue to run and manage your life. In short...

...*Either you manage them...Or they manage you!*

It is when you ignore them, become numb to them, and stop tuning into that internal GPS that you become immune to your talents and you hold yourself back. You settle for mediocrity and a "less than" life.

Jackson State University President Dr. Carolyn Meyers said it so eloquently in the introduction of this book, and I reiterate it here:

"I see young people who have 'it all,' so to speak, but lack the courage and encouragement to stretch beyond that which is within immediate reach. What's more, I encounter erudite faculty who contain themselves and modify their talents to accommodate the limitations of others around them."

She went on to point out that with this book you are being challenged to

> "*...give yourself permission to let your individual light shine, and with that permission, you will undoubtedly free others to do the same.*"

The world is full of mediocrity. Allow your gifts and your talents to shine brightly and help illuminate the world. Hold in your heart the confidence and courage that you need to soar. Manage your PB&Js, so they don't manage you.

Step 6 – Emerge

EMERGE With Clarity

The final part of the process is the actual emergence. You walk through this process, it seems blindly at times, trusting your internal knowing, under a barrage of constant questioning from your old PB&Js. You spend night after night asking yourself just what you are doing, but luckily you stay the course until you make it to the other side.

In my process, I found the best way to gain the clarity I needed to stay the course until I emerged was simply to engage with, and remain engaged with Source—that higher power and consciousness that is all-knowing, that place wherein lies your real truth.

Prepare for an incredible feeling, a sense of liberation, on the other side of your turbulent storm. Having survived the storm, you step out into clear skies... You literally emerge whole, and see a new way to be.

You do whatever is necessary for you to survive and thrive. It may not be pretty but you emerge whole, and more importantly, you emerge in authentic alignment with who you are uniquely designed to be able to live with joy and fulfillment alive in your heart.

For perhaps the first time ever, you are truly comfortable in your own skin, not having to prove anything to anyone anymore. You are at peace with yourself. At last you are in a place where you understand how to use your gifts and your talents fully from a place of service. Gone is the need to seek validation **outside** of yourself because you know you have become your authentic self—and WOW does it ever feel good!

You are no longer living a modified or compromised version of you. You have released yourself from being managed by limiting PB&Js you had imposed or society had imposed on you. Finally, you are in authentic Alignment.

Authentic Alignment

You may remember the analogy I used earlier about a car being out of alignment, how when you take your hands off the wheel the car veers off to the side of the road. Now that you have emerged with clarity, you can take your hands off the wheel. You are in total alignment with your purpose and your passion, heading due north in life, fully aligned.

Your car goes straight even when you take the hands off the steering wheel. Every part of your car is structurally aligned with your core—the chassis of your car.

The structural elements of who you are can be compared to the wheels on your aligned car. One wheel may be your purpose, one is your passion, one is your connection to Source and one your belief in you.

When you reach the point when all of you is in perfect alignment, you are clear about what it is you are designed to do and you remain in right relationship with it, that is authentic alignment. It is from this state of being that you are able to emerge with clarity.

Staying in Authentic Alignment –
The Importance of Mind, Body and Spirit

In order to completely embrace your truths, you must be in good health on three levels—mind, body and spirit. It is there that it becomes possible for you to understand, in their truest form, the voices that represent parts of you—who they are, when they were formed, how they are governing your life and what they believe to be their role in your life. This level of awareness becomes clear only when you are clear—clear of mind, clear of body and clear of spirit.

We talked about and saw firsthand how many people caught in the Gifted Trap resort to self-sabotaging behavior, whether that is in the form of drinking or drugs or other forms of self-abuse. Many forms of self-abuse are an outgrowth of an altering of consciousness that induces a state of being numb and unwilling to embrace truth. You must be consciously aware to maintain your alignment.

Let's return to the analogy of the car to understand how to sustain your alignment. To completely engage with your internal GPS—Guidance Protection System—it is necessary to cleanse and remove all of the toxins mentally, physically and spiritually, essentially eliminating toxic elements from your life. Again, compare it to the car, oil and filter change. In order for the car to run smoothly and optimally, you must replace the oil and flush out the valves. Then, it is necessary to lubricate them with clean oils.

The same principles apply to your body. I personally have adopted a lifestyle of nutritional cleansing as a process for cleansing and fortifying my body nutritionally. To make it easy, I use the all-natural Isagenix system (www.apalmer@isagenix.com). That is my way to maintain heightened awareness and the ability to connect with Source at will. For me it is the optimal way to engage with my internal GPS. I am fully aware of my body and I am functioning on all cylinders. As a result of paying attention to my body, I feel twenty years younger than I actually am.

We are all energy in the universe, and in order to connect to that energy you have to be willing to enter a place of awareness that is only possible in the purest sense of connectivity. That cannot be achieved if you're in a state of altered consciousness through drugs or alcohol. Your arteries and internal plumbing must be clear.

Now I must be fully transparent. I am not a purest in this regard. I definitely enjoy a good margarita, a refreshing fruity glass of Sangria or a marvelous Merlot, but everything in moderation. My motto is "moderation, not deprivation."

Taking care of your body is vitally important.

My practice is to hydrate and exercise regularly. I ensure that I get appropriate amounts of rest and drink a minimum of 64 ounces of water each day. I make it a daily practice to meditate for at least 15 minutes a day. Rarely does a day go by that I do not journal. It is through that practice that I engage in a dialogue with my Source, my parts or my spirit guides. Maintaining healthy, harmonious relationships inside my psyche keeps me in a peaceful state. And finally I set the intention to be consciously aware by practicing my Vocal Awareness rituals every day and by setting intention to be aware. I dream vividly and often find that I am able to interpret important messages that my subconscious is sending to me by having them surface at a conscious level through my dreams.

I attribute much of my heightened state of awareness to the fact that I take care of my body. In the next chapter, I'll discuss self-care in more detail, as ways for you to achieve clarity of mind, body and spirit.

A Shout Out to my Lifelines

My journey to emerge began after waking up, being shaken and realizing that I was in such a deep state of denial and that I was suffocating and withering on the vine. I knew I needed help and I looked around for lifelines to save me. I want to personally thank my mentors for the hand each of them played in my process of fortifying my spirit. They represent an artfully linked lifeline that responded in my state of emotional emergency to help me from my state of emergency to E.M.E.R.G.E. and SEE.

Fortunately, my first lifeline was what seemed to me just the oxygen mask I needed to help me breathe again. I found a therapist to help me untangle the withering vines wrapped around my throat, sort through my contorted thinking and console me in the emotional prison around my head, my heart and my body.

I am so thankful to Dr. Robert Filewich, my behavioral therapist. Dr. Bob took my hand in my most broken state and extended a lifeline to me that helped me examine my behaviors and my beliefs. He taught me the GVLWIDS acronym. That just because I am me, I am Good, Valuable, Lovable, Worthy, Important, Deserving and Strong. What a gift he gave me that allowed me to remember who I am.

The next mentor on my journey is now one of my closest friends— Erline Belton. She's like a sister to me now. Erline is an extraordinarily talented executive coach who in my time of emotional entrapment helped me professionally navigate my way around the landmines and booby traps that seemingly had me stuck in a place that I could never imagine how to get out of.

As part of Erline's nurturing guidance, she challenged me to pick up my pen again to journal and dream my way to a healthier state of being. She challenged me to look in the mirror and see the real me, even under the protective layers that, like paper mache, were a "perfect façade." She encouraged me to trust myself, knowing that the answers were within me, and nudged me to go inside to examine, excavate, peel back the layers and get to the truth that was in my heart.

My next mentor, Bill Mayer, helped me in that examination and excavation process as well. His *Magic in Asking the Right Questions* book and his artful, inquisitive coaching style taught me to ask all of the right questions that would yield all the right answers. That is why, in my opinion, it is essential that you find mentors, coaches, teachers and friends to ask you and help you answer your own questions that will reveal who you truly are. It is through that inquisitive process that I was able to answer my very own questions.

The next link in my lifeline of mentors and coaches who helped me to emerge was Marcia Wieder, America's Dream Coach. Marcia challenged me to dream. I had denied myself the opportunity to dream about and see what possibilities there were for me.

She taught me how to embrace and implement tools that helped me manifest what it was that I truly wanted.

Marcia also introduced me to my next series of "psyche-mining mentors." It was through the joint collaboration and work that I did with Tim Kelley and his amazing "True Purpose" work, along with Jeffrey Van Dyk's wonderful "core wounds work" that taught me to identify and tap into my essence. That was when I learned the truth deep in my heart: I had a being-ness, my "essence", that was "maternal, holy, grace"—an energy longing to reignite itself in the world and to lovingly nurture others to a healthier place of being.

Through an understanding of my purpose I was then able through Jeffrey and Tim to connect with parts of myself that were running my life in ways that I wasn't even aware of. I reconnected with my Wounded Child, Joy, and understood her pain. Through the art and process of "transforming parts work" that Tim taught me, I was able to realign my internal scaffolding and relationships with my parts to create harmony within me.

Jeffrey then led me to Suzanne Falter and together they helped me to gain greater clarity about my gifts and find the courage to own them fully. It was at that point in my journey that I "got it"—the fact that I had been in a Gifted Trap and that it was possible to emerge fully into a more joyful way of being.

And then in walked the ultimate mentor, my Dalai Lama of mentors—or better yet, my own personal Yoda—Arthur Samuel Joseph. Arthur surfaced in my life to give me the structure that was needed. His incredible Vocal Awareness work offered me seven (7) rituals that I practice daily for 7 minutes a day, 7 days a week.

Arthur reminds me often that "structure does not impinge; it liberates," and I'm here to say it definitely does just that. By becoming conscious of my "Self" as Arthur says (with a capital "S"), I am able to access all of me.

Most recently, I have been further blessed to have attracted "The Secret Sauce" (pun intended) coaching attraction, Lisa Nichols—and YES, it is THE Lisa Nichols of *The Secret*—along with the super smart "sexy-systems specialist" Melissa Evans, the "Guru of Implementation" at Live Rich Spread Wealth™. They have both encouraged me to be unapologetic about my brilliance.

Melissa believed in my vision for this book and linked me to the amazing Mia Redrick, who has held me accountable as I worked to manifest my dream to author this work. Mia and the team at *Finding Definitions* have been the ultimate midwives to support me in birthing this book.

So I want to personally thank all of my mentors and all of my other support systems who are noted in my Acknowledgements at the beginning of the book. As a result of all of you encouraging me and by engaging with my higher Source daily I am able to share the E.M.E.R.G.E. proprietary process from a place of authentic alignment.

And my lifeline list would be incomplete without expressing my deepest gratitude to my very first mentors—Father John Sanders and his wife Frances. To this day, over half a century later, I still go to and rely on my deep-rooted knowing that there is, and I have, a deep and direct connection to God. Father John was my pastor as a child. He saw the light within me as I grew, and still, to this day, prays with me and encourages me. With that kind of unwavering belief in me, I know anything is possible.

Throughout my life I have stayed connected with the Episcopal Church and with my faith to keep that umbilical cord to God connected and nourished. The additional spiritual work outside the church has allowed me to align my free will and my faith in a way that is healthy and liberating.

Through the ritual of meditations at dawn, I am able to see my life clearly—I'm able to see new pathways and possibilities. So I end this chapter with, and recommend, the following as a pathway for you to emerge:

- *Meditate each day at dawn.*
- *Find time to be grateful—be in gratitude for all of the beautiful things that there are to be grateful for in your life.*
- *Check in with your higher power—whatever that means for you—as needed, and pray regularly.*

- *Establish a spiritual connection with Source. For me that means that twice-a-week I attend services at my church (when I am in town). This physical house of worship serves as a place where my spiritual energy is nurtured and fortified.*
- *Get in right relationship with the Voices that represent your parts and negotiate a harmonious way of existing with them.*

As I have emphasized repeatedly throughout this book, it is vital to trust Source. Because then—and only through that kind of trust—can you surrender to the knowing that will guide you, help you shift your state of being and allow you to joyfully emerge.

In addition, go a step further. Work on transforming relationships with different parts that come into play and that come up for you. You'll need help with that process, and I'll offer you suggestions in the Resource Section at the end of the book on how you might do that.

Live within your reframed PB&J structure, a state of possibility, of empowering beliefs and joyfulness. It is important to engage all of your parts and encourage them to embrace this new way of being with you because then and only then will they allow you to take your place in the world as it was intended.

As you engage with yourself and ultimately emerge with clarity, allow exploration and expansion to become a way of being until the day you expire from this planet.

A Shift In State

by Anne Palmer

Awoke this morning depressed struggling to handle so much rejection,
That appears to be the result of how others perceive my perfection,

Of how I show up and am viewed as having it always so together.
They see no need to support me—offers to help come almost never.

So, for nearly twelve hours I have been curled up in my bed,
Thoughts whirling around in my dreams and in my head.

Thoughts of desperation longing to understand this plight,
Why these challenges—that make me feel like I'm in a fight.

Even in my dreams, loved ones turn against me—cast me out,
I walk away in silence, while inside I'm screaming—want to shout,

That I too have needs and desires that long to be heard and met,
Simple expressions of caring from someone other than just a pet.

Is the struggle I am wrestling with imagined or is it really real?
In the moment, as I toss and turn, it is honestly how I feel.

As I look at life, in the scheme of things though, it's not really
all that bad,
It's my focus on rejection and loneliness that makes me so sad.

So I stop myself midstream and say… practice what it is you preach.
Live by example—that is the truth that you are meant to teach.

Swing your feet over, pick yourself up, get a new attitude,
these words I say,
The quickest way to shift energy is to focus on gratitude and to pray.

Begin by listing things for which I'm grateful for all around me,
Noticing and acknowledging blessings—yes, that is the profound key.

When attention is switched from what is lacking to the good that exists,
It is virtually impossible for negative thoughts or depression to persist.

Already it seems that the sun is beginning to shine rays of hope,
As though I've finally reached the downhill side of a steep slope,

Where ease and grace will take over as guides again from here.
My role is to "just trust" my sources to lead me,
surrender, let go of fear.

Troubles will vanish and work out according to a divine plan.
What I must do is release the controls into the Master's hand.

I am ever so thankful for this wisdom that arose from
my fetal, curled state,
To shift my depression—revealing the optimism and possibilities on
my plate to be really delicious.

As You Emerge...

Surviving Life's Storms
An Umbrella Offering

Throughout this book, we've explored different perspectives on how PB&Js influence your life and penetrate your awareness positively and negatively from a very early age. The earlier we focus support and encourage healthy emotional growth in our children and young people, the more opportunities they will have to live in authentic alignment with themselves and avoid the Gifted Trap. The primary purpose of this book is to offer you a different type of umbrella to help you withstand life's inevitable emotional storms. Below is a poem I channeled. I offer to all who read it "a more delicious way of being," and an opportunity to give greater meaning to your life.

A More Delicious Way of Being

by Anne Palmer

We ALL have crosses that we carry on our backs and in our hearts.
They rise to the surface as we begin to transform our internal parts.

This pain I know well—it has been inside me for years.
It slices my heart, rips my gut and shows outwardly as tears.

This time is different though because of the work I've been doing,
To figure out why we spend much too much of life stewing,

Over the little things that we allow to upset us so much,
Then create coping skills as defenses we use like a crutch.

The time is now to put aside behavior that does not serve.
It requires that we find courage, honesty and the nerve,

To speak from the heart and share truth as we know it to be,
Willing to detach from the outcome, relax and let things flow free,

In the space of being authentically who you are,
That place of peace where there is no need to spar.

This new place of being is a more comfortable way to be in the world.
It is about removing grit from the oyster shell to reveal the shiny pearl,

To put a stake in the ground for life the way you want it to be,
And to step gracefully from behind the massive trunk of the tree,

Where you have been shielding yourself from any pain,
Of not being understood, or thoughts of being insane.

No, by definition insanity is to keep doing the same,
And staying there is not a very good place to remain.

So the best way to move forward from darkness to light,
Is to openly admit that this has nothing to do with being right,

That what this really is all about are the messages from above,
The single most important message is that this is all about Love—

The love of family and friends, people for whom we deeply care,
A love that we exhibit by finding compassionate ways to share,
What we appreciate, admire and love about each other,
Cousin, aunt, uncle, daughter, son, mother or brother.

When we speak and treat each other with mutual respect,
We create much healthier relationships I suspect.

So consider this pledge, as I have, to speak from a place of love,
And when we miss the mark, to simply nudge with gentle gloves,

Rather than respond with words and acts that hurt and cause
struggle,
Instead be open, willing to forgive quickly, embrace and find ways
to snuggle,

Back into a place where expressing love is more than a mere notion.
It is a way of being, where it is safe and wholesome to share deep
emotion.

This invitation is extended with a sincere and compassionate plea,
That if you feel hurt in any way please accept a heartfelt apology.

Know that as long as intentions are pure and not malicious,
Through communication, relationships can be transformed
to be really delicious.

I firmly believe that part of reaching authentic alignment is to understand the importance of the legacy we want to leave in this world, and how best to use your gifts to leave your indelible footprint.

I come from a long line of teachers. So my commitment to the personal growth of others should come as no surprise. My grandfather, Herbert Hardwick, Sr., was a teacher. My aunt, Dolores Martin, was a highly respected elementary school principal. My uncle, Dr. Walter Lester Henry, taught in the School of Medicine at Howard University. Several of my other aunts and uncles were educators as well. And my pioneer mother trained Head Start teachers to teach.

In case you are not aware of what Head Start was, let me explain briefly. It was a program developed by the U.S. Department of Health and Human Services to provide comprehensive education, health, nutrition and parent involvement services to low-income families and their children. Launched in 1967 by June Sugarman, it was conceived as a catch-up summer school program providing tuition to low-income children to prepare them for kindergarten. It was a revolutionary program in America, and my gifted mother played a role in launching it in Texas.

Later in her career she launched one of the first corporate-sponsored childcare programs in America. She was committed to the personal growth and development of the whole person. She firmly believed in giving children a solid foundation and opportunities to empower them from the beginning.

Yet what I say is this: no matter how many opportunities and experiences we give our young people, **if they are not in authentic alignment with themselves, these opportunities will not bear productive fruit.**

You must align with the truth in yourself in order to evolve into the person you are uniquely designed to be in this world. Without doubt you will know when you are in authentic alignment with yourself because opportunities and resources will come to you effortlessly, and events will flow. It will feel like smooth sailing on calm waters.

Challenging times are an inevitable part of life, but when you experience those times, the strength and support you need to navigate the turbulent tides naturally exists within you… all you need to do is access it.

Part of the message of this book is to assist young and old (or I prefer to use the term "more seasoned") people in reaching their inner knowing that they are **"good enough."** We all have the capacity to learn and grasp one key truth—

Being exactly who you are, and responding to your calling using your gifts is the fundamental lesson to master in life. It is your reason for living.

During the 2012 Democratic Convention I observed President Barack Obama's acceptance speech. He models someone who is clear about his gift and abilities. He is an extraordinary orator and so much more. He possesses the gift of clarity—clarity of thought and an ability to articulate his vision in almost any situation. He combines that with compassion and an extraordinary ability to connect with others where they are. He is in total authentic alignment with himself, his vision, and his values. He has dedicated his life to being the best he can be, doing his best to maintain his immunity to detrimental PB&Js that no doubt storm him and threaten to disrupt his emotional state of peacefulness day and night.

I believe his secret to always showing up as the leader that he is lies in his ability to live in authentic alignment with himself under an umbrella of protection provided by his Source.

Smooth Sailing

If as you are reading this section and you feel the hairs standing up on the back of your neck and a shivering sensation gripping your body, that is because this message is resonating with you. Perhaps you have reached your own place of authentic alignment. It manifests itself in "goosebumps" in the midst of an indescribable "Wow!" moment. To reach this point has taken nerves of steel and reserves of courage you may not have known you possessed that allowed you to ride out the rough waters of life's storms. Kudos to you if you have EMERGED!

For those who are looking for the best surfboards, or heavier vessels to help you navigate the storms, so that you too can stand in stature with confidence on solid ground, I encourage you to read on and also do the exercises in the E.M.E.R.G.E. Lifeline Guide. (www.TheGiftedTrap.com/ LifelineGuide).

Riding the Inevitable Emotional Waves

Let's look at a few case studies that illustrate the reality of what it takes to emerge from life's rough waters into authentic alignment. I share my experience and the experiences of other, so that you will be aware of the inevitable emotional waves you will encounter along the way. Armed with this information, my hope is that you will survive life's rough waves. May these insights serve as surfboards that allow you to ride those waves safely and successfully to shore.

The Undertow – Guts and Grief

The front end of my journey was especially challenging—there were times when I felt my experience was like rough waves of emotions crashing violently against jagged rocks. It took guts to keep going. So, too, was the case for Yolanda Johnson-Peterkin. During our interview together, I asked her to explain what she did once she finished the Shock Incarceration Program and went back into her community. She shared the guts it took to change her life and the choices she had to make to build a new life for herself:

> *"I think I'm having a hard time processing the fact that I chose because I really didn't choose, or I didn't know I was choosing. The only thing I chose not to do was to come back to prison. I really didn't know how life might unfold for me out of prison. I wanted to do different, but didn't know how. I saw there was an opportunity to get out of Shock, but didn't know how it would pan out in the community.*

"Let's go back for a minute, because I actually felt I wasn't going back to prison the day I walked into a maximum security prison and saw people who would spend 50, 75, 80 years in prison. Something then said, 'I don't want to do this,' but I couldn't tell anybody because I was too tough to tell people I was afraid. This was too daunting to me that there were beautiful women who would spend 25, 30, 35 years in prison. I couldn't say anything at that moment in the yard, but I was very young, I was 20 years old thinking 'Lord have mercy, how am I going to do this? I can't do this, let me figure out how this works.' Let me just say that I think my life is governed by a power greater than me. I was given the opportunity to do the Shock program because it was time for me to move on to that phase.

"In each of these phases I didn't think about his glory and his grace then. I didn't see it then, but I can see it clearly now. But in the moment, I didn't think to myself, 'I see an opportunity and I'm going to take it.' I still don't do that. My Executive Director said, 'Don't you wake up every morning with new possibilities?' and I said, 'Absolutely not.' I wake up in the morning hoping I can pay my rent. Hoping that I don't say the wrong thing and get fired. We are on the ground here. Let's get on the ground. We still have women incarcerated with their children; we still have women who are suffering. We have work to do here…that's another story. I came home to people who were still getting high, people who were in my household stealing my pocketbook. I had to sleep on my pocketbook. And I saw things that weren't conducive to what I had just learned in Shock. But one of the things that Cherie did was constantly say, 'You must change your environment.'

"So I went to programs they mandated me to go to. I was one of the first ones to go through the program. I participated in telling people how frustrated I was about being in the same environment. My cousins were robbing me. I put my pocketbook down and they took all of my money. They were still getting high, still doing the same things. I was explaining this to my mom, and my mom got me a two-bedroom and I started to stay there.

"I got my GED inside the program and then when I got out I got a job at Tupperware packing boxes because that's what they told you to do in Shock. There was an After-Shock program that you were mandated to go to, and they helped you find gainful employment. I was packing boxes bigger than you and I—I say that because I remember meeting you. I was making $3.35 per hour and I was proud and felt I was doing something. I did work before I went to prison, but this time I was really working. I remembered getting a check for $78 and I thought I was rich!

"I went on that journey and often ran into individuals. One of the greatest things about Cherie and how she enlightened me is that she taught me to always talk about what the issues were, and always give back. So I stayed connected to that same program Cherie had run on the inside. I stayed connected to that program on the outside. Although we were mandated at first, I stayed connected to it out of choice.

"I was working packing boxes in the day and was eventually given a counseling position at night for the Shock program that Cherie structured on the inside. They called Cherie 'Mama Shock' on the inside, and called me 'Mama Shock Junior' on the outside because I was passing that same message on. I specialized in helping formerly incarcerated women that were coming out with the same issues, children, working, some may not have gotten educated, whatever. It certainly gave me insight to push myself as much as I could."

Yolanda made a conscious choice to make something of her life. She stood up to the PB&J's of her environment, and withstood the tide that could have easily sucked her back into behavior that would have landed her back in prison. She had the guts it took to change the trajectory of her life.

During my own phase of deciding whether to take a leap of faith, I often felt an undercurrent was trying to suck me back out to sea in a storm. It took tremendous guts to embark on the journey, and remarkable willpower to stay the course.

I explained how this felt to me in my interview with Erline Belton:

> *"There is part of the self-discovery process that I refer to as **Guts, Grief, Gratitude and Grace.** You have to have the guts to confront yourself to do the work, which means you may have to let go of something, which leads to the grief. When you start to see the freedom you're really grateful you took the step and then you shift into this more graceful existence emotionally."*

That sounds like an intimidating challenge doesn't it? Aside from the challenges you face in the self-exploration and self-excavation of the emerging process, now you face the ominous sounding "guts and grief."

I can hear the reluctance in your heart as you face yet another hurdle, but without guts you will not reach that desired place of authentic alignment.

To take those first scary steps to face the world, to truly tap into the reserves of courage you've mustered against all odds, you need guts. You must have guts to let go of where you are, to release all that you know that is binding you, to finally relinquish control, and to dare to leave that comfortably uncomfortable place that represents your security. Yet the only reason it represents security is because it is familiar, not because it is emotionally liberating.

In the following extract from my interview with her, Jennie Hernandez shares her own experience of the guts it took for her to make a change in her life with seven children in tow and the grief she endured to get to the other side:

Jennie: *I've joked over the years that what gave me the strength to do what I had to do was knowing I had to take care of my children. Arthur Joseph has made me aware that what took a lot of guts for me was knowing I honored myself enough to embark on this very difficult journey into the fog and take seven children with me.*

It was honoring myself enough to know I would not stay in a relationship where I was being emotionally and mentally abused. I believe that is what really took the strength, to honor myself enough to take a gutsy leap to embark on this journey.

Anne: *When you did that, was there a feeling of breaking away, of denying or killing part of your existence—leaving part of you behind? I also dealt with walking away from a 25-year marriage. Could you speak to the grieving process of that?*

Jennie: *Yes, in the prior months I'd left a church I'd given 100% to for almost 35 years and then left a marriage I'd committed to for 16 years. I was walking away from everything I needed—as I thought—to be safe and secure. As I let go of what was no longer serving me, it was very difficult to do so. There was grief because it feels like jumping off a cliff and it's very difficult emotionally and mentally. Underneath it all was that nugget, so to speak—that universal intelligence of God that I could hold on to and trust that would see me through. The grief was definitely there and many times I felt crazy, stupid and insane to be doing what I was doing, but when I looked back at what I was leaving I knew I couldn't stay there. I knew I had no choice but to keep moving forward and just trust. That was very difficult, but I knew I had to do it.*

Allow me to share a startling perspective with you now—the emotional security in your current situation may not be real. It is quite possibly a mirage, constructed and secured in place by years of emotional entrapment and limiting PB&Js that have flooded your world and assumed control of your thought processes.

If that is the case, to break free requires you to reach deep inside and find that core of connectedness that resides with your inner knowing. It is that inner voice that is desperately seeking an outlet—that voice that is slowly gaining strength to shout…

"You can do this, go for it! Just do it!"

Trust <u>that</u> voice of hope and encouragement; don't allow your inner parts' responses to long-held limiting PB&Js to drown it out. Find inspiration from Jennie's story—bankrupt, with seven children and no one to support her except herself. She went on to explain:

"Before I made these dramatic changes in my life I had been asking Spirit. But I wanted more spiritual knowledge than I was being given through my church. I was asking through prayer for more knowledge and wisdom. Things were becoming difficult and changing, for example, everything felt so hopeless. I had just declared bankruptcy. I had no credit score, no money, no car, no job experience, etc.

"Yet, just as things seemed hopeless, something would come in, such as the welfare program I went on. They also paid for my tuition, childcare and gasoline. I also thought I would be homeless, as my landlady kicked me out. When I was at the point of being homeless, a home came into my life. It was the perfect place for where I wanted to be, although I had to move out of state.

"Although I was going through a difficult process, I continually saw these miracles appear in my life, so I had a sense of gratitude. Despite what was going on, these miracles continued to happen for the next few months and continued even for the next year. There was grief, heartache, tears and everything in between, but gratitude as the process continued."

Jennie's words hint at the next emotion which surfaces in our process—**gratitude**.

When you are willing to do just as she did—whatever it is that requires those guts—you can move forward. In many cases, it may require you to walk away from all that is familiar to you, as it did for Jennie. No doubt that can be scary.

Another frequently used term for this kind of bold action is "radical action." How much more radical can you be than to let go of everything that has brought you to where we are today and reframe it into a whole new life? What is more radical than that? What could be more gutsy than that?

When you are called to follow your heart, it sometimes calls for you to allow elements of your life to fade and die within you. Letting go causes grief. You are walking away from what is familiar—from situations that you've been holding on to so tightly your knuckles are white from the effort you've expended.

I don't want you to have any illusions about this part of reaching authentic alignment.

Grief is an integral part of this process.

The grief I'm referring to is the grief you feel when you lose something or someone that has played an important or pivotal role in your life. It is also a state of being that you experience as you let go of the things and people that no longer serve you. I have experienced both forms of grief first-hand.

I walked away from a marriage that had defined who I was for nearly a quarter of a century. Not only did it require guts, but it also was the source of a lot of grief. Why did I do it?

Opting to remain for the sake of physical comfort certainly would have made others happy. As my ex-husband had pointed out, it worked for him and it worked for our children. There was only one problem… It wasn't working for me. I was living an unhealthy, inauthentic life where my emotional well-being was not valued. That may have been fine with everyone else. It wasn't fine with me.

While it was materially comfortable, it was emotionally barren. I had to make a choice. Was I going to sacrifice my emotional well-being for the sake of others? OR was I going to be true to me?

That fateful morning when God shook me, the truth became frighteningly clear. I wasn't happy. Without radical change, I would suffocate both literally and figuratively. At that moment I knew that I had to summon the guts to make the toughest decision of my life. I had no guarantee of a positive outcome and I didn't know what the consequences would be for the people I cherished most in the world—our children.

In the inner recesses of my soul, I prayed for a miracle to figure out a way to work through the situation and maintain the family unit. Even as I prayed, I intuitively knew that for me to emerge into authentic alignment, I could not remain where I was. I had two decades of journals filled with my pleas and prayers to figure it out. Those journals were written from within my trap and represented my efforts to make where I was work. The time had come to face my gut-wrenching truth. It wasn't working.

Ultimately I had the have the guts to walk away, and with that gutsy decision came grief. I began the process of unraveling the quarter century that I had committed to building what "appeared" to be the perfect marriage and family. However, as the perfect façade of my world crumbled into dust, I was able to open my eyes to the truth and the new possibilities around me. In that state of emergency, I began to EMERGE and SEE a world of possibilities before me. I began to evolve authentically. Emotional self-sacrifice was not an option.

Emotional self-sacrifice seemed to be in my family's DNA and I had witnessed how it could manifest if left to run its course. My brother comes to mind when I ponder the notion of grief and emotional entrapment. In his short life, he struggled to find authentic alignment within himself. He allowed his frustrations to fester within him until his body fought back in the form of a stroke that claimed his life.

Ironically, one of my uncles also passed away at the young age of 57. I find it interesting how God put me in direct contact with him during the final months of his life because for most of my life growing up we had had little contact with him. I visited him frequently during those months. Despite the warm and loving smile he always greeted me with, I sensed a deep pain and unexplained sadness within him.

He had been hospitalized for a heart condition, but seemed to be rallying. I visited him at the hospital during the day and spoke with him the night before he was to be discharged. The doctors had cleared him and said his heart was fine. During that night, he passed away. To this day I wonder if it was painful emotions trapped inside him that caused his young heart to fail. He was my grandfather's namesake and there was a kind of sadness in him that was all too familiar to me. It reminded me of his father—my "Big Daddy."

I've shared how close I was to Big Daddy. Because I was the grandchild who spent lots of time listening to his stories and helping to care for him, he had shared in depth with me how sad and lonely he was. His wife had passed away when they were both in their early forties and he had never remarried.

I will never forget the day I came home from school and he was slumped on the floor outside his bedroom. His mouth was twisted from an apparent stroke, yet he gazed into my eyes as if to say, "Thank you. I love you." We sat alone together in silence for nearly 45 minutes as I waited for help to come. As I held his hand and stroked his brow, I somehow knew, even as a young teenager, that this would be the last time he and I would be together. He was taken to the hospital and passed away within a few days. While I had lost my best friend, he was finally released from his emotional trap.

On many occasions, I think about my brother, my uncle and my grandfather, and I grieve the loss of those three gentle giants. I wonder about what felt like a deep underlying sadness that they each masked so beautifully behind their generous spirits and million-dollar smiles. They each modeled dedication and devotion and stood tall and strong in stature with loving, caring and compassionate hearts—beautiful hearts that seemed to be emotionally trapped.

I urge you now...
Life is too short. You come here to live...so get busy living!

That fateful morning when God shook me, the truth became frighteningly clear. Without a radical change, I would suffocate both literally and figuratively. At that moment, I acknowledged that I had to somehow summon the guts to make the toughest decision of my life, without any guarantee of a positive outcome and without truly knowing what the consequences would be for the people I cherished most in the world—my children.

In the inner recesses of my soul, I prayed to God for a miracle to figure out a way to work through this situation and maintain our family unit. Even as I prayed, I intuitively knew that for me to emerge into authentic alignment meant that I could not remain where I was. I had two decades of journals filled with my pleas and prayers to figure it out. Those journals were written from within my trap and represented my efforts to make where I was work. The time had come to face my gut-wrenching truth. It wasn't working.

Ultimately I had to have the guts to walk away and face the consequences. With that gutsy decision came grief. I began the process of unraveling the quarter century that I had committed to building what "appeared" to be the perfect marriage and family. However, as the perfect façade of my world crumbled into dust, I was able to open my eyes to the truth and the new possibilities around me. In that state of emergency,I began to E.M.E.R.G.E AND SEE a world of possibilities before me. I began to evolve authentically.

Evolving Authentically

Gratitude

Despite the emotional and inner physical pain that I endured every day during that period of emerging, I thanked God for jolting me out of my stupor. I thanked him then, and still thank him today, for waking me up to have the guts to do what I did. Without his intervention I would never have experienced the opportunity to live fully or to understand who I am and why I am truly here.

Without the grace of God, my life would have gradually faded into the oblivion of emotional entrapment. Now, I begin each day counting my blessings and focusing on all that I have to offer this world. I do my best to carry and share God's grace everywhere I go.

That's where **guts, grief and gratitude** play their role in this process, and it affects us all in different ways.

Growing up as students in school, we strive to be popular and accepted by our peers. For those blessed with academic "giftedness" and ability, it may be difficult to fit in at times. Unfortunately, too many young people think it's not "cool" to be smart. You may not be accepted by "the in-crowd." If you're nodding in agreement, my advice to you is: You don't have to fit in! You don't have to be liked. Do the hard work. If you are an "A" student, you are gifted. It may be tearing you apart at times emotionally to feel separate from the crowd, but I invite you to reframe your situation and embrace the thought and reality that your intelligence is what makes you unique. That is your gift!

One man who epitomizes this very point is African-American neurosurgeon Ben Carson.

As a young child, his mother encouraged both Ben and his brother to read and write book reports on a weekly basis—in addition to their assignments in school. Unquestioningly, he complied with his mother's request. Over the years he grew to understand that knowledge was power. He realized that his commitment and dedication to these reports had equipped him with an inner strength that set him apart from his peers.

That situation took guts. It required guts for his mother to insist that he and his brother write those reports. And it took a steely determination for him to comply in the face of ridicule from other students and friends. Today, at the top of his game as one of the world's leading neurosurgeons, he is eternally grateful for his mother's intuitive knowing and understanding of what was possible for him. She instinctively knew what it would take to build empowering belief within her son.

You were given your gift for a reason. Celebrate it. Don't waste it.

For some of you hearing these words, your lives consist of a soulless daily routine of waking up, showering, eating breakfast and going to work, coming home, going to bed, and starting all over again the very next day. Are you merely going through the motions of life to make ends meet and giving no credence to your true desires and passions? Take a moment and look inside yourself.

If these descriptions resonate with you, you are doing yourself a major disservice and it's time to WAKE UP.

Think back to the beginning of this book when we talked about the prison cell with its impenetrable, invisible bars. That person you see in that cell is you.

This is your wake-up call...

Figure out what makes you unique and energizes you. Explore what possibilities exist for you to use your gifts and talents to make a difference. No matter where you are in your life cycle, this is your opportunity to wake up and use your gifts.

It may be your ability to work with children, or if you think of our theme of cars and their alignment, it may be you are a skilled mechanic. What are your hobbies? Your hobbies will give you insight into what will make you feel truly alive. If you haven't done them, go back and do the exercises in the E.M.E.R.G.E. chapter and take advantage of the Lifeline Guide (www.TheGiftedTrap.com/LifelineGuide).

As you begin to explore the options available to you, you will recognize the truth of who you really are. Doors will begin to open for you, opportunities will surface in the least likely of places. Watch those steel bars of that impenetrable prison begin to melt. Finally you will be able to make the transition from that wilderness of simply existing to an oasis of joy. But you must sail across some turbulent waves to get there.

Finally you will emerge into that place of authentic alignment on an island called "Peace of Mind."

Remember Dike's story? Dike was a very successful doctor and for all intents and purposes lived the ideal life. Everyone who met him marveled at his achievements and his success. Yet, as we've seen, Dike was miserable, struggling to hold himself together at his core. How had he reached this place of emotional turmoil?

From his early childhood, Dike's family had bombarded him with genetic PB&Js. His family dreamed of him becoming a doctor and encouraged him overtly along that path, telling him he would be the family's first MD. Through school and college, when asked about his ambitions, his automatic response was "I'm going to be a doctor." To him, all other doors were automatically closed.

Dike's PB&Js weren't all bad. In fact, they were the motivation that produced an amazing doctor. And yet they inhibited him from exploring his truth.

A few years ago, to the astonishment of those around him, Dike walked away from his medical practice. Today he is a life coach and runs a coaching practice called TheHappyMD.com, specifically focused on serving doctors finding themselves in similar situations as Dike.

Today, he works with people to empower them to figure out how to make their passion work for them. His giftedness is his ability to inspire others to claim the life they truly seek.

Dike Drummond had the guts to walk away from what appeared to the outside world to be the perfect life. Of course, it wasn't that simple. In the process his world crumbled before his eyes as he let go of the familiar to replace it with the unknown.

Now Dike lives in a place of joyful gratitude. Emerging into his authentic self required guts and a transitional phase of grief. Today he lives at one with himself and his giftedness and describes his own experience:

"I believe that authentic alignment is when I am sharing what I've learned on my path that might help you that comes from my own direct experience. For me it was impossible to be authentically aligned until I had more water under my bridge, had felt more pain, more heartbreak and survived more things, like the old Greek heroic journey. I've returned home to see it for the first time, I earned gifts of knowledge at great cost. For me to speak authentically and feel like an elder to help you, that's the sense of being authentic. I know what I'm going to be when I'm grown up. I'm grown up now, and this is what I'll do until the day I die."

This is your life we are talking about, the life you only have one of.

Each day that passes with you in a state of denial about who you are, what you want out of life, and where your giftedness lies is one day less you have to live joyfully.

Allow yourself to be shaken! Wake up!

Thank You God For My Ten Toes

The process of emerging allows you to self-excavate and assess what it is that's right with your life. As you awaken, your vision becomes clearer and you can finally seize the life you crave. In doing so, harness the energy that flows around you by counting your blessings.

> *"Where your focus goes, your energy flows."*
> *– Wayne Dyer*

I use a simple exercise every morning before I take that first step from my bed to face the day. It may sound unusual, but it's guaranteed to evoke gratitude.

I open my eyes and I look down the bed to my toes at the end of my long legs that are appendages to my core. That core is in alignment with Source and my self. In turn, that core is sustained by a strong heart sending blood coursing through my veins that tells me without a shred of doubt I'm alive and I have something to offer to the world.

At the top of that core are long slender arms to embrace the world we live in. Above the core is my head, driven by a brain that is perpetually seeking out new opportunities to use my gifts for the benefit of those less fortunate.

Between my heart and my head I have a throat and a mouth to speak from and I have a voice. Every single day I possess the opportunity to speak the truth that's in my heart, a truth that I pray will penetrate the hearts of others and inspire them to make a difference.

If you wake up and see a roof over your head, that's something to be thankful for.

If you stand up and walk unaided to the bathroom, that's something to be thankful for.

If you open your refrigerator and see one morsel of food in there to nourish your body that's something to be thankful for.

If you can open your eyes to see the world around you in all its vibrant colors and you have ears to hear, and fingers to touch and experience the sensations of life you have something to be thankful for.

Some people don't possess even that…yet they are still thankful. Think of the limbless girl we mentioned, who had no perception of any challenges. She saw her state of being limbless as a gift.

Take my advice. If you begin every day focused on what you are thankful for, motivation is effortless. By opening your eyes, you are able to emerge and see what's necessary to use your gifts to benefit others. I compare it to visiting the gas station and filling up your tank.

That is gratitude. It all starts with those ten toes. So as you count each one…count a blessing that you have to be thankful for.

It doesn't end there with you simply counting your blessings. You have to use them.

A great example I want to share is going to watch my son compete in the NYC Triathlon. That experience was deeply humbling. That triathlon consisted of a one-mile swim, a 25-mile bike ride and a 10k run. For most of us, completing that would be quite a feat, to say the least. What made it even more extraordinary was that some of the competitors that day were missing legs and arms. Some were blind and tethered to guides who were leading them through each wave of the triathlon, enabling them to compete and complete this amazing endurance test.

When we consider gratitude, I ask myself often, what did those people say to themselves that morning before beginning their triathlon? The magnitude of their gratitude is beyond the comprehension of most of us and should humble us all without exception.

Here and now I invite you to look around and ask yourself …What am I thankful for? Take time to write down your answers.

That is the essence of gratitude. As you focus on your blessings and truly comprehend your beautiful essence, you are entering the realm of grace. Your blessings are like rolling waves at the surf's edge.

Grace – Rolling Waves

Grace is a generosity of spirit, of genuine kindness, of elegance and appreciation. It is an inner understanding that you are blessed.

I was brought up to say "grace" before every meal and before closing my eyes every night. Many of you who were brought up with a religious underpinning in your life live with that same habit, but you don't need to restrict it to mealtimes. Today I seize every opportunity to say grace and express my gratitude for the opportunity to continually share my gifts. Above all, grace is a way of being, an understanding that you're blessed and in return are blessing others.

Faith

> *"Faith is to believe what you do not see. The reward of faith is to see what you do not believe."* – *St. Augustine*

Faith has been an integral part of my journey. There is no question in my mind that I would not have made it without my faith. It played a major role in the transformation of many of the clients I coach and the people that I interviewed for this book.

In my interview with Troy Vincent it was clear that he had a belief system that was larger than he was—and he is regarded as a giant in the world of football. He is a man of high integrity and great character. So I asked him to cite an example when he had to rely on his faith to pull him through a very tough time. He shared this moving memory:

> *"In my second year of the National Football League, at the time I was with the Miami Dolphins, and we were playing the Pittsburgh Steelers on Monday night. In the first quarter I was hit and tore my knee up—ACL, MCL, dislocated my kneecap, and cracked my femur, all in one shot. As I made my way back to the bench, and then began to move to the locker room to go get x-rayed, there were a bunch of emotions that were running through my mind and my body. It was a soul*

check because, at the time, those kinds of knee injuries weren't just a three-to-six month recovery. At my position, you didn't just come back, you didn't return the same, you were never expected to be the same, and that was what was reported the next day in the media.

"At that particular time there was a check-in in my mind before I even left the stadium. I was 22, my grandmother was living with me in South Florida, and she reminded me that night, 'Just remember the God that we serve', and she rubbed my forehead and that was it. That was a time for me to activate my faith. I made a conscious effort to make sure that no negativity entered into my ear gate.

I didn't read about different people not returning. For me, it was focus, focus, focus. I didn't put a timeline on it. I said I was on God's timeline and I took it day-to-day. During that time it was nothing but faith that pulled me through, because if I had listened to the media, I would have never returned. If I had listened to doctors, I never would have returned. So for me it worked. It was my faith and my foundation that allowed me to overcome one of the most difficult circumstances in my life."

Troy relied on his faith and it served him well. He came back from that injury and had a stellar career playing as a cornerback for the Philadelphia Eagles, the Buffalo Bills and the Washington Redskins. His professional successes include being a five-time Pro Bowl and three-time All-Pro player, and receiving the Walter Payton Man of the Year Award, the "Whizzer" White NFL Man of the Year Award, and the Bart Starr Man of the Year Award. I would say that his faith served him well.

Wouldn't you?

Incorporating your faith as you live in alignment with your gifts is a winning formula. Founder and CEO of Innerlight Sanctuary Dr Niki Elliott integrates faith as a ritual in her professional practice. She shared a prayer that she recites as a ritual before she sees each one of her clients:

"I have a prayer that I say before I see each client, no matter how many that is:

> *"God is the do-er of my life's work. Unlimited energy and resources abound. My path is clear, success is guaranteed. Amen.'*
> *"I put each section of that prayer together for a reason…*
> *"God is the do-er of my life's work. I am just the straw. That affirmation takes the responsibility off of me for how things work out.*
> *"Unlimited energy and resources abound. Everything I need to do this work is coming because I'm showing up with what God has asked me to do. I'll have enough physical energy, too.*
> *"My path is clear. I always kept visualizing people waiting to negate or discredit me. God has sent me to do this work so all obstacles are cleared before I get on it. Now, I don't acknowledge enemies or opposition because God has cleared the path.*
> *"Success is guaranteed. If God is the do-er, success is guaranteed.*
> *"That prayer helped me 'emerge.'"*

As you emerge from the Gifted Trap, your final action in that moment of recognition is an expression of gratitude in the most gracious way you can muster.

Finally, you've reconnected with your Self and with Source. What a sublime place to find yourself in.

As I was writing this section of the book, I had a clear message from Source—that it was vital to be transparent about my own process of emerging and to further explain something I touched on in an earlier chapter.

An integral part of the emerging process is that of the world opening up for you and the pieces of the puzzle falling into place. As part of my process of emerging and my quest to uncover who I really was, I attended a workshop led by two of my mentors, Marcia Wieder and Jeffrey Van Dyk. It was at that workshop that critical elements of my emotional entrapment were revealed to me.

Earlier in the PB&J section of this book we explored the voices of our inner parts. We looked at how the Wounded Child affects you throughout your life.

Jeffrey's gift is his ability to help you connect with your core wounds and the Wounded Child within you. He helped me peel away the layers shrouding my true essence.

During that workshop, all of the participants were divided into groups of three. Each person was asked to answer specific questions while the other members experienced their responses. The exercise was designed to expose each person's true essence. Following a period of meditation at the end of the exercise, we each shared what had emerged for us. Collectively we helped each member of our group unveil his or her true essence.

With the help of my group, as I underwent that sensitive and delicate process, three words surfaced that we all felt clearly described my essence: maternal holy grace.

Upon hearing those words pass through my mouth directly from Source, I experienced what can best be described as an emotional volcanic eruption within my soul. The enormity of that description was too overwhelming for me to hold at that time. All I could do was cry because I knew God was calling me to do something extraordinary.

Yet in that knowing, my Doubter immediately surfaced saying, "Who are you to think that is your essence?"

After all, for so long I'd been living with the question of "Am I Good Enough?" hanging over my head.

In that moment of transcendence,
I finally saw the truth of who I really was.

During that workshop when my essence was revealed to me, and after thoughtful reflection on it, my response to answer the call to claim it was a resounding "YES!" I am passionate about humanity and want to do my part to help people heal emotionally.

YES, my life purpose is fulfilled by empowering others to be the best they can possibly be—just as a mother longs to nurture, love and encourage her children to be all that they can be. So it is true to say, I am Maternal.

YES, I am a deeply spiritual, extraordinarily blessed being—connected to God as my source of strength, guidance and love. So it is true to say, I am Holy

And YES, I am committed to embodying grace—with a generous spirit I work to use my gifts from God to serve humankind. So it is true to say, I reflect Grace.

If that means I have been called to embody the essence of *"Maternal Holy Grace,"* then I respectfully accept the call.

As a result of that truth being revealed to me, I have chosen to humbly claim that with humility as my truth and live it. When people turn to me and tell me they appreciate how much I care and that I've helped them see who they really are and love themselves in ways they had not been able to before, I feel I have achieved my purpose. I've nurtured them on their path to becoming what they are capable of being.

That is why I chose to relinquish control and answer the call to write this book. It is an offering of my gifts to inspire you to own your gifts and claim your greatness.

Relinquish Control

by Anne Palmer

Understanding who is in control,
Who is actually guiding the ship?
That is the message to receive,
The key factor and winning tip.

Ego wants to lead—thinks it is the one,
Making decisions and being in charge.
When actually who determines everything,
Is the more powerful "Master-at-Large."

Once this message seeps all the way through,
And is accepted as a law-abiding truth,
It is then that things begin to flow,
Going down like a well-aged Vermouth.

Smooth sailing is what it feels like,
When the controls are finally released.
When we surrender, stop, and let go,
That's when abundance starts to increase.

Sounds easy and simple enough,
Yet it is hard for this message to sink in.
Sometimes the easiest and simplest concepts,
Are the hardest to grasp and comprehend.

We resist—are bold and determined,
Won't accept that there is a better way.
So inner struggles and constant turmoil,
Lead to exhaustion at the end of each day.

If you seek peace and contentment,
A fulfilling life, one of effortless ease,
It behooves you to get this message,
Surrender to the Divine within—if you please.

Soulful Surrender — The Calm After The Storm

The next emotional wave for me was caused by the tide I call "the state of total surrender"—the rolling tide of surrendering completely deep in my soul.

Soulful Surrender is quite simply learning how to fall apart and surrender to Source. The act of surrendering is loving yourself enough to fall apart if you need to. During this process, your soul needs time to recharge, to heal and to find equilibrium. Give yourself permission to crawl into bed and cry if that is what you need. It is not a sign that you are falling back into the clutches of the PB&Js; it is simply an acknowledgement of your inner emotions. It is a release of the negative emotions, allowing you to enter a new place of calm and healing.

Surrender to the honest voice of your soul and allow it to guide you back to calmer shores.

Carole Martin-Wright defines her "soulful surrender" this way:

> "*The key for me is really not knowing whether you're there or not and always having that question. When I get comfortable with the idea that I may never be able to answer that question, that will be good. It's OK, because one day it's like I have to be back on that ladder, the next day is 'Why on earth would I want to do that?' It's OK to not be sure.*"

Natasha Phoenix is still learning to relinquish control and reach the state of soulful surrender, as she revealed to me during our interview:

Natasha: *It's funny, I don't believe yet that there's an end of the journey. I don't think you get there. If you're the type of person that I am, and because of the core beliefs I was raised with, I feel I'll always be seeking a different place—a healthier place. For me to get to a place where I think I am successful professionally, personally and emotionally, for me it's an effort. I'd like it to be more natural. So I'm not sure that journey will ever be over. Maybe that's not such a bad thing, because having a goal gives people a reason to be alive and to be successful. And that's not such a bad place to be.*

Anne: *Let me say: if you do the work, you will evolve to a place of surrendering, which allows you to embrace a whole other way of being. It has allowed me to be at peace and still be an achiever…not from a place of competitiveness, but from a place of "knowing" what I am called to do…of allowing things to flow, rather than feeling that I have to do everything. It's a "knowingness," rather than a "doingness."*

Natasha: *I understand that because I do feel like that. However, that state is not my regular default yet.*

Anne: *I totally get that. That's where the process of "allowing" comes into play. It is a state of naturalness that I have evolved to that if you'd asked me about it 10 or 12 years ago I would have responded from the same place where you are. You are right. It's a constant process. You are constantly evolving. I believe there's a whole other level beyond where I am now as well. It's that conscious awareness of what you are striving to be and choosing in every moment to show up as that person in your life.*

Natasha: *One of the other interesting messages for me is that I wish I had known in my mid-twenties what I know now!! Most of us carry different personalities and it's self-destructive and difficult to maintain. It's difficult for girls and younger ladies to understand that.*

Anne: *That's my hope for this book, that it shortens the learning curve and stimulates an awakening about how to manage your emotional well-being in a healthy way.*

The desire that I shared with Natasha during that interview captures one of the primary motivating factors for writing this book—to help you navigate the rough seas and turbulent tides in your life. May the principles in this book serve as lighthouse signals to guide you to calmer waters.

Restoration, Renewal and Rejuvenation

Life under any circumstances can challenge you because there is negativity lurking all around you. It has the capacity to drain you dry. In order to survive, it is imperative that you find ways to restore, renew, and rejuvenate your spirit.

In my interview with Yolanda Johnson-Peterkin, she shared her perspective on how to manage the inevitable negative forces you must face:

"There are so many uglies on this earth until you constantly need to be refeeding and refueling yourself both spiritually and mentally, because uglies don't go away. Uglies are waiting, always sitting in the

cut, waiting to take back what God has given us. So always be refueling and recharging yourself, both in his spiritual word and opportunities, but also within yourself and within your work.

"It's not always a constant mindset that 'I'm going forward and I've found my source and I'm keeping it moving.' There are always some things that will come about, be it spiritual, mental health, or physical health and others that will come in and try to steal your joy. But continue to stay rooted and grounded in your process and you are going to be OK!"

Yolanda realized the importance of recharging and refueling and taking time for herself. She chose to surrender to her source of strength, God, to be her source of inspiration and guidance to restore her when others attempt to steal her joy.

When you consciously decide to up-level your life and claim your greatness, it will likely require you to exert energy mentally, physically and emotionally. Until you have harmony among your internal voices and a peace treaty within your psyche with all of your parts, it may feel a bit like an internal tug-of-war that exhausts you.

Understanding that emerging is a process that you must manage your way through will help you get through the storm. It is also important to understand the notion that whatever you are experiencing emotionally will often manifest itself physically in some form. I had to learn this lesson the hard way.

In the midst of my own journey, in 2004 I laid in a hospital bed for 3 weeks with a fever of 105 degrees burning my body up from the inside out. Barely able to raise my head, teetering near death, I was in a constant state of sleep. I didn't know if I would ever wake up.

Fortunately I emerged from my near-death experience with viral meningitis—yes, I WOKE up—victorious in the fight for my life. I woke up with new vision—awakened to a new perspective—a new way of living and being. That physical "wake-up call" was both a metaphorical and pivotal awakening in my life. I learned, among many things, the value of taking time for relaxation, renewal and rejuvenation. I learned how important it is to simply sleep…

Sleep

by Anne Palmer

Sometimes we find ourselves unable to get enough,
Especially when Soul is wrestling with really deep stuff—

Stuff that drains energy—that makes us feel tired,
Internal adjustments happening, circuitry being rewired,

To allow for a much more fluid way of living,
A more even exchange between receiving and giving.

Sleep allows silence a place for Soul to be heard,
Where emotions that matter simmer and are stirred.

They rise to the surface so that they can be addressed,
In plain view we are able to clean up some of the mess,

That over time we created by ignoring our parts,
The true essence of ourselves buried inside our hearts.

This longing to sleep can be confused as depression.
When really it is the result of self-imposed oppression.

For too long we have pushed down that which really matters,
And now it is time to address the resulting inner chatter.

Oh but how masterfully we manage so well to ignore,
The "truth" that Soul knows in fact we are longing for.

So Soul finds a way—it makes us exhausted and tired.
And it is there, in our sleep, we find ourselves mired,

In the mucky and muddy water that we have created,
That yucky stuff that within ourselves we have hated.

To face this ugly stuff we have refused far too long,
And Soul is crying out…"Stop singing that same old song!"

Why not write some new lyrics and add some harmony?
In the silence of this sleepy state we hear a new melody.

So cherish the opportunity to get plenty of rest,
For it is from this state that we emerge at our best.

Think of sleep as a blessing—a time of renewal.
Honor and treasure it like a magnificent jewel.

For without it we are unable to truly function,
Especially when we find ourselves at Life's major junctions.

So shift the way you approach the time spent in your bed.
Think of it as a sacred place to rest your weary head.

Think of it as more than just a place to flop down as one big heap,
Instead regard it as "Sabbath time"—this time we spend asleep.

Sabbath Time

My near-death story is one I share to drive home an important point. Up until that time, I had been a picture of health—and that is probably what saved my life. The doctors that treated me during my three-week-long hospitalization were absolutely dumbfounded. The hospital ran every test imaginable, from AIDS to Lyme. You name it, I was tested for it. There seemingly was no explanation for how I had gotten sick. They discounted stress as a factor and simply said that I had some virus that was dormant in my system.

Maybe it was the "disease to please" virus, or the "I don't matter" virus, or the "I'm not good enough" virus, or the "They'll love me if I'm perfect" virus. All of those viruses had certainly been alive in my system for most of my life.

It happened the weekend that my son was graduating from high school. No matter how hard I tried to push through, I couldn't function for more than a few minutes at a time. The symptoms were that I couldn't tolerate any light, I had to keep my eyes closed, and I couldn't lift my head from a pillow. With a fever of 105 degrees, my body was burning itself up from the inside out. I was delirious, confused, and weak, and I couldn't stand up without support. I had to totally surrender.

The doctors finally figured it out by doing a procedure called a spinal tap. That's right, they took fluid from my spine to figure out what was in my backbone. The diagnosis was viral meningitis. In clinical terms, that means that there were submicroscopic parasites corrupting the membranes protecting my spine and my brain.

My personal belief is that the stress of all that I was going through emotionally was taking its toll on me. I was in the early stages of what turned out to be a decade-long divorce process. There is something about being in the position of defending yourself in a vengeful battle that drains you. I was the target of toxic venom outwardly, while internally I was praying for a peaceful resolution. I was concerned about the welfare of our children.

Certainly our children were aware that the divorce was not pleasant. But much as a mother bear protects her cubs from harm, I was determined to shield them from the battle their parents were in. I made a vow not to say things that would diminish their opinion of their father, no matter how hard it got for me.

It was such a difficult balancing act because I did not have the means to provide everything that my children needed by myself. The court ruled that any decisions that involved the children required participation from both parents. Boy was it hard to honor what they needed, stay in integrity with my vow, and honor what I needed as well.

While I was battling outwardly to survive, inwardly my systems were exhausted from the constant barrage of emotional manipulation and warfare. Literally my body was under attack emotionally, and it manifested itself physically. Similar to the case of my brother, my body found a way to shut down. It simply needed a break.

Lucky for me, because I had been so diligent about taking care of both my physical and spiritual health as a priority in my life, I was able to fight back. It was during the middle of the night, in the darkness of a 4-hour-long MRI, that a bright light within me came forth and assured me that if I just "let go and let God" it would all work out. Armed with my faith, prayer, and a rekindled belief in myself, I knew, in that moment, that I would survive and thrive. I was able to do an about-face at the brink of death's door and fully recover.

My illness was God's way to get me to rest and renew my spirit. As a result, I lived to share one of the most important messages of my journey:

Take time to fortify your faith, whatever that means for you… and take loving care of you!

Ironically, after I recovered, the actual divorce trial took place and as I sat in the courtroom I looked up over the judge's bench and noticed the seal that read…*In God We Trust.* I remember it vividly because I drew a picture of it to reinforce in me that I would never be alone and I would always have whatever I need, so long as I am mindful of the source of my strength and just trust.

Along my road to recovery, I came across an amazing resource that I offer to you as a tool to have in your toolbox. It is Wayne Muller's incredible book entitled *Sabbath: Finding Rest, Renewal, and Delight In Our Busy Lives.*

In his book, Muller offers Sabbath as *"both a specific practice and a larger metaphor to stimulate a conversation about the necessity of rest."*

He goes on to share that, *"Sabbath is a time for sacred rest; it may be a holy day, the seventh day of the week, as in the Jewish tradition, or the first day of the week, as for Christians. But Sabbath time may also be a Sabbath afternoon, a Sabbath hour, a Sabbath walk—indeed, anything that preserves a visceral experience of life-giving nourishment and rest."*

We live in a world where everything moves at lightning speed. It is easy to get caught up in the undertow of life. So, I invite you to take Muller's words to heart as a revolutionary concept worthy of your time and attention…

"Sabbath is a way of being in time where we remember who we are, remember what we know, and taste the gifts of spirit and eternity."

Making time for Sabbath days might just save your life, as it did mine.

Loving Yourself

In one of her most famous records, the beautiful spirit that was Whitney Houston sang a song entitled "The Greatest Love Of All." Loving yourself is a vital part of this process of emerging into authentic alignment. Making time to take loving care of yourself is a concept I strongly encourage you to embrace.

Learning to love yourself is indeed the greatest love of all.

Here, Episcopal priest Susan Purnell emphasizes the importance of love in our lives:

"Love empowers us to grow and change. I know for myself the only life-giving changes that I have made have been motivated first by know-ing God's love for me, then the love of self and others; never out of the need to meet the 'shoulds or have to-s' dictated by self or others.

"Jesus underscores the centrality of love in the following words: 'The first commandment is to love the Lord your God with all your heart,

with all your soul, with all your mind, and with all your strength. The second is this: Love your neighbor as yourself. There is no other commandment greater than these' [Mark 12:29-31].

"It is telling that in carefully reading the second commandment we see it assumes that we love ourselves. Yet there is clear evidence in our world that there are those who suffer the ramifications of the lack of sufficient self-love. So if self-love is not a given, how do we make sense of this second commandment? The key is in the order of the commandments. The second commandment is dependent on our doing the first commandment first. It is in loving the Lord our God with our whole being that we open ourselves to experience God as Love. In this way we put ourselves in the position of first knowing God's love for us, which then enables us to respond in love to God and ourselves. Without first knowing we are loved by the very source of love, how can we love ourselves much less love our neighborhood?

"In my work with people over the years I have repeatedly witnessed that self-love is not something you can tell someone they must learn to do. What we can do, however, is to lovingly encourage them to be open in various ways to experience God's love from the inside out. Once they taste this love, their life begins to change. The transformation process is incredibly beautiful. As God's love draws them closer into the truth of who they are and the gifts they carry, they increasingly are able to let go of the debilitating distortions of themselves, others, the world and God. As their love for God and self deepens, they discover a more expansive vision of possibilities."

Power of Prayer — Wind Beneath Wings

Prayer has played a profound role for me throughout my life and throughout my emerging. When I chose to take the leap into the unknown, I felt the wind from my angels responding to my prayers beneath my wings.

For my pastor, Father Rob Rhodes, the power of prayer is fundamental to his life:

"I couldn't do anything without prayer. I've had a rule of life for sixteen or seventeen years that hasn't changed drastically in that time. I pray for an hour at least every morning, then go to Mass every Sunday and try and make time to understand what's going on in the church and the world throughout the day. It might be paying attention to what God has created as I walk down the street or visiting the soup kitchen. I pray every morning. I don't think I can do anything without it; it's the place where I can let go of the other voices and pay attention to the one that matters. That's really what it's for.

"I have a half hour of silent prayer. Even if I pray for somebody, I'll speak briefly and then go quiet for about a half hour and then do morning prayer. I need both the time with the silence and a time to learn what that voice sounds like. That's where Morning Prayer comes in with psalms and Scripture reading and prayer from Scripture to enable me to recognize God's voice in the silence and in the world around me. I need both aspects of that prayer. Without the liturgical structure of Scripture and the Daily Office that I use as the basis of my prayer ritual, a whole lot of voices might speak to me in the silence. It is the Scripture that helps me to understand which ones to listen to and which ones to ignore."

Having and maintaining a connection with your source through prayer and belief can be powerful. Having faith in something larger than you plays a significant role in your transformation. Yolanda Johnson-Peterkin shared a beautiful example in her riveting story:

"When I couldn't carry myself, my God carried me. When I couldn't bear the burden alone, he carried me. I thought I was being tough and proud and given this opportunity and I was going to change this situation.

"I remember telling my aunt, 'Well Aunt Mary, I've been sentenced to 2.5 to 5 years,' and my aunt said, 'God says you're not going to do that time,' and I remember thinking she was crazy. The judge said I was going to do 2.5 to 5; I'm going to do 2.5 to 5. I'll never forget when

they called me for Shock, because when I said I was going to go I called my aunt to tell her. I'd already done nine or ten months, and told her I was going to a boot camp and I might have the opportunity to get out a little earlier. She said, 'To God be the glory, I told you that when you went in,' and for me it was, 'Wow!' As I went through the process—and I went to services inside of the Shock program—I would always sing. And after a while I started to recognize that I'm being elevated through this process—that God is taking care of me. And I still wanted to take it back, and make it my own. But as I graduated and came into the community, as I started to work in the community, I started to really understand that.

"I really don't like to say, 'If it wasn't for that opportunity, I wouldn't be who I am,' but that's kind of true. If it wasn't for the opportunity, I don't think I would have found my voice. But I absolutely do believe today that the voice and the power that I have—the small power that I have to be able to walk into a correctional facility and look a woman in the eye—it could be 1 to 500 women—and say to them, 'This too shall pass' in whatever way I choose to say it—the words that come out of my mouth. I think I am brilliant, but I believe the words are coming through a force that is his grace and his mercy."

Stay In Integrity With Your Truth

Prayer is simply a form of truth that allows you to take care of yourself. If you live in alignment with yourself and Source, abundance will flow steadily into your life. For it to do so, you must attend continually be aware and in integrity with your truth on every level—mind, body and spirit. Nourish yourself on every level so that you have what it takes to be comfortable in your skin, physically and metaphorically.

Furthermore, my mentor Arthur Joseph taught me many things that proved crucial to my emergence that support me in staying in integrity with my truth. He shared with me that to succeed in life and in business, it is imperative to have Persona, Vision and Mission statements about who you are, the vision you have for your life, and the goals you want to achieve.

As an individual you are your own business, and in order to be successful at being you, you have to establish how you are going to show up, what persona you are going to "be" in every arena of your life. Achieving this requires acute clarity about the gifts and talents you possess, and how you want to share them with the world. With an understanding of how you want to be, you must then establish the personal practices and behavior that supports your ability to make good choices and sound decisions.

Decision making in life is learned behavior. As a result of some of the environmental influences that many athletes have before they come into the game, they haven't necessarily seen good role models off the field. I asked Troy Vincent to share his formula on how an athlete develops good decision-making skills. His response is valuable not just to athletes, but to everyone:

"I always challenge anyone that would use the environment or where she or he has come from as an excuse. We always have our own story. Whether we grew up in South Central LA; Trenton, New Jersey; or Cleveland Ohio, it doesn't matter, nor does our education level matter. The one thing that God has given each of us is the ability to choose and with that ability we all know right from wrong.

"So good decision-making—I'll use the athletic parallel—good decision-making is a habit. Just like in the sport, I'm a good free-throw shooter because I practice shooting free throws. I excelled at my position because I practiced it. It was practice, practice, practice, practice, practice—creating good muscle memory and tremendous habits. There were things that the athletes could do without thinking about it. Why? Because of the repetitive nature of practice. That's the basis of good decision-making on and off the field.

"I practice being a good husband and a good father by what? Making sure I am constantly using the right verbiage, treating my wife the way she is supposed to be treated. That's a habit, regardless of what

I've seen or what I've heard. My parents, outside of my grandparents, were never married. There were a lot of broken marriages inside of my home and in my wife's family. My wife and I have been married 21 years. We constantly practice taking care of one another. So for the athlete, creating good habits, repetitive habits that are good habits, that's how you gain peak performance."

Good decision-making and good habits all boil down to the concept of choice. You have a choice to do something or the choice not to do something. Troy shared some sage advice that he shares with his own children about making choices:

"I go back to what I share often, especially with my own children: 'Control what you can control.' I share with my daughter, 'Hey Desiree, I don't care what happened. I don't care what they said to you. Tell me how you replied.' I'm back to the concept of personal choice again. It doesn't matter what someone said was their perception. Who are you? How did you respond? How did you carry yourself in the meeting? How did you respond to that email? It goes back to personal choice—how you want to be perceived."

Once you gain that degree of clarity, it is vital to make a commitment to yourself to stay true to that persona in every area of your life, no matter what PB&Js are being hurled at you.

Establish your persona statement. It will serve as your North Star, your guiding light and the point you set your compass to. With clarity of intention, the Universe conspires to meet your visceral desires…

Visceral Desire

by Anne Palmer

Soulful Spirit what is it that I desire?
Deep in my heart…that burning fire,

That I locked away and turned my back on,
Afraid of the pain—and the light that comes at dawn.

Allow me to surrender to that which is longing to escape,
From within deep chambers behind my heart's protective gate.

It is a freedom, an experience of genuine love,
That feels like a really comfortable snug glove.

That fits perfectly yet still allows me to move free,
To dance at the oceans edge and sing with glee,

That the shackles and chain-linked armor have fallen away.
I am able to bask in the sunshine and enjoy this new way,

Of serving others and helping them see the truth in their gifts.
In sacred spaces we share channeled divine shifts,

That allow for the release of secret long held desires,
And we enjoy the holy music filling our souls from Divine choirs.

OWNING YOUR POWERFUL PRESENCE

HAVE YOU EVER NOTICED SOMEONE WALK INTO A ROOM and you immediately felt the energy shift? That is what I call "presence."

As you emerge into your new way of being liberated from limiting judgments, it is much easier to embrace a new way of showing up. You are energetically more attractive and the world will respond to you as such. There is an opportunity for you to E.M.E.R.G.E. with a Powerful Presence™.

You do this by polishing the jewel that you are and claiming your power. There are five areas of focus to fully claiming your power—steps to achieve your individual Polished Presence. They are:

- Self-Care
- Style
- Stature
- Self-Confidence
- Self-Mastery

Self-Care

Self-care is the vital first step. All of the hard work it has taken to reach this point requires sustenance and self-care if you are to continue on your journey into fulfilling your purpose. You're only given one body and whatever particular frame that takes, it is your duty and responsibility to take care of it. God doesn't give it to you to treat it with a lack of respect.

Dr. Niki Elliott expands on the importance of self-care in the work she carries out with her clients in this excerpt from my interview with her:

Dr. Niki: *In my work, it's important to ensure people know they have an energy body and that we have different layers that need to be strengthened and cleaned on a regular basis. It's second nature to us to clean our physical bodies from the debris we come into contact with during a shower, yet we don't think of maintaining or cleaning our energy body to ensure we have the boundaries that allow us to experience ourselves as a distinct individualized being who is a part of a divine whole.*

I work with five layers with my clients:

1. *Physical boundaries*
2. *Emotional boundaries*
3. *Relational boundaries*
4. *Psychic boundaries*
5. *Spiritual boundaries*

We do exercises. Activities such as karate and martial arts are good for building the energy body, as well as breathing work, meditation practices and yoga. Going to the ocean, walking barefoot with nature and being with trees—these are all ways in which energy practitioners clear and reset their energy field on a regular basis, daily or weekly at least.

Different systems will have different ways of categorizing the energy bodies. They extend about arms' length from your body in all directions. I also work with the chakra system. They are the two main systems I use to clear and regulate energy in the body.

Anne: *That's a vital step in the process of beginning to EMERGE and claim your whole self.*

Dr. Niki: *You have to recognize yourself as a distinct individualized being sourced of spirit as well as your role in being fully absorbed as part of the one whole. You have to see yourself as a separate 'Self', while simultaneously experiencing yourself as part of the whole. A lot of peoples' difficulties in attracting wealth, maintaining relationships, and having success in their career are often due to damage or interference in the energy field of which many people are not aware.*

What happens when you receive a treasured gift? Imagine that shiny new car in your driveway. Are you going to run it into the ground and discard it when you're tired of it? Of course not; you're going to service and polish it because you've worked hard for it. You want to maintain that sleek, well-maintained image.

The same principles apply to your body—you only get one, so take loving care of it. Keep it in tip-top shape.

In summary, when you commit to self-care as a practice, your life will literally change for the better. With the proper fuel, nurturing and pampering you can accomplish anything you set out to do daily in your professional and personal life.

The important thing to remember is that you are a treasure and you must take care of your treasure CHEST. You do this when you Cleanse, Hydrate, Exercise, Eat Healthy, Stretch, and Take Loving Care of YOU! Learn more in the online course E.M.E.R.G.E. with a Powerful Presence™.

Take Loving Care

Your mind, body and spirit are interdependent. For you to function at an optimal level you need to work continually at taking loving care of all three.

Your mind. Fill your mind with positive thoughts. Surround yourself with positive people. Don't spend a moment longer than necessary with people who do not recognize the unique being that you are, or that express negative ideas in any form. Release them from your life.

Your body. You inhabit a toxic world and periodically you need to detoxify and provide nourishment to your body. Exercise regularly, maintain a balanced diet and ensure you hydrate adequately. Make sure that you observe regular sleep patterns.

Your spirit. I can't overemphasize the importance of nourishing your spirit on a daily basis. I shared how the first activity I undertake every morning is to express my gratitude to Source. Think about those ten toes! Center yourself mentally so you can embrace whatever obstacles the world chooses to throw at you that day. Meditate regularly and keep a journal so you can reflect on the events of the day and therapeutically express your emotions.

We mentioned this part previously, but I make no apology for repeating it.

> *Connect with Source, whatever that represents for you. In my case it is God. It is the single most important part of the process of emerging and to polishing your presence.*

Style

Repeatedly throughout this book I have reinforced the concept that each of you are gifted. You have your own unique style or brand. It is a reflection of your attitude and personality. I like to refer to it as your own personal "panache."

I must stop and share with you that "panache"—which means having dashing style—was one of my brother's favorite words. So I use it as a way of honoring him and to encourage you to honor yourself.

Style is so much more than how you look—what hairstyle you choose or clothes you wear. It is about how you choose to reflect the inner you—how you choose to "BE YOU" authentically in every area of your life and how to broadcast it brilliantly to the world. BE YOU is an acronym I developed that signifies how to best claim your greatness. It stands for:

B – Beam your Beauty, Brilliance and Bravery
- Beauty—the pleasing and impressive qualities that others find attractive, the energetic "Being-ness" of who you are.
- Brilliant light—splendor burning inside you.

- BRAVE enough—courageous enough to step into the world, allowing your unique beauty and brilliance to show in the world.

E – Energetic Way of Being
- Allow yourself to have an uplifting spirit.
- It starts with a smile that is an invitation to the world. "Yes… come experience some of me, and in our exchange allow me to experience some of you!"

Y – Youthful State of Mind
- Age is in fact a state of mind.
- You have a choice every day to set an intention about how you want to show up and how you want to be.

O – Own Your Gifts
- Your Mind.
- Your Body.

U – Utilize Your Uniqueness
- Identify what makes you unique, embrace it and infuse it with your own "verve"—your artistic energy and expression—to develop your "personal panache"—that style you are known for. And then
… Utilize it to show up powerfully in the world.

To step out more powerfully in the world, start today to:
- Identify your unique gifts;
- Infuse verve—artistic energy and expression—into your life; and
- Develop your own "personal panache."

In short, start today to simply…BE YOU!

Stature

How you hold and carry yourself in the world speaks volumes about who you are as a person. The moment you walk into a room, PB&Js

instantly surface in the minds of others. It is a fact of life. Be prepared for them and stand tall and erect—comfortable in your own skin.

Reap the rewards of your self-care personal practices and those hours of abdominal crunches and lunges—ouch! I feel the pain just mentioning them.

It is all worth it when you are able to stand with a strong core, aligned emotionally, physically, and spiritually. There's that mind, body, spirit trilogy again.

To stand firm and proud, you must BELIEVE in who you are and what you have to offer. How others perceive you is a direct result of how you feel about yourself…inside yourself and what you stand for …your values. In the words of Malcolm X…

"If you don't stand for something, you will fall for anything."

Both Dr. Niki in her work at Innerlight Sanctuary and my yoga and Pilates master, Jody Domerstad, participated in my online home-study program *E.M.E.R.G.E. With A Powerful Presence,* in which registrants are reminded of the importance of grounding as a principle to claiming your power. It is available to you as an online home-study course at *www.annepalmer.com/emerge.*

Jody reminds me and I share it now with you to

"claim your place on the earth and be supported by the universal energy. The earth is full of energy and offers unlimited possibilities and nourishment if you are open to receive it."

Give yourself permission to BE who you are uniquely designed to be without apology. Stand tall in stature in that knowing. It's enough simply because it's YOU!

Self-Confidence

When you achieve self-confidence—an unwavering belief in your own abilities—you are effectively managing your PB&Js. You no longer let what other people think take you off your game. Remember Lisa Nichols' grandmother's words of wisdom:

> *"What other people think about you, ain't none of your business."*

Take that to heart and live it. Remember you have reframed your PB&Js in a healthy way. You have a new attitude. Embrace your new PB&J paradigm—**Limitless Possibilities, Empowering Beliefs and Life-Enhancing Joy.** As you emerge into this new place of authentic alignment, your self-confidence will EXPAND and your new beliefs will become second nature.

I offer you my EXPAND acronym as a doctrine to incorporate into your life:

E – Elevate yourself in mind, body and spirit; increase your rank and your opinion of your Self when you enrich your thoughts; take pride in your body and surrender to Spirit.

X – Xtract your essence from Source; exhibit for the world to experience your most important features, those identifying qualities that at your core make you special.

P – Punctuate your positive attributes:
- **Edit out ...**
  Question marks that have been limiting you.
- **Emphasize...**
  What is best about you with periods and exclamation marks.
  Adopt an attitude of "I CAN!"

A – Allow yourself to be fully present, conscious and aware. Grant permission to your Self to be in control of your destiny—no longer distracted by the energy that has been draining you, keeping you off-balance and out of alignment with you.

N – Nurture your Self to flourish. Determine who it is you want to BE and find someone to share your vision with.

D – Dare to be You. Challenge your Self, be courageous and have the audacity to Be YOU. This is YOUR life. Dare to live it to the fullest. Play full out in life!

Natasha Phoenix's journey to claim a more powerful presence has been gradual. She incorporated the personal practices that have become essential elements of her life:

> *"On the outside I've always been the image of control, composure and presentation. I spend a fortune on clothes. I'm always well-dressed, so people wouldn't notice a difference there. In the meantime, I was working like crazy and I was stressed beyond belief and I wasn't working out. I carry weight easily but I gained weight, although people didn't notice it thankfully but I noticed it. In the last three years I invested a ton in yoga and in working out. I've been getting to the gym regularly, and I'm much more focused on my inside and in how I'm feeling. And I thought I was projecting composure and confidence before, but now I'm really feeling extremely good about it all."*

Like Natasha, you have the capacity to up-level and expand your life. You can exude confidence and have healthy self-esteem as well. Look at the EXPAND acronym above again, and then create ways that you can apply that doctrine in your life starting today. Use the exercises in the Lifeline Guide (www.TheGiftedTrap.com/LifelineGuide) to expand your life.

Self-Mastery

We have explored many concepts within the pages of this book that individually may be of value and that collectively have the capacity to change the trajectory of your life if you choose.

To "integrate" is to make something open to all—to make it whole. Integrating into your life the information within these pages—the wisdom that has been shared by the generous people who allowed me to reveal their stories for the benefit of your learning—will ultimately yield peace of mind within your soul.

The path to self-mastery is one that calls you to re-member. The invitation is for you to take the elements explained herein and assemble them in a manner that is authentic for you and yields an energetic alignment that is powerful.

I defer again to my mentor, Arthur Joseph, to drive home the opportunity that lies before you to Be your Self in every arena of your life. Through my Vocal Awareness work with Arthur, I was able to craft a Persona Statement that was the framework for how I wanted to show up in the world. This statement is a creed that I created for myself to live my life by. I no longer feel like I have to juggle several different hats, each one representing a different personality or job description. I just need to live my life and show up as one powerful presence in alignment with the truth of who it is I choose to be in the world.

Now is the time for you to consciously integrate your Mind, Body and Spirit. For support with the process, go to **www.TheGiftedTrap. com** and register for the E.M.E.R.G.E. with a Powerful Presence™ online course. The content-rich program will empower you on your journey to Be and Speak your truth as I have been able to do, so that you can…claim your voice, own your dream, and emerge with your powerful presence.

That is what this process of emerging is all about—**authentically being all you are meant to be…**

Be All You Are Meant To Be

by Anne Palmer

Peel open your heart—reveal your truth—all that there is to know,
The truth that unlocks floodgates and allows abundance to flow.

Wallowing in sorrow, wringing out every drop of strained emotion,
Yields, on the other side, "pulp"—a secret ingredient for a magic potion.

Come to the table now and partake of the body and of the blood,
As a reminder of the sacrifices, and a cleanse to remove
remaining crud,

The residue of any resistance or reluctance to live an absolute truth,
Creating a clearing for the emergence of authenticity—much like a
new tooth,

Breaks through infant's tender gums—teething can hurt so much.
Yet it is an inevitable process—one we must go through to get in touch,

With the inner essentials that make it possible to chew,
Life sustaining food that provides fuel to get you through.

So be patient with this process despite discomfort and pain.
Clarity follows like clear skies bursting through after heavy rain.

Of this I am certain, for this lonely path I too have walked.
It is from a place of knowing that I speak to you and talk,

About freedom that accompanies the truth rising to the surface.
Inside this information is a gift—the gift of your true purpose.

And from that place of purpose a new way of being is given birth,
Unbridled passion is harnessed gently with an "awareness girth."

And off you ride on the winged horse called Freedom.
Galloping across fields surveying an open kingdom,

A new frontier to explore—new horizons you are able to now see.
Go forth with this new wisdom and be all you are meant to be.

THE PB&J DIETARY SHIFT

GOOEY CHILDHOOD SANDWICHES ARE SERVED IN HOUSE-holds everywhere and don't require any culinary skills to make. Throughout the pages of this book, I have shared new techniques and recipes with you to enhance how you prepare a healthier emotional diet.

You've been busy in your internal kitchen, learning new ways to cook meals for yourself with love that will nourish you and enhance your life with flavorful new seasonings.

You don't have to limit your diet to gooey childhood sandwiches anymore. This work offers you an opportunity to transform your basic culinary skills and become your own Master Chef. You now have the skills to create a masterful, soulful soufflé.

In the South, where I grew up, one way of demonstrating love is through cooking good food to nourish your soul…thus the term "soul food." You know it the minute you taste it. It may be good homemade rolls that melt in your mouth like butter, or the perfect fruit cobbler, or it may be a delicious pot of gumbo—a wonderful soup with a melange of flavors of seafood, sausages and tomatoes. Like that pot of gumbo, your gifts and talents are a mix of succulent flavors that together create an incredible soup that is the essence of who you are, the basis for your greatness.

As we used to say in the South when you had an amazing meal that someone had clearly prepared with love, "She sure put her foot in that one." The foot refers to love. And God certainly pours love in us by giving us each incredible gifts. It's now up to you to serve yours up to the world as an incredible soulful soufflé. I extend some Southern hospitality and invite you to serve your soufflé up for the world to enjoy!

And when you choose to do that…you will have truly emerged:
- From Binding Perceptions to Boundless Possibilities
- From Limiting Beliefs to Limitless Beliefs
- From Life-sucking Judgment to Life-enhancing Joy

…From Sticky Sandwich to Soulful Soufflé!

Emerge From The Trap
by Anne Palmer

Emotionally trapped in a world using your gifts to please others,
Overwhelmed, underappreciated, unsure what tomorrow holds,
Longing to course correct and craving another path,
One on which your "authentic self" has not been sold,

Longing for a less frenetic way of being,
Searching for clarity, a sense of calm and truth.
No longer willing to pretend or perform,
This process—this shift—feels like cutting a new tooth.

Calls for taking conscious loving breaths,
Rather for "allowing" heart to deeply breathe.
Releasing from the trap, taking leaps of faith,
Welcoming inner wisdom, as doubt surrenders and leaves.

A soulful journey…less about the "doing,"
More about being in and creating from a nurtured nest,
Where "Self" is lovingly held and embraced,
And finding true passion is part of the quest.

From this altered perch, new insights become aware,
As you begin to polish your own innate presence,
No longer performing as a way of seeking love,
Instead learning to adore your personal true essence.

Explore every inch of your new landscape and horizons
Excavate, expand and watch YOU within grow
With "The Gifted Trap" experience you become enlightened
Empowered, enlivened and simply begin to KNOW

That the talents you possess are unique—intended just for you
To express them with gratitude, generosity and grace
From a peaceful vortex you emerge in "inspired action"
Sharing your gifts—outside the trap—in a brand new space

LIBERATE YOURSELF FROM YOUR TRAP

T HE PROFOUND MESSAGE DELIVERED IN THE FOLLOWING excerpt from Marianne Williamson's *Return to Love* summarizes eloquently what I hope you are taking away from our time together:

> Our deepest fear is not that we are inadequate.
> Our deepest fear is that we are powerful beyond measure.
> It is our light not our darkness that most frightens us.
> We ask ourselves, who am I to be brilliant, gorgeous,
> talented and fabulous?
> Actually, who are you not to be?

Williamson goes on to say…

> As we let our own light shine,
> we unconsciously give other people
> permission to do the same.
> As we are liberated from our own fear,
> Our presence automatically liberates others.

[Often said to have been quoted in a speech by Nelson Mandela. The source is *Return to Love* by Marianne Williamson, Harper Collins, 1992. —Peter McLaughlin]

The journey out of the trap is one that I genuinely hope you see as one worth embarking on to liberate yourself. Embrace the concepts in this book and the resources that are available to you through my website, www.TheGiftedTrap.com and the workbook www.TheGiftedTrap.com/ LifelineGuide. Claim a joyful life outside of the trap for yourself and make your life meaningful by committing to: invest in you; integrate your head and your heart; plug into your Source; leave a legacy; and be unapologetic about your greatness—and the footprint you leave will be indelible.

Invest in YOU...

My mentor Erline Belton, whose wisdom was so vital in my transformation, spoke in-depth in my interview with her about the importance of investing in yourself:

> *"People invest in financial portfolios, other people, relationships, but self-investment—doing the internal work to invest in yourself to become everything you were intended to be—is the most important work of all. It's the work most people don't find time to do. And if you don't do it, you stay trapped."*

Integrate Your Head and Your Heart...

She went on to share her sage advice on the importance of integrating head and heart:

> *"You hear people talk about 'head and heart' and I do that in an extraordinary way because that is what I most care about—having people use their intellect without disconnecting from their heart."*

Plug into your Source...

Allow yourself to connect with the truth in your heart of who you were uniquely designed to be. You are a work of art. **Plug into your Source** of all-knowing—whatever that looks like for you—and yield to that knowledge. It is available to you when you simply take time to **be silent and listen**. There is a reason why both those words have the exact same letters. So listen and let the guidance from Source be your North Star.

Leave a Legacy...

We all want to feel that our time here on earth had reason and purpose. Again I reference Erline's interview as a call to action that we all strive to leave a legacy—a mark that our life mattered in some way. She went on to say...

> *"For me, people create a legacy from moment to moment. The important piece of that message is to be conscious that you do that, so you can make choices about those moments. It's never too late to begin to employ that as the way that you choose to live your life.*
>
> *"For example, I went to a Senior Center, working with seniors 65 or older, and the beauty of the meeting was I was able to say to them, 'What you've done before doesn't matter; it's what you do from this moment on with the time you have left that's important. What legacy do you want to leave going forward?'*
>
> *"It's important for people to get that because people get stuck in what they didn't do or what they have done that they are ashamed of or unhappy about or what caused them pain. When you really think about, what matters is how you want to move forward. What do you want to do with the moments you have left?*

> **"The notion of 'moment to moment' is futuristic—it can give you a guidepost for how you want to 'be' going forward."**

I cherish those wise words of my mentor and hope you will find inspiration from them as well. Wherever you are on your journey called life—at the beginning, in the middle or winding down toward your final chapters—as long as you have breath and health, you have time to claim more of your greatness.

Be Unapologetic About Your Giftedness...

My bright, beautiful, bipolar friend Vasavi Kumar shared with me in her interview (and I make no apology for repeating them here)...

> *"First of all, you have been bestowed with everything you possibly need to create anything that you want to be. And secondly, don't apologize for your existence. Never apologize for the creation that you are, whatever it looks like."*

I echo those words to you now because it is crystal clear—and as a clarity coach I do understand what it means to be clear—it is clear that we have all been blessed in some unique way.

You have been given so much. And ultimately, what you want at the end of your life is to leave an indelible footprint that shows you were here and made a difference. There is therefore no reason for you to ever apologize for claiming your greatness.

Yolanda Johnson-Peterkin is a shining example of what it looks like when you accept and embrace your gifts and use them to impact the world around you. She shared with me what that looks like for her.

> *"Sometimes it doesn't matter if it's incarcerated men or women. It could be a room of women period. If I open my mouth and talk about this journey, or any part of my life, I always get an overwhelmingly powerful response. It's just like being in a room with Sandra Yancey or Lisa Nichols—I never realized that people actually share their stories to motivate people for real, because I've done it so much just being who I am. "It doesn't have to be a room full of people. It could be one person. It could be a homeless person I just found in my neighborhood and took to the local shelter. It's a power that...you can't get that grace and that power from anyone else but God. That's how I see it. I like to think I'm brilliant,*

but I know…I know…I hear. I can be very calm and silent so I can listen to what my next journey is all about. Often I even hear my next journey come to me through other people.

"For instance, I was speaking at a school a couple of years back, and I have to say that kids get on my nerves a little bit. I was talking to ninth graders about my prison experience and who I was. I never try to 'big me up' (as we used to say in the street). Instead, I always make a point to 'big up the process.' So I was talking to these kids and one of the guys stood up and said, 'Can I hug you?' I said, 'Sure you can hug me.' Then he said, 'My foster mother always told me that my mother and father were animals because they are both in prison. You have helped me see that my mother and father are human beings.'

You can't pay me for that experience; there's no payment large enough. And I've had so many of those life-altering conversations that are so powerful that you can't bottle them up—you just can't bottle them up. I know the ability to have that kind of impact is not because of me. There is only one explanation and that's because of my Lord and Savior. I just continue to do his work and his will and I make no excuses. I am unapologetically doing what I was called to do with the gifts and blessings I have been given.

Yolanda is fully claiming her greatness. She uses her voice to change lives. By simply sharing her story she is leaving her indelible footprint.

Your Indelible Footprint…

I opened this book with the story of the indelible footprint my father left. I end our journey together here with a call to action for you to…

**Use your gifts to leave a legacy—find fulfilment
in the life that you live.**

GO FORTH AND...

JOYFULLY CLAIM
YOUR GREATNESS!

AUGUSTUS L. PALMER, SR. WITH DAUGHTER ANNE

...TAKE LOVING CARE!

Appendix A – Interview Profiles

Erline Belton
Executive Coach and Organization Healer

Erline's unique input and advice is vital throughout this book. Erline discusses the reality of emotional entrapment, together with the three common symptoms of those caught in the Gifted Trap. She also provides insight into the E.M.E.R.G.E.™ process, while emphasizing the importance of joy and the value of legacy.

Erline's Book, *A Journey That Matters: Your Personal Living Legacy*, focuses on how you move forward in your life, creating a legacy that is defined by you and not others.

Carol Callan
Women's National Team Director for USA Basketball

Carol provides invaluable insight into the PB&Js™ that pervade the sporting world and explains how world-class athletes remain at the top of their game, despite the ubiquitous pressures. She also reveals how the Gifted Trap affects those athletes driven to succeed and the vital role of coaches in reinforcing positive beliefs.

Rainbow Chen
Career and Relationships Coach

The brilliant, Ivy-League-educated Rainbow shares the story of her struggle with the culturally and personally imposed PB&Js™ that have dominated her life. Her interview is also provided as an example of a case study of a gifted young woman still in the process of emerging, negotiating with the voices of her internal parts, learning to love herself, and celebrating the rich diversity of her big heart, artistic talents, and intellectual horsepower.

Rainbow is happy to share that she's finding a sweet balance coaching brilliant students and Ivy League graduates to be more alive in their careers and their love lives, as well as teaching dance workshops to help smart professionals connect to themselves and others joyfully and lovingly.

Cheryl L. Clark
PhD in Health and Human Services

Dr. Clark's pioneering efforts lead to the design of revolutionary transformational learning environments called Total Learning Environments™ (TLE™) in prisons and in drug treatment programs that have been fundamental in turning lives around.

Dr. Clark's work speaks to the PB&Js™ we see so often in society that affect ethnic groups and prison populations, while simultaneously demonstrating how it is possible to emerge from seemingly inescapable circumstances.

The TLE™ involves physical, emotional, mental and spiritual dynamics of the human environment. More information, including Dr. Clark's dissertation entitled *12° of Freedom: Synergetics and the 12 Steps to Recovery*, are available at www.socialsynergetics.com.

Dike Drummond, MD
www.thehappymd.com
Physician Burnout Prevention Coach and Trainer

Dike's story is a classic example of the multi-generational PB&Js™ that keep people firmly in the Gifted Trap. To the outside world, Dike lived the perfect life but inside he was caught in a classic case of emotional entrapment. Dike discusses his journey, including his slide into the Gifted Trap, his experience with his internal parts and how he reframed his beliefs before emerging into authentic alignment to claim his greatness.

Niki Elliott, PhD
Founder and CEO of Innerlight Sanctuary
Web : www.innerlightsanctuary.com

Niki Elliott, PhD is Founder and CEO of Innerlight Sanctuary. The purpose of Innerlight Sanctuary is to create a safe space where families, children and adults can safely discuss the concepts surrounding energy and intuition and how these powerful characteristics of our natural being impact our ability to function and survive and thrive in our daily life.

Dr. Niki's combination of mainstream "normal" professional degrees and her intuitive healing arts energy expertise creates a palatable balance of two extremes of judgment. This allows people who might not otherwise open themselves to her gift to accept it and explore the possibility that they have it as well.

Please tune in to the "Nurturing Intuitive Children with Dr. Niki" radio show to learn more about her innovative work. The radio show airs live on the second Sunday of each month at 8pm ET/5pm PT on AM 1510 Boston NBC Sports Radio. You may also visit www.dreamvisions7radio.com to listen to archived shows.

Melissa Evans
The Guru of Implementation
Founder of Live Rich Spread Wealth™, LLC
www.melissa-evans.com

Known as The Guru of Implementation, Melissa draws on her wisdom as a successful business woman who has been in business for over three decades, and has served over 5,000 entrepreneurs and business owners in 239 different industries, helping them to identify their soul purpose and monetize it.

For years, the supremely gifted executive suppressed her giftedness to make others feel more comfortable around her. Her story is a classic example of the "light being too bright" for some people, yet she continues to claim her greatness unapologetically.

Marie Guthrie
CEO of The Legacy Track
http://marieguthrie.com
The Legacy Track develops consciousness intelligence strategies for leaders in business, education, science and technology.

Marie mentors spiritually conscious executives who lead with the best interests of others at heart and are struggling with advancing unique solutions to today's complex issues while engaging the cooperation of even the toughest critics. Instead of allowing adversities to make one unhappy or discouraged, her Relationship Technology and Quantum Leader Foundation System teaches how to transform any difficult situation into an advantage and to make heart-centered decisions with a calm peaceful state of mind.

Marie provides essential insight into the effects of emotional entrapment typically seen in corporate America. She believes firmly in the importance of the inner GPS and encourages all of her clients to spend time focusing on this area every day.

Jennie Hernandez
www.jenniehernandez.com

As an incredibly gifted author, motivational speaker and teacher, Jennie Hernandez has had a life that, in her own words, has been one of *"change, possibility and growth."* During the journey of her life, Jennie has developed a parenting process based on effective business principles that eventually became an internationally published parenting book.

From a long period of emotional entrapment caused by cultural and self-imposed PB&Js™, Jennie emerged from a period of welfare and bankruptcy—supporting seven children alone—into authentic alignment. The story of her journey is an inspiration to all of those caught in the Gifted Trap.

Yolanda Johnson-Peterkin
Director of Operations For The Women's Prison Association, New York City

Yolanda's story is an incredible inspiration of how to reframe your life and emerge to claim your greatness. Formerly incarcerated herself, she was selected to participate in the Shock Incarceration Program pioneered by Dr. Cherie Clarke, Yolanda has transformed her life and is now the Director of Operations for the Women's Prison Association in New York City. Her story is riveting and compelling.

Vasavi Kumar
www.vasavikumar.com

Inspirational coach Vasavi speaks candidly of her struggle with bipolar disorder, societally and self-imposed PB&Js¨, self-sabotage and the problems with being "too good." Her journey through the E.M.E.R.G.E. ¨ process lies at the heart of this book.

Vasavi's *Keepin' It Real* weekly video series was created to share positive messages to keep people moving forward, support them on their journey and push them to take action to maximize their true potential. In her series she shares inspiration, tips and tricks to overcome obstacles, action steps and motivational messages from her personal stories like those she shared here in *The Gifted Trap.*

Carole Martin-Wright
Currently a Senior Consultant,
Previously VP, Information Systems for
Large Fortune 100 Company

High flying executive senior consultant Carole confesses she is still emerging from the PB&Js™ experienced in the Gifted Trap and still suffers from the effects of burnout. Her experience of emotional entrapment epitomizes the issues faced by many gifted individuals in corporate America.

Gina Maria Mele
http://ginamariamelems.wordpress.com

Belief expert Gina Maria Mele has chosen to merge the disciplines of traditional medicine, holistic medicine and the study of how we view our reality together to challenge those PB&Js™ and enable her clients to undergo what she describes as a "Thrivable Transformation"™. Her contribution and extensive work on Beliefs is essential reading in this book.

Natasha Phoenix
Program Delivery Executive

Natasha is a yet another gifted corporate star whose experience of the PB&Js™ in corporate America manifested itself in an emotional breakdown. Today, Natasha is emerging from the trap and encourages everyone to seize their gifts and follow their dreams.

Susan Purnell
Ordained Episcopal priest Living in Southern California

Susan's contribution speaks to the divine throughout the Gifted Trap. Her advice on learning to love yourself and trusting God, together with the story of her incredible ordination experience and how she learned to reframe her PB&Js™, are an inspiration to everyone.

Father Rob Rhodes
Grace Episcopal Church in Westwood

Father Rob has been pastor of Grace Episcopal Church for four years and was ordained to the priesthood in June 2003. Deeply spiritual, Father Rob explains why, for him, faith is so important in emerging from the Gifted Trap and his own belief in the power of prayer.

Troy Vincent
Senior Vice President of Player Engagement
National Football League

Troy discusses candidly the effect of PB&Js™ on athletes both during their career and as they transition into a new life after retirement from active sport. Above all, Troy's life epitomizes the impact that a complete trust in God can have, regardless of your environment and opinions of others.

APPENDIX B - RESOURCES

A Letter to Agnes De Mille

There is a vitality,
a life force,
a quickening
that is translated through you into action,
and because there is only one of you in all time,
this expression is unique.

And If you block it, it will never exist through any other medium and be
lost.
The world will not have it. It is not your business to determine
how good it is
nor how valuable it is
nor how it compares with other expressions.

It is your business to keep it yours clearly and directly
to keep the channel open.
You do not even have to believe in yourself or your work.
You have to keep open and aware directly to the urges that motivate YOU.

Keep the channel open...
No artist is pleased...

There is no satisfaction whatever at anytime
There is only a queer, divine dissatisfaction
a blessed unrest that keeps us marching
and makes "us" MORE alive than the others.

Martha Graham
(– a letter to Agnes De Mille-)

Resources about Communication & Self-Mastery

Books by Arthur Samuel Joseph about Vocal Awareness™
http://wwwl.vocalawarenes.com

*VOCAL POWER – Harness Your Inner Voice to Conquer Everyday
Communication Challenges (Featuring the Vocal Awareness Method™)*

*VOCAL LEADERSHIP – 7 Minutes a Day to Communication
Mastery*

Resources about Leadership & Legacy

TRUE NORTH – Discover Your Authentic Leadership
By Bill George with Peter Sims

GOOD TO GREAT
By Jim Collins

A JOURNEY THAT MATTERS – Your Personal Living Legacy
By Erline Belton

Resources about Love:

THE FIVE LOVE LANGUAGES
By Gary Chapman

THE POWER
By Rhonda Byrne

UNDEFENDED LOVE
By Jett Psaris, PH.D. & Marlena S. Lyons, PH. D.

Resources about Rest & Renewal:

SABBATH – Finding Rest, Renewal, and Delight in Our Busy Lives
By Wayne Muller

Resources about Spiritual Success Principles & Purpose:

THE SEVEN SPIRITUAL LAWS OF SUCCESS
By Deepak Chopra

THE FOUR AGREEMENTS
By Don Miguel Ruiz

GETTING INTO THE VORTEX – The Teachings of Abraham
Guided Meditations & CD
By Esther & Jerry Hicks

THE UNIVERSAL MIND MEDITATION CD SERIES
By Kelly Howell

Resources about Purpose & Beliefs:

TRUE PURPOSE – 12 Strategies for Discovering the Difference You Are Meant to Make
By Tim Kelley

Gina Maria Mele, M.S. – ginamariamelems@gmail.com

THE PASSION TEST
By Janet Bray Attwood & Chris Attwood

**Release yourself from your gifted trap…
Reach for a lifeline to lift you out
of your emotional quicksand.**

Download your **FREE**
E.M.E.R.G.E. LifeLine Guide at
www.TheGiftedTrap.com/LifelineGuide

Put a stake in solid ground and tie a lifeline to it. Use the
principles and exercises that are available to you for FREE.
Your personal guide will be delivered immediately to your
e-mail address. In it will be valuable strategies that help you
E.M.E.R.G.E. AND SEE how to:

- Gain greater clarity about what really matters
- Explore new possibilities for your life
- Reframe limiting beliefs into empowering beliefs
- Establish a new relationship with the chatter within
- Release judgment and embrace joy
- Own a more powerful presence
- Find your voice
- Claim your greatness

INJECT INSPIRATION INTO YOUR ORGANIZATION...
CLAIM INDIVIDUAL AND COLLECTIVE GREATNESS:
EMPOWER YOUR PEOPLE WITH AN
E.M.E.R.G.E. From Gifted to Great™ WORKSHOP

Empower your employees, managers, members and students to be the best they are capable of being. Powerful transformations are possible when they experience an E.M.E.R.G.E live group training or workshop.

In theses content-rich experiences your people will be energized and inspired to harness their innate gifts in ways they may never have imagined. They will be equipped with new insights and awareness that allow them to embrace a new level of excellence for themselves.

The alignment of their personal mission, vision and values integrated with your organization's mission, vision and values will yield for them...greater feelings of self-worth...more passionate commitment to excellence...improved performance and productivity...and that allows you to claim your collective greatness!

An E.M.E.R.G.E. From Gifted to Great™ Workshop includes a customized curriculum complete with training tools for all attendees. More intensive, long-term leadership and communication strategy trainings to improve presence and presentation skills are available and can be designed to meet the specific needs of your organization. E.M.E.R.G.E. Workshops and trainings are perfect for a wide variety of groups such as:

- Executives and Entrepreneurs
- Executive leadership programs
- Women's Leadership & Empowerment Groups
- Non-Profit Executive Teams & Boards
- Executives in Transition
- Professional Athletic Programs
- Collegiate Athletic Programs
- Graduate & Professional Institutions
- Educators and Students
- Youth Leadership Organizations
- Faith-Based Organizations
- MLM Organizations and Teams
- Holistic Healing Organizations
- Trade associations
- Military personnel, spouses and families

For more information on these valuable trainings contact:
Trainings@TheGiftedTrap.com
www.TheGiftedTrap.com/Trainings

MORE PRAISE FOR ANNE

As a former butcher turned millionaire, I understand what it takes to live up to your potential. We each have the gifts and the capacity to do extraordinary things. Anne uses her gift of clarity to help you tap into your own vision to see, wisdom to understand and courage to pursue what is possible. Make the decision to claim your greatness and let this valuable tool, **The Gifted Trap,** be your guide.

Jimmy "The Butcher" Smith
Isagenix Millionaire

• • • • • • • • • •

"I am awed by Anne's depth, wisdom and ability to plug into her inner knowing in profound ways. She is committed to living a purposeful life, with authenticity and grace. No doubt, however you engage with Anne, it will yield greater clarity for you, your organization and your relationships."

Marcia Wieder
Founder, Dream University

• • • • • • • • • •

"As an international trainer of trainers, speakers and presenters, I rarely encounter the natural talent, ability presence and charisma that Anne Palmer exudes every time she steps on the stage. She is as comfortable, genuine and caring when speaking to thousands as she is one-on-one."

"The way I describe Anne is a beacon of light who impacts the lives of every person she encounters, whether on stage, through her CD's, on Television or standing in a line up at the grocery store or walking down the street"

David Wood
www.davidtraining.com

. . . .

To be a great coach you need to ask the right questions and be a compassionate listener. Anne has mastered both these skills. It is no coincidence, that those who are blessed to be mentored by Anne, have joyfully created quantum transformations in their personal and business life!

Bill Mayer
Author, *The Magic in Asking the Right Questions*

. . . .

Anne Palmer is a remarkable and unique person who uses her gifts to bring out the best in others. She is an outstanding coach, and speaker whose wisdom comes from her heart and touches the soul of others. I'm thankful that she has touched my life and you will be too.

Erline Belton
CEO Lyceum Group
Author of *A Journey that Matters*, Boston, Mass

. . . .

Anne encourages me to see my truths while honoring myself as she coaches me through the process. She masterfully guides me and provides me with the tools I need to anchor myself in my core values so I can be the 'designer of my life'!

Paul Interval
Master Hair Artist, New York City

. . . .

Anne has a unique ability to see through unspoken beliefs and limiting behavior that people and organizations lack and provide them with key insights to help them transcend obstacles thus empowering them to soar and take flight."

Christine Regan Lake
Artist & Author, Heartylicious LLC, Cave Creek, Arizona

. . . .

Anne guides me in what I consider to be a Crème de la Crème coaching experience. Her velvet-like voice is gentle yet her message and mentoring is firm – challenging me to take control of my life. Becoming a well-respected actress is one of my life long dreams. I am performing again, after 33 years of not being on stage.

Rhonda Oliver

. . . .

Coaching with Anne is like having a safe, secure support net holding you. She lovingly encourages you to bring out the best in yourself. She has a laser-like ability to help you get to what is blocking you and then comes back at you with honesty in an amazingly humanitarian way. Anne helped me find the courage that I wasn't quite sure I had.

If you want results … If you are ready to shift your life for the better … You'll get where you want to go with Anne guiding you. She simply helps you get it done!

Lauren S.

• • • • • • • • • •

Few people in the world today have Anne's unique gift to speak. The effortless delivery of her words opens your heart, motivates and inspires you. The vibrational frequency of her voice is healing. Simply being in her presence brings you into alignment and connects you to who you really are so you then have a foundation to manifest your dreams. Anne is A-list, world class … Extraordinary!

Nicholas Pratley
Intruessence.com

• • • • • • • • • •

Anne Palmer is the best speech and communication coach I've ever worked with. As a medical director for a Fortune 100 health insurance company, great communication skills are crucial. Within minutes of working with Anne, she improved my voice quality, pacing and breathing tremendously. Without question, I'm a much more effective speaker thanks to Anne's teaching and leadership

Virgie Bright Ellington, M.D. New York, NY,
Author of *What Your Doctor Wants You To Know*
But Doesn't Have Time To Tell You